YOUNG MAN OF CARACAS

The author at the age of eighteen

T. R. YBARRA

YOUNG MAN OF CARACAS

Foreword by ELMER DAVIS

ILLUSTRATED

IVES WASHBURN, INC.
NEW YORK

COPYRIGHT, 1941, BY T. R. YBARRA

All rights reserved including the right to reproduce this book or portions thereof in any form

PRINTED IN THE UNITED STATES OF AMERICA
BY THE HADDON CRAFTSMEN, INC., CAMDEN, N. J.

in memoriam:

E. R. de Y.

A. Y.

Foreword

THIS is news to me, this book—as much as to any other reader, even though I have known Tom Ybarra for twenty-seven years. For the young man of Caracas hereinafter depicted is the person known to me as a young man of Manhattan, Boston, Paris, Berlin and way points. (No nasty cracks from the back row, please; twenty-seven years from now, you won't be as young as you used to be, either.) His North American friends were of course aware that he was half Caraqueño and half Plymouthroqueño, that the person known around New York as Thomas Russell Ybarra was known in other localities as Don Tomás Ybarra Russell, with heaven knows how many saints' names interpolated besides. But not till later, when I met in Paris his brother Alejandro, wearing out chair bottoms in boulevard cafés while he revolved schemes for slipping back to Venezuela some dark night and overthrowing the Tyrant, did I realize how far Tom had traveled from his starting point; for whatever his inward feelings may have been, it seemed to make no more difference to him who was President of Venezuela than who won the world's series, and considerably less than who won the Harvard-Yale game.

But it appears from these reminiscences that the two natures in him have been perpetually in conflict; and while Caracas lost, it was not Boston that eventually won. To me, as perhaps to a good many other people, Tom Ybarra first made himself known as a Manhattan boulevardier . . . This was back

FOREWORD

in those days, along about 1907; when I was in college in Indiana, and had no reason to suppose that I would ever see New York. For it was my intention to become a Hoosier schoolmaster; and if I were diligent in my business, I might hope to rise some day to the dignity of superintendent of schools in some county seat. Which, if I could become besides a Shriner, an Elk, and a trustee of the First Baptist Church, seemed the utmost to which human ambition could aspire.

But once in a while I relieved my studious preparations for this future by reading a fiction magazine; and in that magazine I was likely to find a story by one Thomas R. Ybarra. A story, usually, about some gentleman of Broadway leaning up against a bar, engaged in philosophical discussion with the bartender before going out to spend an evening of excitement and romance. For all I know Tom never wrote more than two or three stories like that in his life; but they were the stories I read, the stories that stuck in my memory, associated with his name. And I used to think, What a glamorous life this man Ybarra leads! Maybe it might be more fun than being superintendent of schools in Rushville or Veedersburg . . .

Well, maybe so; Broadway, I later discovered, has its points if taken in moderation; but you can't have everything, and I never found out how it would have felt to be a school superintendent in Rushville or Veedersburg. The life Tom led (or at least wrote about) in those days seems to have had some characteristics of a perpetual-motion machine; leaning up against a bar and talking to the bartender he got the material for a story, which he sold for enough money to enable him to lean up against another bar and talk to another bartender

FOREWORD

and get material for another story, which he sold, etc., etc. But I suspect that he leaned in order to write, rather than wrote in order to lean; for in my recollection leaning up against a bar was no more than a minor and incidental activity in his life, even though he showed no ambition to emulate his father's record of never taking a drink from the cradle to the grave.

Which has some bearing on this subjoined narrative. Caracas as he recalls it was a romantic and exciting place; yet not romantic enough, not exciting enough, to keep him from going back to Boston instead. Boston too failed to hold him; by the time I first knew him he was already a blown-in-the-glass New Yorker who went to Boston, like most New Yorkers, only to see his aunt. (Some young anthropologist could earn a Ph.D. by a study of this well attested but inadequately analyzed phenomenon, that aunts flourish so luxuriantly in Boston, and nephews in New York.) New York has held him—aside from long sojourns in Paris and Berlin, while those cities were still fit to live in—but that proves nothing in particular; for as John dos Passos has observed, if New York turns sour on you, where is there to go? And it seems that now Tom Ybarra's thoughts more and more turn back to Caracas. No wonder; as a certain poet phrased it long ago, the garden spot is where you're not.

ELMER DAVIS

Contents

CHAPTER		PAGE
I	PRE-TOM	1
II	MORE PRE-TOM	19
III	STILL MORE PRE-TOM	33
IV	MILITARISM!	52
V	MORE MILITARISM	67
VI	"YESSIE"	84
VII	MY CARACAS	101
VIII	EL CEDRAL	117
IX	REVOLUTION	132
X	UNDER THE SURFACE	148
XI	"DIPS" AND OTHERS	162
XII	THE LANGUAGE OF THE TRIBE	178
XIII	WILLIAM TELL AND TERESA	198
XIV	LA FAMILIA	212
XV	MORE OF MY CARACAS	233
XVI	MORE REVOLUTION	252
XVII	EARLY BUSINESS LIFE	265
XVIII	FROM MACHETE TO PEINILLA	279
XIX	UNDER FIRE	293
XX	CUSTOMS OF THE TRIBE	307
XXI	THE BOSTONIAN RETURNS	319

List of Illustrations

The author at the age of eighteen . . . . . *Frontispiece*

FACING PAGE

General Alejandro Ybarra, the author's father, at the time of his marriage 40

A favorite picture of the author's mother, Nelly Russell de Ybarra 40

Family group (including "Yessie") in front of the Ybarra home, Monte Elena 96

The Plaza Bolívar in Caracas showing statue of the Liberator and the Cathedral (*Underwood-Stratton photo*) 113

General Ybarra in uniform as Military Governor of Caracas 192

Monte Elena, the Ybarra home in El Paraíso, just outside Caracas 209

A view of Caracas from El Calvario (*Underwood-Stratton photo*) 240

The Pantheon in Caracas where national heroes, including Simón Bolívar and two members of the author's family, are buried (*Underwood-Stratton photo*) 257

YOUNG MAN OF
CARACAS

Chapter I

Pre-Tom

It all goes back to 1874, six years before I was born. Judge Thomas Russell, Collector of the Port of Boston, returned one afternoon from his office to his home. The latter was on Hancock Street, directly behind the Massachusetts State House, which perches so impressively on the top of Beacon Hill. Walking into the drawing room of his house, Judge Russell abruptly asked his wife and his three young daughters:

"How would you like to go to Venezuela?"

Their immediate answer is not on record. It probably consisted mostly of dropping whatever they were doing at the moment and turning their eyes, in expectant amazement, on the Honorable Thomas Russell. Having achieved his effect, in accordance with the ancient rules of drama, the head of the family gave the following explanation:

General Ulysses S. Grant, President of the United States, had seen fit to request his acceptance of the post of United States Minister to Venezuela. This was as a reward, I have since gathered, for yeoman service done the Republican party in Massachusetts politics.

After eager inquiries and excited discussion as to where and what Venezuela might be, the reply to his question resolved itself into a collective family O.K. to President Grant's request. But that request elicited no family enthusiasm, especially from Judge Russell's three daughters. They were having too good a time in Boston. Besides, they had been led to expect that if they *must* leave their friends and the daily round of amusement and youthful love affairs, it would be in order to go to Spain or Italy. In one of those countries (rumor had been saying) Thomas Russell was to represent the United States.

But Venezuela! Dreadful! The Russells—Mary Ellen, wife of Thomas, aged forty-four; Minnie (Mary Ann), aged twenty; Nelly, aged sixteen; and Dora, aged thirteen—when they heard Thomas Russell's news, felt as if he had been appointed United States Envoy Extraordinary and Minister Plenipotentiary to the Forest Primeval. Nelly wrote in her diary: "Oh, ye scorpions, tarantulas, centipedes and cockroaches! I feel so tingly all over!"

But they soon recovered from the first shock. Love of travel lay in their blood. Mrs. Russell was a daughter of "Father" Taylor, Boston's renowned apostle to mariners, who, in his youth, before he became a preacher ashore, had long faced the dangers of the sea. Her two older daughters had already been abroad; once, in a sailing ship, to the Azores. All three of them, like herself, were soon thrilled at the thought of coming change and adventure. Especially Nelly Russell, aged sixteen. I am convinced that within a very short time after the explosion of her father's bombshell she was speaking of mysterious Venezuela with the sparkle of pure joy in her brown eyes, and dancing with excitement at the idea of going there. You see, in later times I got to know Nelly Russell pretty well. She was my mother.

Decision having been arrived at, Judge Russell and his wife and daughters circulated the news among their kin and friends

PRE-TOM

in Boston—also in Plymouth, for the Russells were of Pilgrim stock, descendants of Myles Standish. I can imagine the excitement and shock occasioned among conservative Bostonese. I can imagine the impact of the news on staid Plymouthians, who had come to believe that adventure had ended for them and theirs with the disappearance of the last Indian from Plymouth Woods—or, if not quite so early as that, with George Washington, or, possibly, Abraham Lincoln. What had Venezuela to do with Thomas Russell, born within a stone's throw of Burial Hill, who had left home for Harvard on one of the old Plymouth-Boston stage coaches?

While the astonishment created by their report was at its height, the Russells sailed away toward the land of mystery to the southward, which fate (in the bearded and clamlike person of Ulysses S. Grant) had designated as their new place of residence. That land, to one of them at least, was to mean romance and thrill, happiness and heartache, grief and adventure and fruition.

The Russells set out for Venezuela on a steamship called the *Claribel*. She may have considered herself a passenger boat; but, according to all that I have been able to piece together from my mother's descriptions, the *Claribel* was no better than a tramp, with sketchy accommodations for a few nonmembers of the crew. On her way southward, she distinguished herself by running aground on a reef somewhere in the West Indies. Adventure Number One for Nelly Russell.

"I can't write well," remarked Thomas Russell in a letter home, "as we are on a coral reef and thumping hard. . . . We were soon surrounded by Negro wreckers more anxious to help themselves than to help us. They came like crows when a horse dies. . . . The children hope to live on the little island for ten days, in tents made out of sails. But we may get off. I hope so, for the captain's sake. Otherwise, I should like the experience and the extra time for learning Spanish. . . . Min says: 'Isn't it just our luck to have all the good of a shipwreck without its discomfort?' "

The just-appointed American diplomat also chronicled:

"There was a deckhand who, in a panic, when the ship ran aground, kept wailing, 'Oh, I shall never see my wife again, God damn!' "

Soon the *Claribel*, having been eased off the reef, proceeded to La Guaira, in Venezuela, the seaport of the Venezuelan capital, Caracas.

Today, modern steamships make the run from the United States to La Guaira in four or five days. The *Claribel* must have taken, counting in her sojourn on the reef, several weeks. At La Guaira, today, Americans, including thousands of tourists every year, land at a regular breakwater-wharf. There, steamers tie up in regulation style and put down a regular gangplank to let passengers go ashore.

But when Judge Russell and his wife and daughters reached La Guaira, there were no such conveniences. They had to climb down a rope ladder lowered from the deck of the *Claribel* into rowboats awaiting them. Then the rowboats were propelled shoreward by dark-skinned *Guaireños*, who shot them deftly through the pounding surf and landed them, with a bump, on the beach. Adventure Number Two for Nelly Russell—met by her, I feel sure, with squeals of delight.

In those days the boats monopolizing the passenger-landing business were run by a rough Spaniard with a flair for making money and no respect for anything savoring of culture, not even a boiled shirt. Twenty years later, in the Venezuela of my childhood, that boatman's daughter and son were socialites. She got dresses from Paris. He spent most of his time in boiled shirts.

Today, Americans who land at La Guaira proceed to Caracas mostly by automobile along an excellent macadamized road, chockful of thrills. Or they go by rail. Road and railway wind in long spirals up the steep side of the mountain range that separates the Venezuelan seacoast from the interior of the country, turning the beeline distance of six or seven miles into something around twenty-five miles.

But when the Russells were dumped on La Guaira's waterfront by one of the boats of that Spaniard, there was neither carriage road nor railroad to take them on the next lap of their journey. For them there was only the old Spanish muletrack. You can still see it from the La Guaira waterfront. It goes zigzagging up the mountain behind the seaport, past the forts of El Vigía and San Carlos, which, since the days of Spanish overlordship, have frowned over La Guaira and dropped cannonballs on unwelcome visitors.

In the Caracas just about to enter the last quarter of the nineteenth century, the Russells met a welcome that was royal in its sincerity. The Caraqueños eagerly sought the acquaintance of the new American Minister and his family. Formal calls were made on them by ladies and gentlemen of sonorous Spanish nomenclature. These calls were duly answered by Thomas Russell, by Mary Ellen, his wife, and by Minnie and Nelly, his two older daughters. And Dora Russell, aged thirteen, was soon playing in patios rich in southern flowers and topped by graceful palm trees, with little playmates answering to names never heard in the Old Bay State—Mercedes and Solita and María del Cármen.

With it all went fine touches of Castilian courtesy. To his brother-in-law, Marston Watson (bosom friend of Emerson and Thoreau), on the Watson estate of Hillside in Plymouth, Thomas Russell wrote: "Here in Caracas one meets delightful hospitality. Already a dozen gentlemen have placed their horses at my disposal."

The Russells were soon deep in the life of their new home. So busy were they socially during the hours of daylight that, as the head of the family put it in a letter: "We are never quite ready to have the sun set." As for the hours of darkness!—well, Thomas Russell and his wife soon lagged far behind Minnie, Nelly and even little Dora as that active trio jumped delightedly into the nocturnal festivities of Venezuela's effervescent metropolis.

"The nights are made for sleep," wrote the American Minister, who had reached that portal of sedateness, his fiftieth year, "with the cool breeze from the mountains, of which you can be certain every evening. I am beginning to understand why people become fascinated with Caracas and love to stay here."

He marveled at the polyglot foreign acquaintances who soon bobbed up around him. Among them he found persons who could speak—besides Spanish—French, German, English, Italian and even Dutch.

"The time which I spent on Greek," he remarked enviously, "would have enabled me to talk in two or three of these languages. If I had money to leave for public purposes, I would give it to lecturers to advise young men not to go to Harvard College."

Now and then, in the midst of his growing liking for Caracas and its ways, the visitor from Massachusetts found something that jarred him. For instance, the fruit known as "lechoza" (pawpaw). He hated it. (So do I.) It grew in the garden of the house that he had rented as a residence. "The lechoza makes a sickish sweet," he informed Marston Watson, "that is much better to give than to receive." And he refused to be weaned away from loyalty to the delicacies of Massachusetts. "People coming to the tropics," he wrote home, "think of tropical fruits as the chief luxuries. But *we* place Indian meal first and fish balls second. . . . I believe our servants think it is a mark of Protestantism to eat 'fish cakes.' . . ."

Nor did Mrs. Russell abandon the New England cooking for which she was famous in the circle of her kinsfolk and friends in Boston and Plymouth. Caracas became acquainted with pie. Also with turkey stuffing, Massachusetts style. Indeed, Judge Russell's wife produced the latter in such superlative excellence as to cause her husband to report that the German Minister had sent a dispatch about it to Bismarck.

The Russells found themselves in a typical Spanish colonial capital. Its Spanish masters had left it scarcely half a century before. Aged men still walked along its streets who had fought against Spain under Simón Bolívar, the renowned South American Liberator. Younger men took off their hats in reverence to these old fellows, the *próceres* of Venezuela's era of glory. Everybody listened with respect to their tales of what they had done in the battles that had freed Venezuela and other parts of South America at the beginning of the nineteenth century—Carabobo and Boyacá, Pichincha and Junín and Ayacucho.

Caracas, when the new American Minister and his family first saw it, had narrow cobbled streets. After a heavy rainstorm, a torrent of muddy water swirled over some of these thoroughfares, since the city slanted downward toward the river Guaire from the foot of the mountains that cut it off from the sea. At such times, enterprising members of the lower class kicked off their sandals, rolled their trousers above their knees, and offered their services as human ferries for taking citizens and citizenesses from one sidewalk to the other. The ferrying charge was a few *centavos*. Many possessors of the fare availed themselves of this impromptu ferry service. If they did not, the only alternative was to remove one's shoes and socks or stockings, and plunge into the yellow flood—an expedient out of the question, of course, for ladies in that formal little Spanish community. Or pedestrians could wait—for these sudden inundations never lasted long. In a few minutes the sun would come out again, the streets would dry off, and the ferryman's occupation would be gone.

Caracas soon took revenge on the Russell girls for the reluctance to make its acquaintance that they had shown in Boston. It completely won their hearts. They took to its friendly way of life with the zest of their youth.

Minnie, aged twenty, with a formidable record of seriously disturbed Massachusetts hearts already to her credit, soon began to add pining Latins to her list. Once—her father reported to a doubtless greatly shocked Plymouth—she almost provoked a duel. It was prevented, fortunately, by a "Cuban gentleman" who stepped in between "two of Min's friends who were going out from a ball to fight on the spot, and so decide some question as to dancing." Furthermore, Plymouth learned that "Min has driven a second lover into an engagement. They make a final attack on her, threaten to marry someone else, and then rush off and offer themselves. It is much better than suicide."

Minnie and Nelly and Dora proceeded to adapt themselves most successfully to their exotic environment. "The children look very Spanish," wrote their father, "perched up behind the window bars, and still more so when they go to mass in their black lace veils."

Despite her conquests, Minnie Russell remained love-proof. In Caracas, as in Boston and later in Europe, she smiled on her swains and went her way untouched by Cupid. She lived until she was forty—to die, still unmarried, in Munich. To the end she agitated men's hearts.

I remember, when I was a small boy in Munich, shortly before my Aunt Minnie's death, how the members of the family were thrown into convulsions of merriment by a letter addressed to my grandmother. It was a solemn letter, from a Munich matrimonial agent. A German client, of unimpeachable family, character and solvency, had seen Aunt Minnie and fallen for her at first sight. Nothing would calm his tumultuous heart but marriage. Therefore, as became a respectable suitor of the eighteen-nineties, with honorable intentions raging in his bosom, he had asked that matrimonial agent to present to my grandmother a formal offer for her daughter's hand.

My grandmother, whose sense of humor was impish, shrieked with joy. So did Minnie Russell's two sisters. The honorable Teuton, let us hope, found consolation elsewhere. And Aunt Minnie died a few months later without having stood at the altar with an honorable Teuton or anybody else. Nor did she carry to the grave (as I suppose she should have) a sense of frustration. "Never in all my life," she confided to her sisters, in the days of her devastating progress from one lovelorn suppliant to another, "have I met a man with whom I would like to take breakfast."

Bustled along by his energetic young daughters, the new United States Minister to Venezuela saw the sights of Caracas, especially the churches. They searched eagerly for old jewelry and other relics of the days of Spanish rule in Venezuela. These, however, were difficult to find; most of the treasures of Caracas had been given by the patriotic citizens to Bolívar to help the Liberator finance the war of independence against the Spaniards. But now and then the Russells ran across a rich prize.

"I had the most beautiful rosary and cross offered me for its weight in gold," Judge Russell wrote to his Aunt Jane in Plymouth, "but I haven't any use for it, and Min declined to regard *AM* (Ave Maria) as *MA* (Mary Ann)."

Nelly Russell, aged sixteen, sparkling and vibrant, drank deep of the strange life around her. And little Dora—a severe and aloof New Englander even then—picked and chose from the impact of foreign manners and customs such impressions as pleased her highly discriminating nature. A native of Caracas asked her once whether the people of Boston were Christians or Protestants. "Most of them," replied thirteen-year-old Miss Russell, "are both."

The Russell girls valiantly tackled the Spanish language. For the two eldest, a highly respectable old Caracas gentleman was employed as a teacher. To every lesson the giggling young things brought tales of their daily adventures in the exotic city

PRE-TOM

where their father was representing the United States. For instance, Minnie and Nelly told the solemn pedagogue that when they had walked past a certain street corner, a group of young Venezuelan males had addressed a remark to them.

"What remark?" asked the teacher.

"Those young men," replied Minnie and Nelly, with wide-open eyes, "said, as we went by: 'the buzzards!'"

"Impossible!" exclaimed the old gentleman, outraged to the core of his Spanish soul.

"That's what they said," insisted the two sisters, vigorously nodding their curly heads.

"Tell me in Spanish exactly what you heard."

"*Los zamuros.*"

"Impossible, *niñas*, absolutely impossible!"

"But that's what those men did call us."

"Say it slowly."

"*Los za-mu-ros.*"

The teacher's eyes lighted up. He smiled in overwhelming relief.

"What they said was '*los amores!*'" (Whereas "*los zamuros*" means "the buzzards," "*los amores*" means "the loves," or, better, "the sweethearts.")

Judge Russell also wrestled manfully with the local language and customs. He was much struck by the exuberant rhetoric dished out by Venezuelans to one another and to foreigners, especially in official correspondence.

"Their main idea," he confided to Aunt Jane, "is to tell polite falsehoods in words of six syllables." He also informed her: "Transitive verbs in Spanish must govern something. This reminds me that, as a rule, active Spanish verbs, though they govern things, can't govern persons without the aid of a preposition. It is a queer streak of politeness and respect for humanity. We are now accustomed to the invariable use of the third person. 'You' is a lost word, and everybody is addressed as 'Your Honor.' 'Will Your Honor unbutton the trousers of Your Honor' is the preface to a spanking in this country."

In another letter he wrote, with perfect gravity, about the puzzled American visitor in Caracas who had called at the Legation for advice on a knotty problem: should he or should he not accept the invitation of a Venezuelan gentleman who had "put his house and goods and family" at the disposal of the gentleman from the North.

"I prefer to stay at the hotel," that American explained plaintively to the United States Minister, "but I don't wish to offend." He was much relieved, Judge Russell announced, "on learning that the phrase meant nothing—no more than the offer to kiss her feet, with which any note to a lady should end."

Minister Russell soon became acquainted with Antonio Guzmán Blanco, the dictator of Venezuela, whom he found a very ornamental and forceful individual. At that time, Guzmán —one of the most remarkable figures in the turbulent history of Venezuela—was on the crest of the wave. Four years before he had vanquished his foes in a spectacular campaign culminating in the capture of Caracas street by street and house by house. He was busily decreeing reforms, announcing the building of roads, opening schools, and otherwise trying to live up to the grand titles that he had officially bestowed on himself— *El Ilustre Americano* (The Illustrious American) and Regenerator of Venezuela.

Guzmán was an exceedingly good-looking personage, of martial carriage and distinguished bearing, capable of impressing even the least impressionable foreigner. Thomas Russell,

PRE-TOM

anything but unimpressionable, absorbing all the novelty around him with avidity, was much struck by the dictator. Marston Watson, Aunt Jane and other regular recipients of letters from Thomas were soon learning a lot about Venezuela's Big Boss.

"Last Sunday," Thomas told Aunt Jane, "I called on President Blanco" (later Judge Russell learned to say either Guzmán or Guzmán Blanco, in correct Spanish-American fashion). "I have never seen a handsomer or more elegant man. He was very pleasant and introduced me to his beautiful wife. A group of bright children were playing in the room, no more afraid of their father than mine are of me. Yet he must be a bad man for his enemies to meet in battle—or just after one.

"He has asked the Dutch government to drive one General Díaz from Curaçao (an island belonging to Holland, off the coast of Venezuela), where he is plotting a revolution. The Minister (of Holland) says that General D. shall be sent away if there is as much proof against him as there was against General Blanco when he planned *his* revolution in the same place. In the meantime, General D. keeps a boarding school. For, when these generals are not ruling or rebelling, they teach, or sell charcoal, or go out wet-nursing, or turn their hands to something else that is useful."

Describing another call that he and his wife paid on the dictator, Judge Russell wrote home:

"We were glad to find children more thoroughly spoiled than ours."

After that came a big official reception, given, in honor of the new representative of the United States, by Guzmán Blanco.

"He wore," wrote Thomas Russell, "a beautiful miniature of Washington, which has a history. The Washington family, after Washington's death, placed his miniature and a lock of his hair in a medal, which Congress had voted to G. W., and gave it to Lafayette. He sent it to Bolívar, telling him that G. W. would have honored him (Bolívar) more than any other man alive or dead. And now a nephew of General Bolívar has given it to Guzmán. . . . It is too precious for any man to own or wear. I have never seen any likeness of G. W. so pleasant."

In the same letter, Judge Russell added:

"A little girl, a friend of mine, always calls me George Washington, associating his name with the U. S. We asked her what she knew about him, and she attacked a tree with an imaginary hatchet. So that fable of Mr. Weems has come here also, but apparently without the moral."

The American Minister derived much amusement from Venezuelan ways. He quotes the following officially announced reason for the postponement of a religious ceremony: "To allow the people to attend the horse race, and *because King Herod has a cold.*"

In the early eighteen-seventies, the convents scattered all over Caracas by the Spaniards had mostly disappeared, owing to Guzmán Blanco's strong anti-clerical tinge. After becoming Venezuela's supreme ruler in 1870, he started a private war against the Pope. The Russells found the most important convents and monasteries already emptied of the pious men and women who had occupied them for generations. But the ecclesiastical air of other days still hovered over the city. One of its principal corners was known as "The Nuns." The name of another was "The Carmelites." A third was "The Ragged Brothers." Still another recalled a long-dead priest, Padre Sierra. These names persist to this day. Nuns and monks have

PRE-TOM

vanished, but the memory of their serene lives still clings to the places where, scores of years ago, they prayed and fasted and moved in contempt of worldliness.

When the Russells lived in Caracas, Dictator Guzmán Blanco was not confining himself to chasing nuns and monks out of town. Already he had started an ambitious modernization of the pretty little metropolis dozing in the shadows of its towering mountains. Old houses of the Spanish era were being torn down to be replaced by a pretentious *Capitolio*. Plans were under discussion for a fine theater. There was to be a carriage road to La Guaira. Even a railroad was talked about, which some day was to link the hot little port, where the Russells had landed, with Venezuela's capital.

Judge Russell, though a native of the great republic of push and progress, looked askance at these projects. In the midst of his delight in studying old customs, derived from a Spanish past of grace and leisure, he was afraid that Guzmán's "improvements" might spoil the fair land in which he found himself.

"There is much talk of a railroad now," he wrote home, "but the same Providence that has saved this city before will probably interpose—Providence aided by bad credit."

Of another threatened "improvement" he registered this opinion:

"There is one great advantage in living here which doctors don't appreciate. There is no telegraph. Nobody knows the blessed effect on the nerves—besides, think of the time you lose, and the wear and tear in reading news, true or false, three times a day. Here, a Weekly [Boston] *Advertiser* three weeks old, or a St. Thomas Times, of a fortnight ago, furnishes a gentle stimulant with sedative tendencies."

However, only a few signs of coming revolutionary upheaval in architecture and other directions were as yet visible in Caracas. Judge Russell and his wife and daughters still drank in an atmosphere that was essentially Spanish, untouched by modern progress, utterly different from the air they had breathed in Massachusetts.

Everything they saw and heard was new and strange—the horsemen clattering over the cobblestones—the red tiles on the low roofs—the ladies of Caracas, walking slowly, with pride in their eyes and mantillas on their heads, to early Mass at the Cathedral or La Merced. These ladies were followed, a few steps behind, by female servants, in deference to the unwritten law that, laid down by Spain hundreds of years before, was still faithfully obeyed by these descendants of the Spaniards, despite the fact that they had emancipated themselves from Spanish rule.

Though the Russell sisters, particularly Nelly, were delighted with the exotic milieu into which they had been pitchforked, they remained stubbornly loyal to the free-and-easy customs of Massachusetts. At home, they had been in the habit of harnessing a horse to a carriage and driving alone for miles through Plymouth Woods. They could see no reason for not acting the same way in Venezuela, though that abode of Spanish tradition had never allowed its young ladies to do anything so shocking. But Minnie and Nelly and Dora—with an "honi soit qui mal y pense" toss of their pretty New England heads—got hold of a carriage of sorts, had a horse placed between the shafts, and started off on a career of convention-shattering driving that is talked about in Caracas to this day.

Tongues wagged furiously. Some of them, especially if they belonged to sour old *beatas*, self-appointed female guardians of

PRE-TOM

the proprieties as ordained by the Spaniards of the seventeenth and eighteenth centuries, were barbed and cruel. "*Pero, niña* —have you heard about *las hijas del ministro americano?*" Other tongues, however, buzzed in delighted approval. The Russell girls had a way with them. And many of the Caraqueños, with a gallantry worthy of their courtly Spanish ancestors, smiled and chuckled and took off their hats as the carriage of the three *americanitas* went bumping over the city's narrow streets.

One day the horse snorted, stuck its tail straight up in the air, and ran away. It dashed past horrified shopkeepers gesticulating frantic advice from their doorways. It sped around sharp corners. It galloped past grand old mansions, while beautiful young señoritas, leaning on the iron bars of their front windows, turned pale with apprehension and acid old beatas muttered an apocalyptic "I told you so."

Finally, the careering horse, with the carriage and the three girls from Massachusetts careening dangerously behind him, hove in sight outside the portal of the San Pablo barracks. There the Venezuelan artillery had its quarters. At the front window, its commander was seated, young General Alejandro Ybarra.* He was a dashing young veteran of many fights and a favorite of Dictator Guzmán Blanco. The instant he saw the carriage of the *americanitas* approaching, he shouted to an orderly in the doorway to hurry into the street and stop the runaway.

The orderly ran out in obedience to his commander's directions. But he was too late. Nelly Russell was too quick for him. With her brown hair flying and her brown eyes flashing from

---

* The "j" is like our "h," the "y" like "ee" in English—thus, *Alehandro Eebarra*.

the thrill of the thing, she had jumped from the carriage, without the slightest tremor of fright, scampered to the horse's head, seized the bit, and thrown the panting animal back on its haunches. Such a stunt was nothing to her. Again and again, in the past, she had coped with similar emergencies in Plymouth Woods.

But young General Alejandro Ybarra had never, in all his life, seen a young lady act like that. It just wasn't done in his Caracas. Nelly Russell's madcap action flew straight in the face of the old Spanish traditions upon which that Caracas was built. It simply took the young warrior's breath away. It stunned him. "Shocking!" said one or two of the officers around him. For a minute he was speechless. Then, turning to his companions, he said:

"I am going to marry that girl!"

Chapter II

More Pre-Tom

AT a grand ball given by President Guzmán Blanco, the twenty-six-year-old commander of the Venezuelan artillery was formally introduced to the sixteen-year-old *americanita*. He asked her to dance.

Dispensing at once with formality, he began to make ardent love to her—100 per cent Spanish love, except for the fact that it wasn't in Spanish. Nelly Russell's knowledge of the language of Don Quixote, though it was progressing, was still entirely inadequate for coping with Spanish-speaking admirers (witness "los zamuros"). And young Alejandro Ybarra's English was not far from nonexistent. So he said pretty things, and she parried them, in French.

He conveyed his meaning, however, with perfect clearness. He wanted her to be his wife. He wanted her to marry him without absurd delay of any sort. And he said so. He said so to the rhythm of a waltz. He said so in polka tempo. He said so between the figures of a quadrille. And, on days after the President's dance, he said so to Nelly repeatedly, as he leaned against the iron rejas of a front window of the United States Minister's residence, and she sat on a cushion inside that residence, with a big Spanish fan to hide her coyness, just as if her ancestors had sailed from Andalusia instead of Devonshire. There was no resisting such an onslaught. Nelly Russell flipped her fan in a way that could not be misunderstood. And Alejandro Ybarra, in his delight, almost bent the iron rejas.

But the thing could not be done in the haphazard fashion of the informal North. The young general belonged to a family of prominence in Caracas. It was a family whose members held their heads high and walked with dignity and bowed to Spanish traditions brought to the New World by ancestors with the imprint of Spain on their features and the seal of Spain on their souls.

One day, shortly after that big dance, Dictator Guzmán Blanco in person, resplendent in his full military uniform, alighted from a carriage at the door of the American Legation. With him came a straight and stiff old gentleman—also a third visitor, much younger. The dictator and the old gentleman asked politely to see el señor Don Tomás Russell. (They pronounced it Rossell.)

Judge Russell's second visitor was Dr. Alejandro Ybarra, rector (or president, as we would say) of the University of Caracas. He was famous locally as a savant, as a man deeply versed in mathematics and philosophy and astronomy, as a genuine cultivator of the human spirit, unworldly and wise. Behind him walked that third visitor—young Alejandro Ybarra, Jr., a very important youth in Venezuelan military circles and in Venezuelan political life—and in his own estimation. He was reputed to have been chosen by Guzmán Blanco as heir to the latter's dictatorial power. But, as he stood there by the door of the American Legation, in the shadow of his austere father, he was most obviously not only playing second fiddle but playing it pianissimo. Venezuelans of that time may not have heard the old French saying, "il y a toujours la manière," but that's the way they acted, just the same.

The visitors were taken into the sanctum of the American Minister. There they were courteously greeted by Judge Russell. The dictator and the professor seated themselves on big chairs close to their host. The young general seated himself on a small chair in a far corner of the room.

"I have come to you," announced the rector of the University of Caracas, with immense dignity, "to ask that you do me the honor of consenting to bestow the hand of your daughter, la señorita Nelly Russell, on my son Alejandro." (Here the old savant gave a casual nod in the direction of young Alejandro, who fingered the gold buttons on his uniform, fidgeted with his sword and looked uncomfortably at the carpet.)

The atmosphere was pretty overpowering for cheerful Thomas Russell. But he did his best to live up to it. In language which, he hoped, would pass muster with his courtly guests, he replied (Thomas Russell was not without knowledge of what had been going on between Nelly and the tongue-tied warrior in the background) that he deemed it an honor indeed to bestow the hand of his daughter on the son of such a distinguished father and the scion of such an illustrious house—or words to that effect.

The old professor stood up. So did the dictator. They bowed. Judge Russell bowed. They shook hands. The distinguished guests stalked majestically toward the door. Behind them, Alejandro Ybarra, Jr., general of artillery, veteran of fifty fights, prime favorite of Dictator Guzmán Blanco, followed unobtrusively, respectfully, like a puppy with its tail between its legs.

In his next letter home, dated June sixth, 1875, Thomas Russell said:

"I shall write to you this time to tell you of Nelly's engagement to General Ybarra. . . . He is decidedly the first young man in Venezuela. . . . He was made a general . . . for courage in a battle, and, when he was twenty, saved a campaign by carrying the artillery over a country supposed to be impossible and then fighting seven days. . . . He also brought a war steamer here with the crew all bribed to destroy her, so that he had to stand by the wheel, with one pistol pointed at the pilot's ear and another pointed toward the engineer's room. He talks English enough to be understood—by Nelly, at least. . . . He plays on the piano and composes music sometimes, and he has served in the army since he was fifteen, without taking a glass of wine. . . . He is now major-general, in command of the artillery. . . . The family is a very old and good one, which is of no consequence anywhere else, but means here that the men and women have been gentlemen and ladies ever since the days of the Moorish wars in Spain, and a few odd centuries before, I suppose. . . .

"It is not pleasant to think of Nelly's living so far away. But if, after coming home and spending some time among old scenes, she wants to go, then she loves her General enough to live with him and there is nothing else to be done. . . .

"It is not strange that she should be pleased with General Y., for he is far superior to the Harvard youths who were her friends in Boston. Of course, his age and variety of experience make the comparison unfair to them. The whole city is gratified with the compliment which she is supposed to have paid to Venezuela, and they are all delighted with the hope of having her live here. She never could find a place where she would be more appreciated. Last night there was an exchange of rings. Gen. Ybarra gave her a diamond which his godfather gave him when he was confirmed, at the age of five, and which he then declared he would keep for his bride."

Judged strictly from the Massachusetts standpoint, young Alejandro Ybarra was beyond doubt a strange specimen of humanity. He was the sort of thing that just wasn't done in Boston and Plymouth. Behind his impeccable Spanish manners there lurked a cowboy and a daredevil and a swashbuckler. That handsome youth, of classical Spanish features, endowed with a Spanish dignity of carriage that came to him as naturally as sleeping when he was tired and eating when he was hungry, had seen men shot dead beside him in hand-to-hand combat. He had been struck by three bullets. One of these, he casually informed his fiancée from the calm North, was still somewhere in his leg, just above the ankle. He had been hit by that bullet in a rough-and-tumble fight in the Venezuelan town of Barcelona. There he had stood on a barricade and blazed away with his pistol point blank at charging assailants. In that same encounter he had been wounded by a second bullet. That one, however, had been extracted.

"In a field hospital?" inquired Nelly.

"No—in the drawing room of my father's house here in Caracas, after I had been brought there from Barcelona."

"You felt no pain, of course?"

"No pain?" The eyes of the young man opened wide. "What do you mean, no pain?"

"Surely, the anesthetics . . ."

"Anesthetics? There weren't any!"

The third bullet that had hit him, he told Nelly, was a spent one. It had struck him right over the heart and fallen to the ground beside him without leaving a mark. "If it had had any force behind it," he used to say to me in later years, "you would have been somebody else."

Shortly afterward, young General Ybarra's prospective father-in-law told Aunt Jane in Plymouth:

"I live in retirement, and cook my doughnuts by an alcohol apparatus in my room, far from the excitement of the parlor, so that I don't realize what is going on as much as I otherwise should. However, if Nell is to marry anyone, I like the General as well as I should any man, and this is the only place where that young woman will be considered an angel just from heaven."

Nelly's mother also approved. She wrote, in allusion to her son-in-law-to-be: "You would have such a good time watching his splendid eyes as he doubles over Nell's hammock and hearing him make plans as gravely as if they were already married. After they have been engaged six months, he says, he is going to ask 'when may I be married?'—and, if he is put out of the house, he will stand on the street and say it until papa will be very glad to get rid of him by giving him Nell."

I am inclined to believe that the young soldier pulled the long bow occasionally in telling Nelly Russell about his adventures in and between battles. After all, he was trying to fascinate a girl who came from a milieu that knew nothing of revolutions. And no story ever told by Alejandro Ybarra—then and always an admirable raconteur—ever suffered in the telling. No matter how much he embroidered, however, the truth about him was enough to thrill any young girl from the North or any other point of the compass.

His education—like the dress of the ladies of a certain tribe in the Philippines, described by Mr. Dooley—had been "hurried and incomplete." Until he was fourteen years old he had received schooling of a vague sort in his native Caracas. Then he ran away from home to become a soldier. He joined the Liberals, who were, at that time, deep in a particularly bitter civil war against the Conservatives. The story I remember best about that first phase of my father's military career was of how he butted into a circus performance, at a small town in the interior of Venezuela, and spent the evening playing the bass drum in the band.

His father lured him back home with a promise that he would be allowed to enroll himself in the artillery school of Caracas. That is the last I ever heard of his education. I don't even know how long he attended the artillery school. I do know, however, that a very short time after his enrollment there as a student he was firing cannon instead of learning how to fire them.

After his engagement had been formally announced, General Ybarra was on an entirely different footing with the Russells. According to Spanish-Venezuelan custom, he could now enter their home with the informality that became one who was practically a son to Thomas Russell and his wife, and a brother to Minnie and Dora, the sisters of his fiancée—both of whom had been watching the unrolling love drama of Nelly and Alejandro with twinkling eyes and concentrated attention. The young soldier no longer had to stand out on the street with the iron rejas between him and Nelly when he wished—as a flirtatious friend of mine used to phrase it—"to blow sugar in the ear" of his ladylove. Instead, he could now actually seat himself by her side at a front window of her home, where all Caracas could see him in the full tide of his happiness.

Of course, being ardent and devoted, he rolled his flashing eyes at Nelly. And he twisted his splendid mustache (to the end of his days he never shaved it; he merely trimmed it, keeping, until his death, what he termed "the original silk"). He urged his fiancée, in flowery Castilian, to make a doormat of him, to command him to do whatsoever she pleased that he might rush to obey. She took it all, I feel sure, with her customary humorous aplomb. Nelly Russell refused everywhere and at all times to take life seriously. On the Day of Judgment, I know, she will crack jokes with the Angel Gabriel—and make him like it!

As the young general uttered his amorous eloquence in deep resonant tones, she dubbed him "The Boomer." After they were married (probably to curb disrespect toward him on the part of their children) she dropped this appellation. Her favorite names for him, in my childhood, were Alito and Tico (both pronounced with the "i" as in Puerto Rico).

In those early Caracas days, her betrothed was a chain-smoker. His daily quota of cigarettes was something phenomenal, even in tobacco-enslaved Venezuela. At first Nelly tried to be bighearted about it; she wasn't going to be a meddler, a kill-joy; most certainly not! After a while, however, that eternal cigarette, dangling from under those silken mustachios, began to annoy her. Finally, when she and her young chain-smoker were seated behind the rejas one afternoon, Nelly blew up. Pointing to the cigarette in his mouth—probably his fortieth for that day—she said, with as much severity as she could muster:

"There's that nasty thing again!"

He snatched it from his mouth, tossed it through the rejas into the street outside.

"Never again, as long as I live," he vowed dramatically, "will I smoke!"

Grand stuff. Typical lover's stuff, you will say. Anything to impress the loved one favorably. Old stuff. But now comes the surprising part of the story:

Alejandro Ybarra never smoked again. He who had puffed at cigarettes, until his fingers were stained brown and nicotine seemed to have entered into his blood, never again put a cigarette between his lips. Also, he never made any compromise. Unlike many men who get into the habit of smoking cigarettes to excess, he did not substitute cigars. Nor did he start smoking a pipe.

What he had said that night, in the gust of a young lover's adoration, he meant for a lifetime. That was a real vow he made, at the reja of his beloved in Caracas, under the stars and moon of a lover's skies, with care far away, and youth throbbing, and many years ahead of him for savoring the solace of tobacco. I knew him for nearly forty years. Not only did I never see him smoke, but I never heard him talk about how he had loved to smoke. There was steel in Alejandro Ybarra, steel worthy of the steel in Nelly Russell.

Of course, Nelly went much to his home, the old *casa solariega* (so called because it was built on a *solar*, or plot, granted by the King of Spain) of the Rivas family, a daughter of which old Dr. Ybarra had married. It was a big house of the eighteenth century, with two stories, a rarity in the Caracas of those days. It had high ceilings and spacious rooms, and two big patios. There was also a damp, dark corridor, with little cubbyholes opening off it, where—the Ybarras told Nelly, in tones of mystery—"the slaves used to live."

In that old mansion Nelly got to know her fiancé's learned father, who liked her from the moment he first laid his solemn eyes on her. . . . She also met his wife—*Misia Merced*, as people called her—who never really liked Nelly. Misia Merced, somehow, resented her. The barrier between them was religion. The least that a daughter-in-law could do, opined my father's mother—and she had generations of Caracas tradition to back her—was to have been born a Roman Catholic. And here was Nelly Russell, who didn't even know exactly what she was —one day she thought herself an Episcopalian; the next she woke up feeling symptoms of Unitarianism.

Clash of religion, by the way, pursued my mother all through her married life. In Caracas, some relatives and friends simply could not reconcile themselves to her Protestantism, though Heaven knows it sat lightly on her shoulders. And, in the North, that husband of hers was strange enough from any point of view, but what seemed strangest of all to some of Nelly's people, grouped in their cold homes under the shadow of the State House dome, was that, on her exotic travels, she should have fished up a Roman Catholic for a spouse. Such things, as Beacon Hill saw it, were proper only in remote foreign lands, or in the still remoter South End.

But Nelly didn't care. When, after her marriage, her husband requested that the Ybarra-Russell children should be reared as Catholics, she answered, "Why, of course." And it was my Protestant mother, and not my Catholic father, who used to say to me, when I, aged five or thereabouts, would go racing through my Roman Catholic prayers: "Tom, you simply must NOT mumble when you pray!"

Meanwhile, Minnie Russell refused to allow the engagement of her younger sister to eclipse her own importance in the family home and beyond its portals.

MORE PRE-TOM

"Did Nelly tell you of Min's grandeur at the ball?" asked her father in a letter to Plymouth, apropos of a formal function at the dictator's palace. "As the other married diplomats are only chargés, Mrs. Russell is at the head of the female wing. In her absence, Min takes her place, and is, next to Mrs. Guzmán Blanco, the first lady. So the President sent a general to take her in to supper first and seat her at the head of the diplomatic table. . . . Min is not so set up that she can't work. She cut out a white dress yesterday and the young lady in the next house sewed it."

Continuing his quizzical contemplation of people and things around him, Thomas Russell told Aunt Jane:

"Congress here is very funny. They all wear dress coats and white neckerchiefs, and they all speak well, but have no occasion to speak much, except in eulogizing Guzmán and Bolívar. When they adjourn for the day, the country members go to the Singer Sewing Machine store and learn to use the machines, so as to teach their wives. For each one invests part of his pay in a sewing machine to carry home; and so, by degrees, civilization is carried among the Andes and up the Orinoco."

To Marston Watson, Thomas remarked:

"It is pleasant to live in a country where the President is a gentleman (not for publication). . . . Everything is queer and picturesque, and the people are the kindest and most courteous that I ever heard of. The commonest sort, who don't know us or expect to know us, learn just enough English to salute us when they meet us on the street. To be sure, they say 'good night' when they mean 'good evening,' but that is more amusing. . . . Religion is not prosperous here, but the music and shows are fine, and there is not a church in Venezuela where such a man as Henry Ward Beecher would be allowed to officiate for a day."

Young Alejandro Ybarra continued much in evidence. "We went to a great party at the Ybarras'," wrote the American Minister. "It was the greatest collection of old Caracas families that I have ever seen, but I was satisfied to leave before 12, and did not envy Min and Nell their nine hours of dancing from 9 until 6 A.M. General Y. left at the same time, to ride over the mountain to La Guaira, where he was serenaded by the military, and, next night, by the citizens. They are fighting from time to time in La Guaira in preparation for a greater fight—like olives before dinner. Perhaps General Y. will stop it, as he is a favorite there. Nobody knows what it is about, but peace makes them uneasy."

After Nelly and her young general had been engaged for a while, he was made military commander of La Guaira. He held sway over the forts of El Vigía and San Carlos, and over the gloomy old *bóvedas*, dungeon beneath sea level, where the Spaniards used to imprison political prisoners—a custom continued by their Venezuelan successors. The Russells also moved from Caracas to La Guaira, in the hope that the sea breezes might improve the health of Mrs. Russell, who had been ailing almost throughout her sojourn in the Venezuelan capital.

The whole family were delighted with the change. Like good Old Colony folk, it did them good to smell salt air again.

"It is a great thing to live on the sea once more, or, rather, to live on the sea for the first time," wrote Thomas Russell, "for there is no harbor to hide the ocean, or break the force of the waves, or collect bad smells. We get fresh south winds from the open sea all day and a mountain breeze all night. There is no place in the world where the sea and the mountains meet in a grander way." His wife, also, waxed enthusiastic about "quaint houses perched on slopes, as if they had settled after a long flight, and were only resting."

Nelly and Minnie were ardent admirers of Charles Kingsley's *Westward Ho!* At once they started expeditions of research to discover where the Rose of Torridge had been imprisoned and where Amyas Leigh had performed the deeds so excitingly recorded by Kingsley in his celebrated novel about the Spanish Main.

When asked for his opinion on the subject, the young military commander of La Guaira blurted out the Spanish equivalent of "It's all nonsense!" When the Bostonians produced their worn copy of *Westward Ho!* he remarked, *de haut en bas*, that it was "just fiction."

Just fiction! Minnie and Nelly snorted in contemptuous disagreement. They were as sure that the Rose and Amyas Leigh had really existed as they were of the indisputability of the Bible. In vain Alejandro reasoned with them in lordly male superiority. They just snapped their fingers at him. (In later years, I also drank deeply of *Westward Ho!*, egged on by my mother, and I must confess that I also had a sneaking idea for some time that the Rose of Torridge really had put in a lot of boresome days and monotonous nights in La Guaira.)

During her engagement, both in Caracas and La Guaira, Nelly Russell did her best to live up to the complicated Spanish etiquette in the midst of which her young general had been reared. But now and then she slipped. Once, at a dinner, she remarked to a visiting foreigner:

"Yes, my fiancé's family is descended from the first archbishop of Caracas."

Hardly were the words out of her mouth before she felt a tug at her sleeve from a Venezuelan fellow-guest, seated on her other side—Félix Rivas, a cousin of young Alejandro. Leaning close to her ear, Félix—whose liking for Nelly ran neck and neck with his fear of what she might say next—whispered:

"*Connected with*, Nelly, *not descended from!*"

Years later, after Nelly and Alejandro were married, he got hold of a tombstone, which had stood, in the eighteenth century, over some of the remains of that first archbishop—not over *all* of them, for he had been so eminent that, after his death, he was divided up. My father was immensely proud of that tombstone. But my mother was against it. The inscription on it, she insisted, was too gruesome to have in plain sight around the house.

Her efforts to have it removed, however, were in vain. It long occupied a prominent position in our home. The inscription to which my mother objected ran thus:

UNDER THIS STONE

LIE

THE HEART AND EYES

OF

DON FRANCISCO DE YBARRA

FIRST ARCHBISHOP OF CARACAS

Chapter III

Still More Pre-Tom

EVERYTHING was going beautifully with love's young dream when, with appalling suddenness, international politics lifted its head and threw a bomb at the romance of Alejandro Ybarra and Nelly Russell.

As usual with revolutions in the South America of those disorderly days, the one that had landed Antonio Guzmán Blanco in the presidency of Venezuela had caused financial loss to a number of foreigners, who forthwith bellowed loudly to their governments for redress. Included in this chorus were several Americans. They felt that they had been badly mulcted by the hostilities that had preceded the dictatorship of El Ilustre Americano. So they promptly put in claims for large numbers of dollars.

These claims were among the headaches besetting Thomas Russell as United States Minister to Venezuela. They had been dragging along throughout his tenure of office in Caracas. Finally, the State Department at Washington urged upon him the advisability of prompt action.

Thomas Russell was nobody's fool. Behind all the gaiety and courtesy of Caracas he knew perfectly well that political corruption lurked. He knew that feathering one's nest was looked upon by many local politicos as the main reason for holding office; that, as a nest-featherer, Guzmán Blanco was a champion. He was fully aware that the Illustrious American had already laid the foundations of a great personal fortune.

So he decided to tell the government at Washington exactly what he was up against. He wrote a confidential dispatch to the State Department. It called a spade a spade. Unfortunately, the contents of the dispatch were made public. That ended the career of Thomas Russell as the representative of his country in Venezuela. The Guzmán Blanco government, extremely hot under the collar, requested him to leave Venezuela without delay.

Judge Russell informed his prospective son-in-law of what had happened. The young man rushed around to the dictator and protested stormily. The dictator also put on a stormy sketch. The story got all over Caracas. It took rank among the juiciest bits of gossip of its era. It was told to visiting foreigners. It got into print in the United States. It is actually enshrined between book covers.

I transcribe below the version of the scene between Guzmán and his young favorite given by William Eleroy Curtis, a famed American journalistic globe-trotter of those days. It appeared in that author's *Venezuela; A Land Where It's Always Summer*, published in 1896. Curtis appends it to a description of the overturning, by a Caracas mob, of statues put up by Guzmán Blanco to himself. Here is what the American author wrote:

"Another statue, which Guzmán erected in his own honor, in the plaza between the university and the Capitol, was twice pulled down, and the leader in the first indignity was the dictator's own nephew, the general in command of his army, and the man he was said to have chosen as his successor in power.

STILL MORE PRE-TOM

The circumstances were quite remarkable and involve a romance in which an American girl figured as the heroine.

"Mr. Russell, of Boston, was United States Minister to Venezuela during the Hayes administration. Being directed by Secretary Evarts to press for the payment of the claims of certain American citizens for losses incurred during the war by which Guzmán came into power, he replied that there were only two ways by which the money could be collected. One method, he said, was to send a man-of-war to bombard La Guaira. The other was to offer Guzmán a share of the money. This indiscreet dispatch, by a blunder of a clerk in the Department of State in Washington, was published, and, when an official translation was sent to the Illustrious American, he very promptly sent Mr. Russell his passports and ordered him to leave Venezuela instanter. There was a New York steamer in the harbor of La Guaira, and Mr. Russell was escorted on board by a file of soldiers.

"The Minister had a pretty daughter to whom General Ybarra, the nephew and favorite of Guzmán was engaged, and when the young man heard of the affair, he went to headquarters to protest against the indignities offered his prospective father-in-law. The President gave the young man his choice between the girl and the official honors and prospects he enjoyed. Breaking his sword over his knee, Ybarra threw the pieces at Guzmán's head. That afternoon a decree was issued relieving General Ybarra from the command of the army and canceling his commission.

"That night Ybarra gathered a few of his cronies and sawed through the bronze legs of the horse on which the effigy of his uncle sat, and, hitching a rope around the body, hauled it over.

Then, saddling a mule, he rode down the mountain path to La Guaira, joined his sweetheart on the steamer, and sailed for New York before his act was discovered. He married the girl and was too wise to return to Venezuela until his distinguished uncle had left the country. This was the greatest humiliation Guzmán Blanco ever suffered, and no one has dared to mention the name of Ybarra in his presence since."

That tale has some misstatements. Guzmán Blanco was not Alejandro Ybarra's uncle. There was no family connection between the two except that the dictator's wife was a cousin of the young general of artillery. Her maiden name was Ana Teresa Ybarra. Furthermore, Alejandro Ybarra was not commander of the Venezuelan army. Finally, he did not sail from La Guaira to New York with the Russells; he left Venezuela just before they did and waited for them on the island of St. Thomas (then Danish), where they stopped off on their way home.

Here is Thomas Russell's version of the quarrel with the Venezuelan dictator and the romantic episode that followed—contained in a letter from the ousted American diplomat to one of his kinsfolk in Plymouth:

"St. Thomas, Feb. 23, 1877

"We have come to St. Thomas on account of a little rupture between the U.S.A. and Guzmán Blanco. About two years since, said G. B. stated in his message that President Grant, in *his* message, had spoken of Venezuela with such disregard of truth that he (G. B.) had withdrawn his Minister. I felt as an American does when he hears his country abused in a strange land; and, being unable to complain of the message, made some unpleasant suggestions to our government and stated some disagreeable facts—requesting, of course, that they should not be published. They were omitted from the published dispatches. But, last July, the Democratic Congress wanted all the correspondence, and the President let them have it. For five months G. B. has brooded over it (without hatching). He has been quite friendly, especially when he wanted any favors; but, at last, roused by the obstinacy of the U. S. Minister in urging the rights of his countrymen, or provoked by seeing the letters copied in a European paper, he bursts out, and says he will no more deal with the said Minister. So we pack up and sell out and come here.

"Now comes the romance—G. B. sends for General Ybarra and tells him to choose between the service and his engagement, adding that, if he did not break the engagement, he would lose his pay for seven years, $15,000, which was already counted out and ready for him. General Ybarra answered: 'You, as a man of honor, cannot doubt what a man of honor will do. I resign my commission and ask a passport to leave this country.'

"It required some stratagem to get away, but he succeeded in reaching St. Thomas. Otherwise, he would have been put in prison. It is a hard thing for his family, and one old servant is paying him the compliment of dying of a broken heart. Caracas and La Guaira, where the General is much loved, were wild. . . . Even G. B.'s sister said 'Thank God for a man in Venezuela!' General Vicente Ybarra called to congratulate Dr. Ybarra, saying he had always been proud to be the son of Bolívar's first aide, and he was now proud to be a cousin of Alejandro. There are so many such people that G. B. cannot imprison them all. You have no idea how much courage it must have required to do what General Y. did.

"That brilliant wedding in our garden is to be exchanged for a very quiet one here. . . . We have come here after settling our worldly affairs and selling our goods. You have no idea what saleswomen Min and Nell are. They could make a fortune by keeping a fair for the heathen and dividing between themselves and the Hillsiders. By the way, Nelly figures as a Protestant in the Pope's Bull (or bull-calf), which he has issued for her marriage with a Catholic.

"We had a delightful voyage here, with a flavor of elopement about it, as the marriage is supposed to have been postponed indefinitely—only our family and the General's father and mother knowing his intention. His sister cannot know, for she is married to a general who would betray the secret. All General Ybarra's precautions would have been in vain if G. B. had suspected it; and I believe his (General Ybarra's) audacity would have detained us if G. B. had known. . . .

"Nell and the General will go to Europe. . . . And, of course, Nelly will not postpone the marriage for the reason that General Y. has sacrificed his home and some of his money for her."

In the diary kept by Nelly Russell, at the time of her departure from Venezuela and her stay in St. Thomas, she treats her fiancé cavalierly. She hardly mentions him. She was far too much concerned with the feelings of the Russells as a result of their dramatic exit from the land of El Ilustre Americano. (Nelly, by the way, like a good Bostonian, calls him the Illustrious *South* American.) She was particularly concerned with the feelings of her sister Minnie, who was abandoning a troop of supposedly heartbroken admirers.

In the diary, a whole page is devoted to an imaginary apostrophe, addressed to swains left behind in Caracas. (It is written, by the way, in Spanish, which is proof of the great progress made by the Russell girls in that language since the days of "los zamuros.")

"Farewell, angel of my eyes!" the apostrophe begins. "Farewell, Prösch of my affections! [Prösch was a young German diplomat who had been most devoted to Minnie.] Farewell, Félix of my soul! [That was my father's cousin, Félix Rivas.] Farewell, all the others! That sad word 'farewell' breaks my heart. I can endure no more. Tears blind me. All I can write to all of you is 'Farewell forever!' But, to you, my angel, to you whom I have really loved, I cannot say this bitter word. . . . No! I shall see thee again—if not in this melancholy world, in another world that is better. Yes, my angel, in Heaven I shall meet thee again!"

To this ardent outburst is appended, in Nelly Russell's handwriting: "This is Min's farewell to her beloved Caraqueños—as translated by me."

At the hotel chosen by the Russells in St. Thomas they had—wrote Nelly—"three luxurious rooms, each with two double beds. Into one of these [rooms, not beds] stepped a very radiant-looking Boomer, whom we had great difficulty in turning out so we could dress."

Miss Russell's delightful sojourn in Venezuela prejudiced her against the Danish West Indies.

"I don't like St. Thomas—not a bit," she wrote in her diary. "I hate the Negroes, who are big and black and nasty and insolent, and jabber and fight all day and all night (poetry), and are as different from Caracas Negroes as so many gorillas. . . . We have walked through the town—it is not at all interesting." Later on, she gets more tolerant. "We have had some nice moonlight walks. But, as the town runs up hill, the trouble is that you have to run after it—99 steps to reach one house! It's fearful."

After more lively chronicles of doings in St. Thomas, during a three weeks' sojourn (conspicuous for their lack of allusions to Alejandro Ybarra or to the fact that he was about to become her husband), Nelly Russell abruptly concludes the entry in her diary dated March fifteenth, 1877, with these words:

"Papa and Dora leave in the Royal Mail steamer for Havana the 17th or 18th. I probably leave the 23d, and am to be married tomorrow night. This doesn't seem a bit fun. How different from the pretty wedding they thought to have in Caracas, when the struggle was to keep the number of guests under 100. Here there are to be five—Mamma and Minnie stay here till April 28th."

Then comes this:

"March 16th, 1877. Good-bye. Nelly Russell."

And then:

"March 19th. Well, Madame Ybarra, you've been married three days and how do you like it? It's about the same as 'twas before. We sit all day in our parlor, and the Boomer lounges in and out and looks a trifle more radiant than he did before. . . . An English priest married us, in Latin. The General was sure there was to be no ring, because it isn't used in Caracas, so I had to take off the plain gold engagement ring and be married with that. It was put on the right hand, but I changed it to the left after the ceremony was over."

Apropos of this marriage of an American to a Venezuelan, on a West Indian island, by an English priest, who performed the ceremony in Latin, I wish to add that I have since seen the marriage certificate—which is in Danish!

General Alejandro Ybarra, the author's father, at the time of his marriage

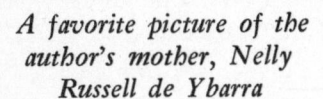

A favorite picture of the author's mother, Nelly Russell de Ybarra

STILL MORE PRE-TOM

After that last-quoted entry, the diary ends abruptly. At the foot of the same page there is merely this:

"Alejandro Tomás Ybarra Russell. Born, Rome, Italy, January 16, 1878. Died, Granada, Spain, June 3, 1878."

Then:

"Arrived in La Guaira, Dec., 1878. Elena Dolores Ybarra Russell, born Curaçao, W. I., April 4, 1879."

Those terse notes chronicle the birth of a baby brother of mine—who lived a brotherless, sisterless life of less than five months—and that of my elder sister, usually known as Nelita, who died before she was seven. I barely remember her—I was about five at the time of her death. My mother gives the name of her first two children, it will be observed, with "Ybarra" first and "Russell" after it, according to Spanish and Spanish-American custom.

The honeymoon of Nelly Russell and Alejandro Ybarra took them to England, France, Switzerland, Italy and Spain. Operating with a bachelor's independence, the young bridegroom added a side-trip to Egypt and the Holy Land, unusual enough for a Venezuelan even nowadays, but almost unknown among Venezuelans of the eighteen-seventies. He went with a fellow-countryman called Saavedra, who turned up in Rome and persuaded him to park his bride there with her mother—who, in the meantime, had journeyed from Boston to be with Nelly. This oriental expedition of her husband gave his wife a grand opportunity to tease him, of which she availed herself generously in later years.

"A fine thing to do, abandon your wife on your honeymoon!" she would say.

"Bot, Nelly, eet eess good for a man to see Yerusalem. . . ."

"That's all right. But you abandoned me, just the same."

As peace offerings, he brought to her water from the Jordan and a crucifix made of wood from the Mount of Olives; also fine albums of photographs, ranging in subject all the way from Calvary to the Pyramids, which, later, were copiously thumb-marked by me in my early boyhood.

He also acquired a lot of good stories. The one I remember particularly dealt with how he and Saavedra, both expert horsemen, watched an exhibition of horsemanship staged by some wild Arabs of the desert for the benefit of the Cook's Tour to which the two Venezuelans had attached themselves, and then proceeded to stage a similar show of their own, to the delight of their fellow-tourists and the chagrin of the Arabs.

From their honeymoon the bride and bridegroom went to Boston, where young Alejandro got his first taste of the United States. He was always of two minds about this country. The speed and practical nature of American business methods pleased him; and they continued to do so all through his life. In spite of his essential alien-ness, he had a remarkable understanding of this side of American life.

Only when beset by an especially black fit of gloom—and when he grouched he grouched!—did one hear from him anything along the lines of the usual stereotyped Latin criticism of *los yanquis* and their blood-relatives, *los ingleses*. "Americans have no soul." "They worship only money." "The only Anglo-Saxon who wrote anything worth while was Shakespeare." All that sort of thing issued from his lips, as a rule, only when they were blue with cold from Boston's east wind. But he did have a lot to say, east wind or no east wind, about American cooking.

STILL MORE PRE-TOM

Meanwhile, in Venezuela, Dictator Guzmán Blanco continued to reign. One day he decided to take a trip to Europe as a self-invited guest of the Venezuelan Treasury. That was one of several such trips in his colorful career. Other Latin American dictators have dipped into the national treasury and then skipped abroad. But it remained for Guzmán to invent a new system.

He would make long stays in Paris while a pinch-hitter kept his presidential seat warm in Caracas and obediently honored the absentee's staggering drafts on the nation's cash on hand. Then, when homesickness hit him, he would return to Venezuela. Now and then this pretty scheme struck a snag. The pinch-hitter would be pushed out of the way by Guzmán's foes, or he would develop ideas of personal aggrandizement and refuse to cash drafts from Paris. But, for years, Guzmán managed to arrange matters so that he could live in Europe, whenever he desired, without losing his job at home.

When young Alejandro Ybarra, heroically trying to establish a *modus vivendi* with Massachusetts cooking and cold, heard of the first flurry between the dictator and one of the latter's pinch-hitters, he leaped aboard a steamer bound for Venezuela in order to offer his sword (not the one he had broken across his knee, but a new one) to the anti-Guzmán cause. That was at the end of the eighteen-seventies. But his stay in Caracas was short. Operating from Paris, Guzmán discomfited his enemies. My father was obliged to flee to Curaçao.

During the next five or six years he oscillated back and forth between the United States, Curaçao, and Caracas, according to whether the Venezuelan dictator's stock was up or down. If it was up, Guzmán's ex-commander of artillery became active in the importation into the United States of Venezuelan coffee, cocoa and chocolate. If it was down, he rushed back into Venezuelan politics, leaving pinch-hitters of his own in the bleak North to attend to his business commitments.

This life was rough on Nelly Russell de Ybarra, but her copious supply of philosophy enabled her to face it with calm and to extract from it an immense amount of amusement.

In Boston, she serenely resumed life à la Massachusetts. In Curaçao, she tried to learn Dutch until she had to give it up because her throat, always delicate, refused to gargle the gutturals of that ponderous language. And, during brief stays in Caracas, she mastered the technique of being the wife of a rabid anti-Guzmancista.

This included holding herself in readiness to dash, at short notice, up the mountain-slope over Caracas and down the opposite slope to La Guaira, with little more than a toothbrush as luggage, in order to catch the next boat for Curaçao, or New York, one jump ahead of the police of Guzmán Blanco. Also, she was initiated into the mystery of how a Venezuelan opposed to the government can stay in Caracas and, at the same time, stay out of jail.

One way to do this, as Nelly soon learned from her young husband, was by means of a local form of disappearance act which was an old custom in Venezuela. When things get too hot there for those playing the intricate game of politics, they go into hiding. This often consists merely in canceling all one's appointments, vanishing from one's official place of residence and all one's favorite haunts, and waiting modestly for the squall to blow over, at the house of some friend—sometimes no further away from one's official habitat than around the corner.

STILL MORE PRE-TOM

Shortly after my father's first visit to Caracas after his honeymoon, it became advisable for him to go into hiding. He had thought that the pro-Guzmán elements wouldn't raise their heads for some time. But they did—most emphatically. What is more, they became top-dog in the government of the moment and began to growl threats of putting my father in prison and leaving him there indefinitely. So he "disappeared."

My mother and his mother and his sister, my Aunt Inés, all knew exactly where he was, just half a block down the street, at the home of an individual of the same political hue. But, officially, his whereabouts were supposed to be a tremendous secret.

For a while nothing serious happened. The family almost began to believe that the government would forget the whole matter and enable my father to keep a dinner date a week from Wednesday.

But suddenly there came a heavy knock on the big front door of my grandmother Ybarra's home. A servant opened it.

Outside stood an officer at the head of a dozen soldiers, armed with muskets. Officer and soldiers trooped into the big front hall. The soldiers formed in line behind their commander. The latter, after saluting politely, took a step toward my mother and my grandmother and my Aunt Inés, who had clustered about at the sound of the invasion.

"The government has been informed," said the officer, still very polite, "that General Alejandro Ybarra is in hiding somewhere in Caracas. Can any one of you ladies inform me whether this is true."

There was a worried silence. Then one of the trio—my grandmother, I think—replied:

"General Ybarra is not in hiding. He is not in Caracas."

The other two nodded in corroboration of this remarkable statement. The officer bowed again.

But, just at that moment, my father's orderly came bustling through the front door. Absolutely ignorant of the crisis unfolding itself before his eyes, he turned to my mother and blurted out:

"General Ybarra told me to ask *la señora* to send him the pair of slippers that he left under his bed."

Nobody said a word. Nobody moved. The ladies of the family, including Nelly Russell de Ybarra, stood in silence. Their knees sagged. They waited, trembling, for words of rage and catastrophe to issue from that officer's mouth.

But he proved himself both an officer and a gentleman. He never so much as moved an eyelid in skeptical reaction. Once more he saluted. Once more he bowed. Then, without so much as a look at the orderly, by this time petrified with fear, he said courteously to my mother and my grandmother and my aunt:

"Thank you. If you ladies say that General Ybarra is not in hiding, and not in Caracas, that, of course, is the truth." He turned to the soldiers lined up behind him.

" 'Tention. Shoulder arms. Left face. Forward—march!"

They all trooped through the doorway and onto the street. In their relief, my mother and my grandmother and my aunt almost fell flat on the stone-paved floor. What they said to that orderly is not on record.

After the foregoing and similar adventures in post-honeymoon Caracas, Alejandro Ybarra and Nelly, his wife, were forced to flee from his native land to Curaçao, where my sister Nelita was born. Then the family proceeded to Boston.

In that city I made my appearance as a new member of the

STILL MORE PRE-TOM

human race. At a little Catholic church there I was duly baptized and entered in the parish records as Alejandro Tomás Simeón Mariano de las Mercedes Ybarra (Tom to my friends).

At the time (late in 1880) my father was leading a triple life: in the daytime he worked at the coffee business; in the evening he gave Spanish lessons; in the morning, at noon, during the afternoon, in the evening, and at night, he yearned to get back to Venezuela.

When I was about two years old, his chance came. Guzmán Blanco was again in difficulties. So we all hotfooted it to Caracas. In a few months, however, we all hotfooted it out of Caracas—that confounded nuisance, Guzmán Blanco had regained the upper hand.

Seven years or so I spent as a human pendulum, with the Venezuelan or the American or the Dutch flag flapping over my head.

Finally, the dictator of Venezuela took his final grand tumble—thanks to Pinch-Hitter Juan Pablo Rojas Paúl, who suddenly decided to stop pinch-hitting, keep the contents of the national treasury at home, and tell the dictator to go to hell.

As a result of this colorful line of conduct, my father, in 1889, once more stopped being a coffee-cocoa-and-chocolate merchant in the United States and rushed down to Venezuela, in order to take up his Guzmán-ridden political career where he had dropped it. At our house much was said about the shining patriotism of Rojas Paúl, but I was too small to appreciate his merits. All I remember about my cursory contact with him is that he had a lot of hair draped around his face and that we leased a house formerly occupied by his Vice-President, whose name was Jesus Muñóz Tébar. Jesus, by the way, is fairly common as a name in Venezuela. It is bandied about there without a trace of the shock that such casual use would cause in the United States. Standing one day on a Caracas corner, I heard a dusky mother, emerging excitedly from a grocery store, shout to her brown brat, playing happily in a nearby gutter:

"Jesus, get out of that puddle!"

The Rojas Paúl régime ushered in my longest Venezuelan sojourn—three years. This stay—and the shorter ones that had gone before it and came after it—were rough on the Bostonian inside me. But, somehow, he managed to survive.

From the moment of my first landing in Venezuela, as a very little boy, my Anglo-Saxon self was on the alert. He armed himself cap-à-pie against my Latin self. On favorable and unfavorable terrain he fought. Sometimes he was badly mauled; sometimes he drove my Latin self to ignominious retreat. Always, pursuing or pursued, he remained full of pugnacity. Always he looked upon the circumambient Latinity of my early years with the cold eyes of a codfish. Always he battled to preserve me for my temporarily abjured New Englandism. At times it became a tremendous tussle, with my Latin self snorting like a hurricane and my inner Bostonian intent on cutting the ropes that bound me to Caribbean shores and towing me northward, in order to make me fast to the spiritual waterfront of Boston.

All through those years of my Southernism, of that life of Latinity, of warmth and light, glamourous and richly tinted, there shone within me a steadfast resolve that I was and would forever stay of the North, Anglo-Saxon, true to that current in my bloodstream which was Massachusetts. This resolve endured, with a stubborn intensity, unimpaired and unquenchable, like a sun in my sky.

STILL MORE PRE-TOM

It never left me. Through thick and thin it remained latent inside me. It tempered my thoughts and actions even when the Latin current in my blood ran quickest and hottest. At the time, I did not realize this: for those were the days of early youth, and, to the young, the moment has compelling appeal. Now that I am much older, I fully understand how, in my father's warm South, it was my mother's cold North that radiated real warmth within me. In Spanish Caracas, ringed by the brooding and beautiful mountains of Venezuela's coastal range, I persisted (now I can see it) in steeling myself against local impressions that might be decisive to my future. Invariably, though unconsciously, I was turning my heart and mind to horizons north of the Caribbean.

The languors of Venezuela encompassed me, the violences of Venezuela caught at me—and both of these things are of formidable power, as I now realize, from having observed how they have dominated the northern part of the soul of my younger brother, whose blood is exactly the same as mine. But I stood firm. In sudden gusts of passionate homesickness, I would yearn for all those un-Latin portions of my international heritage, which, to me, possessed heat and color and texture: Boston, with its wind-swept streets; Boston's frigid brick façades; Boston's stiffness—quintessentially northern, and, to me, perennially fascinating. Externally, in those early years of mine, I was of the South, internally of the North.

Before I came of age, my northern self, apparently, stood supreme on the last battlefield of my personal war. My southern self could no more emerge definitely victorious in that struggle than the flaming sun of Venezuela could melt Plymouth Rock. When I went up the gangplank of the Red D Line steamer that was to take me northward, in the twentieth year of my life, toward Boston and Harvard, a door was slammed shut on my Latinity. The lad who walked up that gangplank—Spanish in feature and carriage, as fluent in Spanish as in English—was already lost to Latinism. Again and again, after that, I have returned to South America—but each time I have taken back with me less and less of my real self.

Yet, at long last, my father's Venezuela has had its revenge on my mother's Massachusetts.

Today, after many years of building up within myself a fortress of North Americanism—after playing and learning and working and wooing in the United States—I am amazed, constantly more amazed, to discover that all sense of warmth and color and beauty, exuded by my memory, has fled southward, to hover, in tantalizing radiance, over the fleeting epoch in my past when I was exposed to becoming a Latin. My allegiance to Massachusetts has been renewed—buttressed by a kindred allegiance to New York, and a strong feeling of affinity for Europe. To knowledge of Boston and Cambridge I have added intimacy with Broadway and Fifth Avenue, with London and Paris, and much else in Europe.

But it's no use! Always, my mind-pictures of these places fail to concentrate into themselves the glamour of my mental Venezuela.

There, *only there*, does shimmering color tint my memories. Never, except when I muse on Caracas, and the short dead era of my Caracas life, am I shaken to the core by inexplicable nostalgia. When I came north—to stay—I found Reality. But I lost Romance.

Not entirely, thank God! Deep down inside me, beyond the reach of reality and environment and practicality and common sense and matter-of-fact New Yorkishness, my lost other life

STILL MORE PRE-TOM

still goes on, my lost other self still swaggers, in imperishable Latinity. In a remote stratum of my being—a stratum which, I uneasily suspect, is a basic layer of my soul—the Caribbean sun has melted Plymouth Rock.

I shut my eyes. I hear palm trees swaying. I see low roofs covered with red tiles. Around the corner of one of the streets of my memory slouches a squad of Venezuelan soldiers. They are little and swarthy. They wear baggy blue-and-red-and-yellow uniforms. Ahead struts an officer, with drawn sword.

He shouts: "*Alto—descansen—*ARMAS!"

Sweaty brown hands bring heavy rifles thudding against cobblestones.

"*En su lugar—descanso!*"

Officers and soldiers relax. They grin at me, like old friends. Good night, Myles Standish!

Chapter IV

Militarism!

WHILE I was a little boy, savoring my first real taste of life in Venezuela, grim militarism reached out for me and gripped me in its clammy tentacles. It dragged me from home. It snatched me from innocent domesticity. It dimmed the effect of early studies at school and obtruded itself rudely on childish contemplation of my enviable status as a native of Massachusetts. It swept me away to an existence encompassed by barracks, guns, trumpet calls, and the martial atmosphere of imminent battle. And how I loved it!

It was all because Guzmán Blanco's long dictatorship (as asserted either from Caracas or Paris) was over at last. Somewhere in the vicinity of my tenth birthday, my father was appointed by President Andueza Palacio *Comandante de Armas*, or Military Governor, of Caracas and the Federal District surrounding it. "I am ungrateful," wrote my mother in her diary, "because I wanted him to be Minister of War. But that comes later." As for my father, he was delighted. "He has gone off to take command of forces, order uniform, etc.," continued the diary. "He is so pleased to be a *militar* once more, poor boy."

The appointment opened for me new and gorgeous vistas. Within a few weeks after my father had taken up his duties, I had decided, without fear of successful contradiction from him, or my Massachusetts mother, or anyone else in the world,

MILITARISM!

that I was going to become a soldier at the earliest possible moment and stay a soldier until my death. That, I decided, must take place, if possible, on some particularly sanguinary battlefield, with my side victorious and the enemy running away in panic from the scene of my heroic démise.

My father officiated during military business hours at the *Comandancia de Armas,* a big building dating back to the eighteenth-century days of the Spaniards, two or three blocks from the home of my family. He wore (unless required to be especially resplendent) a double-breasted blue military coat, cut like the Prince Albert of our grandfathers, reaching to his knees. It was garnished with two rows of gold buttons (I still have a couple of specimens), blue trousers with a gold stripe, and a cap with a tortoiseshell visor and much gold braid spread over it in intricate arabesques. As he was all through his life a very handsome man indeed, with dark, flashing brown eyes and clean-cut Spanish features ("Your father has the most beautiful chin I ever saw," my mother used to tell me and my young sister and brother), he cut quite a dash around Caracas, even in his workaday military garb.

But when big militaristic matters were afoot, he became a sight for the gods. On occasions invested with the maximum of pomp—and they weren't infrequent, for Venezuelans love a show—he would don headgear like an admiral's, pointed fore and aft, surmounted by a plume and bespangled with insignia in the yellow-blue-and-red of the Venezuelan flag. With this went a blue tunic covered with black braid, floppy cream-colored trousers, and big boots of black patent leather that reached above his knees and had been shined to dazzling brightness by a soldier-valet.

Followed by his children, and possibly by two or three small nephews and nieces, in an admiring troop, he would swing himself, with an elegance that a growing paunch never succeeded in lessening, onto the back of a fine, sleek horse—those were the days of splendid horsemen in Venezuela, and my father, up to a short time before his death at the age of seventy, remained one of them. And off he would prance, acknowledging the salute of the sergeant detailed to sit at our front door, to join the President of Venezuela at some military review or take part in some solemn ceremony at the tomb of Simón Bolívar, Venezuela's revered Liberator.

We children looked on in high satisfaction. And my mother, from behind a lattice in the front part of our house, watched until my father had rounded the corner. And she doubtless thought about the Alejandro Ybarra of the 'seventies, about youth and courtship, about the Caracas of her impressionable girlhood, still more remote from her Boston and her Plymouth than the Caracas in which, fifteen years later, she was now living, married to that same Alejandro Ybarra ("Nelly's general," as her father had been wont to call him, in letters home to Marston Watson).

At the Comandancia de Armas, my father had the only desk. To the Venezuela of the late nineteenth century, desks, as we know them, were strange monsters from other climes. They rarely reared their heads in Venezuelan homes or offices. Other local officials, military and civil, usually sat behind large tables, covered with cloths of gay colors and long fringes, anything but allergic to ink stains. From his desk, my father issued orders to the Caracas garrison with martial earnestness. The effect was somewhat marred every afternoon, around four, by the arrival of a servant from our house bearing a pink pitcher

MILITARISM!

of water flavored with brown sugar, especially prepared by my mother.

In the same big room with my father, at a table of conspicuous inkiness, sat General Boza, *Ayudante de Plaza*—which may be freely translated Chief of Staff. Boza was an individual of such mild manner and seeming unworldliness that I have since wondered how he had got as far as he had in Venezuelan military life—which is, to put it mildly, rough. But there he was. And in the enthusiasm of my boyish militarism, I accepted him as unquestioningly as I accepted other prominent local militarists, who were genuinely hard-boiled.

Some of the latter had awful battle scars on their faces. They garnished their Spanish with positively dreadful profanity. When forced by my father, in a burst of deference to Europe, to take fencing lessons from an itinerant Frenchman—who said he had been an officer in the French army—they lunged and parried with elaborate contempt for the whole business. And they would whisper in my ear (devoutly hoping the message would get to Papa) that such stuff was effeminate and useless, that what they wanted was good machete practice—cut instead of thrust; skull-splitting whacks, delivered from above, instead of neat little jabs with blunted foils on the breastbones of equally inhibited opponents, and pretty cries of "touché," uttered when those opponents delicately brushed one's own breastbone. (I duly transmitted the messages of these tough friends of mine to my father. But he was adamant. The fencing lessons continued.)

Boza, his face almost hidden by a grand set of whiskers, as remote from machetes as a priest at the altar, executed the orders of his chief in a military Prince Albert coat as long as my father's. He transmitted them to officers, high, medium and low, of the Caracas garrison, via swarthy orderlies, in sandals and soiled white suits, who shuffled in and out of the Comandancia all day. Even these lowly youths were invested in my eyes, despite their humble station, with a military glory such as urchins of the Paris of the beginning of the nineteenth century must have bestowed on the orderlies of the Grande Armée who ran Napoleon's errands and held his stirrup. Now and then, bewhiskered Boza would come to our house. There he would consume a cup of tea with my mother and unload upon her courtly platitudes, neatly wrapped up in Spanish verbal vegetation.

At another table, in that inner room of the Comandancia where my father reigned, sat Colonel Chavero. Chavero—to my great satisfaction—had a scar on his face. But, when I knew him, he had long since hung up his sword and relapsed into innocuous, well-nigh civilian, desuetude. He was a good fellow—with a bad habit. In his spare time he used to concoct works of art in lavish coloring—lists, for instance, of all the Comandantes de Armas of Caracas, straight down from the earliest days of Venezuelan independence to my father. These were drawn up in the most elaborate lettering, all scrolls and flourishes and gilt and blue and red, within a wide margin of many hues, alive with cannon and coats-of-arms and stacked muskets and crossed swords.

As soon as such a masterpiece was completed, Chavero would respectfully lay it on my father's desk and draw back a step, awaiting commendation—just as he had done under my father's predecessor and the predecessor of that predecessor. My father, of course, would burst into lyrical praise. And he would see that the artist received a suitable bonus. So far, so good. But

MILITARISM!

the masterpiece would thereupon be sent around to our house, by orderly, and hung up, in all its garish colorfulness, at some conspicuous point, where it killed every surrounding attempt at house decoration—to the intense disgust of my mother.

In a big outer room, with a high ceiling and deep window embrasures, encased in iron rejas, dating back to Spanish colonial days, the young aides-de-camp of the Comandante de Armas lounged about, awaiting assignments. They wore handsome uniforms, with swords at their sides and revolvers on their hips. Every one of them was an intimate—and enormously admired—friend of mine.

But their boss could detect in them little of the martial spirit. He surmised (and rightly) that they were just attractive loafers who had got themselves transformed into captains and majors because they knew that a military uniform was a short cut to amorous conquest. From his seat in the inner room he would fix upon these butterflies a frigid military eye and set himself to thinking up something militaristic that would both annoy and harden them.

Once, I remember, several members of a garrison in the interior of Venezuela, who had indulged in a little local mutiny, were brought in irons to the Comandancia. They were forthwith locked up in one of the many big, unused rooms in the bowels of that big edifice. The mutineers were to be court-martialed in the approved military fashion handed down by Spain to Venezuela. Under ordinary circumstances, a jury would have been chosen from among veteran officers of the troops garrisoning Caracas. But my father decided on a jury of butterflies.

He informed a group of his trifling young aides-de-camp that they were to be jurors. The announcement had a sobering effect on the bunch—on lively Arturo Uzlar, descended from a German veteran of the Napoleonic Wars, who had fought under Bolívar; on handsome Blanco Uribe, that distinguished ornament of the Caracas younger set; on dapper Alejandrito Plaza Ponte; on swaggering Godoy and smiling Tinoco Salazar, who looked and acted as if nothing serious had ever swum into their firmament (except from the direction of Venus).

During the court-martial, those butterflies officiated (in the big room where they had been loafing and posturing) with a gravity of demeanor befitting the United States Supreme Court. With knit brows and somber eyes, they listened to evidence—while the accused uneasily shifted their handcuffed hands and shackled feet. When the young jurors filed in to give their verdict, they were deadly pale. They seemed to be weighed down with the destinies of the world, suddenly entrusted to their keeping.

The mutineers got a few years each in the Castillo Libertador, the grim old Spanish fortress that flanks the entrance to the Venezuelan harbor of Puerto Cabello. But if they had all been condemned to be shot at sunrise, the sentence could not have had a more tremendous effect on gay Uzlar and handsome Blanco Uribe and dapper Plaza Ponte. My father observed the proceedings sternly. He felt not only that justice had been done but that a bit of much-needed iron had been injected into the veins of his butterflies.

Then he thought up another trick.

Every day, detachments of soldiers belonging to the various units of the Caracas garrison were selected to mount guard at a number of points dotted over the city—the Yellow House (where the President lived); the *cárcel*, or prison; the military

MILITARISM!

hospital; the "*pólvora*," on the outskirts, right under the mountain-wall fringing the Venezuelan capital, where large amounts of gunpowder were stored against the ever-present possibility of outbreaks against the government. All these detachments (except the President's guard, which was of too high standing to be mixed up with other less distinguished squads) would march to the Comandancia de Armas every morning and line up on the street in front to get the countersign of the day and whatever special instructions the Comandante de Armas might have for them. Then they were dismissed to their respective assignments by some regular officer detailed for the purpose.

"Regular officer, my eye!" mused my father one day. "I'll make those butterflies of mine put in a real morning's work, for a change. Uzlar! Blanco Uribe!"

The butterflies, fluttering into the inner sanctum, perched apprehensively around the desk of their chief.

"On each day of next week," proclaimed my father, "one of you is to dispatch the guard detachments to their posts. Boza will give you the details." And he bent over the papers on the desk before him. The butterflies fluttered unhappily over to Boza.

The necessary arrangements were made—to the immense delight of a little boy of Massachusetts ancestry, who spent hours tagging after those aides-de-camp as if he were one of them.

A leading socialite was chosen as Victim Number One. For hours on the day before his new task, that youth, in a panic of nerves, pranced up and down in a hidden room of the Comandancia, rehearsing his duties of the morrow before an audience of one—me.

"Tom, how's this?" he asked.

He took a step forward, unsheathed his sword, drew himself up with martial effect, put a military flash into his eyes, and roared—to imaginary soldiers drawn up before him:

"*Guardia de cárcel!* Shoulder arms! Left face! Forward—march!"

While the imaginary guardians of the city prison went marching off, he would turn inquiring eyes on the lone young spectator.

"Tom, did that have the right military touch?"

"Well," I replied judicially, "I liked the roar. But the rest wasn't much."

The crestfallen officer would then do it all over again—and still again—until I pronounced him perfect.

But—next day! Oh, what a fall was there! In the presence of several companies of tough, sandaled soldiers of the army of Venezuela, with rifles and bayonets shining in the sunlight, with hundreds of grinning members of the Caracas public looking on, my friend's martial aplomb deserted him. Instead of swaggering, he slunk. His action, as he started to draw his sword, rather conveyed the impression that he was fumbling for a handkerchief. And the menacing roar with which, on the previous afternoon, he had admonished the dream-troops parading before him, gave place to a hesitant and conciliatory twitter, less reminiscent of a battlefield than of a Sunday school.

In colonial times, the Comandancia de Armas had been the *Intendencia*, the headquarters of the *Intendente* of the Spanish Kings, that royal official of lofty rank and mysterious activities, who used to stand at the elbow of Spanish viceroys and

MILITARISM!

captains-general in the great domain of Spain in the Americas and do his mysterious job with true Castilian pomp and dignity.

The back of the Intendencia abutted on the garden of a grand colonial mansion presided over by an ancient, haughty and flawlessly well-connected female grandee whom I shall call Doña Francisca. She ranked very high indeed in the social life of Caracas.

At the pinnacle of Doña Francisca's social importance a new Intendente was sent out from Madrid to Venezuela. He was a Spanish don with a roving eye. He so far forgot the dignity of his official post, and the reverence due the social prejudices of so exalted a local personage as Doña Francisca, as to get himself entangled in a love affair with a pretty young servant girl attached to her domestic staff. The ardent Spanish official used to climb the rear wall of the Intendencia, in the dead of night, and keep lover's trysts in Doña Francisca's garden while Caracas slept in silence under its tropical canopy of stars.

One night, just as the Intendente, having torn himself from his enchantress, was about to climb back in secrecy over the wall to his official bedroom, his way was abruptly barred by a startling apparition. It was the mistress of the mansion in person —arrogant Doña Francisca.

In a voice cold with contempt, contrasting violently with the rage gleaming from her eyes, she said to the amazed royal official:

"Your Excellency has chosen to enter my home in a way far from befitting a noble representative of His Spanish Majesty. It is not meet that Your Excellency should retrace his steps over the same path. Were he to do so, I should deem myself woefully lacking in the respect due to our royal master beyond the seas. Your Excellency—please give me your arm."

Utterly confused and embarrassed, the Intendente proffered his arm to the icily polite old lady. Together they paced through silent rooms, toward the front of the house. As they stepped into the main patio, girdled by the principal apartments of the ground floor and by the lofty tiled balconies of the second story of the mansion, the unhappy Intendente halted in shamefaced astonishment.

Across the patio, all the way to the grand front portal of Doña Francisca's mansion, stretched two rows of her servants. Each held in his hand a lighted torch.

"Thus," said Doña Francisca, "do I show my respect for Your Excellency. Only thus should a high official of His Majesty be speeded on his way when he departs from my house."

Red with shame, relentlessly gripped by the haughty lady at his side, the Intendente walked falteringly between the silent rows of torchbearers. In the flickering torchlight, his face turned pale—he lowered his eyes, his cheeks burned. He dared not look at their faces; well he knew that every one of those servitors was fully aware of the humiliating trick which their proud mistress had played on him; well he knew that Caracas would be ringing with the story next day.

At the front door, he remembered his good manners sufficiently to bow to Doña Francisca. She acknowledged the bow with a curtsey that was insulting in its studied politeness. Then, almost at a run, he stumbled past the last two torchbearers and found himself in the street. As he slunk around the corner, to the Intendencia, he heard behind him the slamming of the great doors of Doña Francisca's mansion.

MILITARISM!

From the Comandancia de Armas del Distrito Federal, successor to the Spanish Intendencia, no such amorous expeditions set out, to the best of my knowledge and belief. Two or three of the aides-de-camp of my father's staff slept there, also a few servants; and, after the doors were officially closed, they surreptitiously introduced damsels unafflicted by morals—to be summarily ejected at an early hour next morning. But the general air of the place, in my boyhood, suggested grim militarism, not Cytherean joy—Mars unsolaced by Venus.

My father believed in discipline. He knew perfectly well that injecting such a thing into the lawless breasts of the Venezuelans of those days—and giving them, along with discipline, some sort of *esprit de corps* and a spark of humaneness toward the men in the ranks—was a tremendous task. But what could be done about it he did, with a zeal worthy of a Von Steuben, Beau Brummell and Florence Nightingale rolled into one. One of his first official acts as military governor was to abolish flogging as a punishment for members of the garrison under his command.

Under his régime, the garrison of Caracas was well-drilled, well-uniformed and well-treated. My father despised petty graft, always rampant in the Venezuelan army. He did what he could to prevent grafting subordinate officers from profiting, while he was boss, at the expense of the rank and file. He went to real trouble to make sure that the men in the ranks—brutally recruited by press-gangs, without regard for constitutional rights and no better than slaves under less humane commanders—really got the meager daily pay officially allowed them. He saw to it that they should be free to spend it as they pleased, without forking over a goodly cut to predatory powers higher up.

YOUNG MAN OF CARACAS

In the Venezuelan army of my early boyhood there was an especially neat grafting trick known as *imaginarias*—imaginary soldiers. It was worked as follows:

Commanding officers in quest of illicit graft would deliver to the army paymaster's office what purported to be the full list of the soldiers of a certain battalion. The first and last names of each noncom and private were duly recorded, and an engaging air of honesty was diffused over the document. The trouble was that only a part of the men listed were actual human beings serving in the Venezuelan army. The rest were purely imaginary.

Now, each private got thirty centavos a day—corporals and sergeants a little more. So, if a dishonest high officer listed, say, thirty imaginary privates, together with several imaginary noncoms, he was able to divert from legitimate channels more than ten dollars a day for one battalion alone—a sum not to be sneezed at, even if he had to share it with other grafters.

My father went after the imaginaria trick with great energy. He worked hard to bring the lists of battalion personnel into harmony with the number of men actually serving in each battalion. He ordained that a special inspection of each unit of the Caracas garrison was to be held every few weeks. And he made a point of being present in person at every one of these functions—accompanied, as a rule, by an absorbed little boy-spectator.

The inspection I remember best was held at the big *Cuartel San Carlos*. There the Third Battalion, 360 strong, exclusive of officers, was lined up in the long corridor fringing the square central patio. At a table sat my father, flanked by several of his aides-de-camp, by some of the officers stationed in the cuartel —and by me. I felt very important indeed.

MILITARISM!

An officer, holding in his hand the list of men supposedly in the battalion being inspected, called out their names, one by one. He used only the first name of each soldier. At the summons, each man would step in front of my father, raise his rifle from the ground, bring his left hand over to his right shoulder, and give his last name. Thus:

"Antonio——!"

A swarthy private steps out of the ranks. He stands at attention.

"González!" he shouts.

"Manuel——!"

"Lozada!"

And so on, until the entire battalion has been called. Meanwhile, the officer with the list in his hand checks off name after name. At the end, if all is well, the 360 names on the list—with the exception of soldiers legitimately absent because of illness or some other valid reason—tally correctly with the actual battalion present in visible human form. This system was pretty rough on the imaginaria trick.

At the inspection in the Cuartel San Carlos there was a sawed-off little soldier of the Third Battalion, with bright black eyes and brown skin, whom I shall never forget. His name was Encarnación Lara. He had a deep, booming voice, of tremendous volume and resonance, which was his special pride.

The officer holding the list would call out.

"Encarnación!"

The little sawed-off would prance forward. He would pull his gun up to his shoulder. Then in tones that might have inspired envy in a bull of Bashan—that shook out of place, I feel sure, some of the tiles on the roof of the barracks—he would roar:

"LARA!"

The thing became a regular part of inspection ritual. Everybody chuckled when Encarnación left the ranks and started toward the table at which my father sat. Everybody laughed when he let out that crashing bellow. And Encarnación would go slouching back to his place in the *Batallón Número Tercero*, with a satisfied smirk on his face, like an opera singer conscious of having knocked them cold out in front.

While he was Comandante de Armas, my father also did his best to see that the men in the ranks got eatable food at the cook-shops installed inside the barracks. Accompanied (as usual) by me, he would go from one barracks to another in order to sample the victuals dished out by the impresarios who had been awarded the cook-shop concessions. As I stowed away garlicky soup and stew and beans—the regulation diet of the Caracas garrison—I used to smack my lips. The stuff tasted good.

Chapter V

More Militarism

WHEN I wasn't at the Comandancia de Armas, I spent as much time as possible at one or another of the various barracks in which the Caracas garrison lived.

One of these was the *Cuartel San Mauricio*. It was the headquarters of the particularly distinguished and well-uniformed Battalion of the Guard. To that battalion exclusively was entrusted the privilege of furnishing the daily guardians of the President's official residence.

Then there was the *Cuartel de Carmelitas*, in a big building that had been a convent in the days of the Spaniards. There, Battalion Number One was quartered. It was under the command of handsome General Fernando Pacheco, a leading recipient of my boyish hero-worship. Pacheco's force included one company, the Sixth, commanded by a most particular friend of mine, Captain Riera, a swarthy soldier of delightful toughness. Riera's company proved itself again and again, in martial competition, the best-drilled and best-turned-out company in the whole Caracas garrison.

General Pacheco used to stage big *terneras* in the spacious central patio of his barracks. These were barbecues, at which a whole roasted steer was served up. The meat was flavored with *guasacaca*, a native Venezuelan sauce hot enough to make the hair stand up in protest on any North American head. Yet my fifty per cent Massachusetts ten-year-old self consumed that sauce manfully, licking it from hunks of dripping meat handed to me by those of Fernando Pacheco's soldiers who were temporarily acting as waiters.

Furthermore, I was intimate at the Cuartel San Carlos. That one was the biggest of the lot. It was a huge one-story structure, near the Pantheon, where lies the body of Simón Bolívar.

The Cuartel San Carlos was the residence of the Second and Third Battalions. It also housed the Half-Battalion of Artillery, whose stock of cannon was assembled in the big patio facing the main doorway of the barracks, ready for anything. In his early days, my father, I have remarked, had been a commander of artillery. That fact kept alight in him forever afterward a special interest in cannon and everything concerning cannon. So he lavished on the *medio batallón de artillería* a benign fatherly regard, and the medio batallón throve and swaggered in consequence.

The Battalion of the Guard, when in gala attire, wore long blue coats of coarse cloth with yellow epaulets, high leather headgear bearing the coat-of-arms of Venezuela in brass, and—to the disgust of sandal-loving privates and noncoms—tight leather shoes. But the other outfits composing the garrison were allowed no such splendor. They wore thin white coats and trousers—grimy ordinarily, clean on festive occasions—faced with yellow, blue or red. They also had dark blue or red caps, which no amount of disciplinary admonitions could force them to wear at anything but a rakish angle. And—to their unbounded satisfaction—their feet were usually encased in *alpargatas*, the national sandals of Venezuela. Without alpargatas, a Venezuelan of the humbler classes considers himself cribbed, cabined and confined in the unwelcome prison-house of a fervently undesired civilization.

MORE MILITARISM

Each battalion of the garrison consisted of six companies of four officers and sixty men each—except the Battalion of the Guard, which, faithful to its obsession that it must be different from the rest, had eight companies. The half-battalion of artillery had either two or three companies, I forget which. It was under the command not of a general but of a major—a peculiar state of affairs in a country where generals outnumbered all other officers, and vied, when added up, even with privates.

Of the various high officers in the Caracas garrison of those days, I particularly remember two, General Leopoldo Sarría, in command of the Battalion of the Guard, and General Higuera, who presided over the destinies of the Second Battalion at the Cuartel San Carlos.

Leopoldo Sarría was a tough egg. He had a long beard and a short temper. He would sit scowling for hours in the staff headquarters of the Cuartel San Mauricio, so much so that I used to tiptoe past his office and vanish hastily into the interior—where I had many close friends, officers, noncoms and privates—hoping that I need not stop to greet Leopoldo and get that scowl of his fixed on my small self.

In later years—after he had chosen the losing side in a Venezuelan civil war—Leopoldo Sarría was exiled to New York. There, having conceived a violent dislike for all things North American, he was installed, by apprehensive friends, in a little Italian hotel on Union Square, in the hope that the Latin atmosphere might soften his grouch. But it didn't. He was always discovering that he had been insulted by some Anglo-Saxon and planning sanguinary revenge. He even talked darkly of duels.

Soon after, to the intense relief of his New York acquaintances, Leopoldo was allowed to go back to his native land. But there he remained as grouchy as ever. Even on his deathbed he played true to form. Throughout his life he had scoffed at religion; nevertheless, his wife, terrified at the thought of what might be awaiting such a husband in the other world, introduced a priest into the room, where, it was believed, Leopoldo was already in the coma preceding death. But Leopoldo wasn't. One glance at the priest made him sit bolt upright.

"Throw that rascal out!" he roared. "Kick him out, I tell you, the damned ruffian!" And there was nothing for it but to remove the priest immediately, whereupon Leopoldo fell back on his pillow and died as he had lived—a typical Venezuelan militarist of the eighteen-nineties.

The commander of the Second Battalion at the Cuartel San Carlos, General Higuera, who was just about as tough as Leopoldo Sarría, once gave me a grand opportunity to strut with pride before my father's aides-de-camp and the rest of my military cronies of the period.

Mounted on my little gray donkey (named Don Rodrigo), I was on one of my regular afternoon tours of the strategic points of Caracas. I blew into the Cuartel San Carlos, handed over Don Rodrigo to the care of one of the soldiers on guard, and started out to see what there was to see. On the way, I ran into General Higuera—dark and chunky and severe of countenance. He beckoned me into his quarters, where a group of his aides and an assortment of other officers attached to the barracks were sitting around.

"Young man, I hear big stories of what a grand little soldier you are," said General Higuera, with heavy banter. "I understand that you know the names of every officer of every company of every battalion in Caracas. [I did.] I have been told that you can even put a soldier through the manual of arms

MORE MILITARISM

from start to finish without a single mistake. Bah, I don't believe it!"

He went over to a rack of arms in one corner of the room, took down a rifle and bayonet (General Higuera had risen from the ranks), stood in front of me, girt with the bayonet, and holding the rifle at his side, said contemptuously:

"Come on now, my lad. Put me through the manual of arms."

I squared my shoulders. I began to give orders. Amid the absorbed attention of the officers clustered about, I made portly General Higuera carry arms. I made him shoulder arms and present arms. I made him right wheel and left wheel. I made him march forward and step back. I made him unfix and fix his bayonet. Soon I had him puffing as he hadn't puffed in years, to the delight of his subordinates. From beginning to end I didn't miss a trick. No veteran Mulvaney, no drill sergeant anywhere, could have surpassed my performance in precision and correctness.

When it was all over, amid the enthusiastic praise of my audience, General Higuera, panting heavily, walked over to the rack and put the rifle and bayonet back in place.

"My boy," he said, when he had assembled enough breath to talk with, "you're all right." When I rode away that afternoon from the Cuartel San Carlos, I sat Don Rodrigo with the easy assurance of El Cid.

Apropos of my knowing the names of all the officers stationed in Caracas: I used to study the set-up of the garrison as if my life depended on accurate knowledge about it. I could run off the list of officers as correctly as I could go through the Spanish manual of arms. I kept track of every change, of every transfer, in the officer corps. I stored it away in a memory that retained useless things like that as easily as it cast off all sorts of other things that might have done me some good then, and more in later life.

On one occasion, I recall, a certain second lieutenant of the Third Battalion was superseded by another. I don't remember exactly what my grapevine arrangements were for getting news of this sort, but I most certainly had them, since I knew the name of the new officer about as soon as it became known anywhere in Caracas. The aides-de-camp of my father thought that, at last, they had caught me napping. When I walked into the Comandancia, three or four of them rushed up to me.

"What is the name of the new second lieutenant of the fifth company of the Third Battalion?" they asked in malicious chorus.

"Ramón Antonio Cordero," I answered instantly. They were flabbergasted. They looked at me blankly. I strutted proudly away from them into the inner office where my father sat.

And apropos of that donkey of mine: it had been given to me at a time when I was deep in admiring perusal of Washington Irving's chronicles of Spanish history, of Moors and Visigoths. (I was an inveterate little bookworm.) So I had named my braying steed Don Rodrigo, after Spain's last Visigothic monarch. In view of that royal Visigoth's lamentable record in combat with the Moorish invaders of his kingdom, my choice was more appropriate than I realized at the time.

In those days my ideas of the proper nomenclature for pets were high-flown, to say the least. In the back yard of our house there were two chickens, which I appropriated as my own, and dubbed *Cristóbal Colón de la Concepción* and *Federación*. When one of them was hauled off, squawking, by our cook, and served up at dinner, duly fricasseed, I refused glumly to swallow a single mouthful.

MORE MILITARISM

"What's the matter?" asked my mother.

"How can you expect me," I answered in an outraged voice, "to eat Christopher Columbus of the Immaculate Conception?"

My father ordained that on Sundays the battalions of the garrison, in rotation, should attend military Mass. This was a most impressive ceremony, one of the main delights of the militaristic phase of my childhood.

The chosen battalion, with uniforms and weapons all spruced up, would march to the venerable Church of San Francisco, alongside the Capitol, in which Venezuela's woefully disused Congress was occasionally allowed (to its great surprise) to meet. The procession through the streets toward the church was headed by the *Banda Marcial*, the army band, a really meritorious aggregation, sixty strong or thereabouts, of Venezuelan, Italian and French tootlers and blowers and pounders.

On arrival in front of the Church of San Francisco, all verbal commands ceased. Officers and soldiers filed into the church in silence, their movements directed solely by muffled drumbeats. One beat—they would halt. Another—down they would go on their knees, their accouterments clanking strangely through the dark aisles. Another—they would stand up again—while priests chanted, and acolytes swung fragrant censers, and the organ, above the bowed heads of the soldiery, rolled out the magnificent harmonies of great composers of the past who had placed their genius at the service of the Roman Catholic church. I drank in with avidity every drumbeat, every bit of ceremonial, every peal of the organ. To make me miss a military Mass, a catastrophe of the first magnitude was needed, such as whooping-cough or the mumps.

After the priest had pronounced his benediction on soldiers

and civilians, the battalion (looking disappointingly unsanctified) would file out into the street again and resume subservience to hoarse verbal commands. And the Banda Marcial, no longer inhibited by religion, would march again at the head of the homeward parade, playing a gay quickstep. (A few years later, in Munich, I saw the German idea of military Mass and found it less impressive than its counterpart in Venezuela. The soldiers just piled into the church like ordinary worshipers—and they sat in pews!)

The Venezuelan and Italian and French maestros who played in the band didn't think of themselves as being in any way connected with such an uncouth thing as militarism. They were artists, one and all, in tune with the infinite, *au dessus de la bataille*. Once, while heading the return parade from the Church of San Francisco, they went wool-gathering in the realm of their dreams to such an extent that they forgot entirely to keep step or alignment. Playing deplorably out of tune, they straggled around a couple of corners like a troop of happy-go-lucky sheep. My father immediately flew into one of his towering rages—which, while they lasted, were superb.

Peremptorily, he halted the procession. With eyes flashing fire and his big mustache bristling with anger, he strode to the front of the Banda Marcial.

"You are a disgrace to the Venezuelan army!" he bellowed to the astounded maestros. "You are under arrest—every one of you!"

"*Pero, oiga, general*——" quavered a Venezuelan clarinetist.

"*Ma, noi non siamo soldati,*" protested a soulful Italian trombonist, "*siamo artisti*——"

MORE MILITARISM

"*Mais, dites, mon general, écoutez——*" began a French cornetist.

My father stamped his foot on the cobblestones.

"Silence!" he roared. "Not another word! I arrest every one of you! Proceed immediately to the Cuartel San Carlos and await further orders."

The band straggled dejectedly to the Cuartel San Carlos. After a couple of hours, my father showed up there (with me at his elbow). And he gave every musician, Venezuelan and European, a terrific dressing-down.

While my father held that post, a strong tinge of militarism settled down over the abode of the Ybarras. It was situated in those days between the corners of El Conde and Piñango, two doors from my grandmother's old mansion, and a short distance from the Plaza Bolívar. In Caracas, to this day, they have a quaint custom when they tell you an address: they don't say on what street it is, but between which two corners. And the corners have such racy names that I hope the custom will never be given up, in spite of the difficulties that it presents to foreigners.

Here are samples: Little Steps, Deep Shop, Holy Chapel, Heart of Jesus, Dead Man, Little Balcony, Green Cross, Box of Water, Little Birds, Ball, Fan, Palm Tree, Old Barracks, Fat Woman, Gaze-at-the-Sky. These are interspersed with numerous corners named after saints or families that have long resided in the city. The corner of the Ybarras owed its name to a big house where, my father remembered, two old great-aunts of his used to live in his early boyhood—hence the name of that corner was *las* not *los* Ybarras, in deference to the female of the species.

YOUNG MAN OF CARACAS

One block, in a tough section of Caracas, lay between the corners of Danger and Keep-Your-Eye-Peeled.

At our house, between El Conde (the Count, after a local nobleman of Spanish days) and Piñango (enshrining the memory of a family of the same era) we had, to emphasize how military-minded we were, a succession of private soldiers as servants. If qualified or teachable, they waited on table; if not, they confined themselves to odd jobs around the house. Soldiers liked these assignments, which brought variety into the years of their military service, put them in the way of tips, and gave them a chance to see a bit of the world beyond the barrack portals.

One importation from the barracks, José del Cármen, showed such adaptability and efficiency that he was made the family coachman. At that time (highwater mark in the fluctuating Ybarra political fortunes) my father acquired a neat little victoria with a high-spirited horse called Comandante. José del Cármen, with a red-and-blue livery in place of his soldier's uniform, was perched on the box of the equipage and entrusted with the task of driving one or both of my parents about Caracas, sometimes in company of one or more of their children. He was so successful that, after things weren't going so well with the family exchequer, he set up as a regular hack-driver —having finished his military service. I used to go down to the cab rank near our house, where about twenty victorias were lined up awaiting customers, and have solemn talks with José del Cármen Martínez, licensed cabman.

In those martial days, no toys interested me as much as lead soldiers. I used to get a lot of them from a *padrino* (godfather) of mine, the head of an important hardware emporium, who would affably hand me squads of toy soldiers free of charge

MORE MILITARISM

when I happened to be passing his place of business.

My soldiers were from France; and, of course, they were in bright uniforms that aped the regulation garb of the French army of that period. This made them, to my mind, altogether too neat and civilized. I had seen Venezuelan soldiers in campaign garb, and they had fascinated me. So I got hold of a lot of rags, cut little pieces out of them, and made a small opening at one end of each. Then I draped them over my lead soldiers —in imitation of Venezuelan cloaks—until their pretty French uniforms were entirely hidden by grimy diminutive garments for which the garbage can was the only proper place. I also tied soiled wisps of straw over their shining European caps to simulate the unappetizing headgear of Venezuelan soldiers on the march.

With some building blocks acquired by me as a birthday present, I erected a barracks in a strategic part of the back patio. The servants kept stumbling over it. Finally, a short-tempered cook swept the whole mess into a corner, along with dust and paper scraps, alleging that it was a menace to domestic traffic. I was furious. In Vesuvian language, I told that cook what I thought of her. But my mother took her part. After that, my home outbreaks of militarism were relegated to the back yard.

In the course of this alarming phase of my career, my young sister Leonor, from the age of four onward, was constantly being pressed into service by me to play a leading part in martial games of my invention. Sometimes she would have to sit astride a chair while I (five years older and many pounds heavier) charged her ferociously and upset her in what was supposed to be sanguinary battle.

At other times she had to play a game that I called "battlefield." The patient child, all rumpled and disheveled, would be forced to lie on the floor in a pose suggesting that she had just died a violent death—with her arms spread out and her legs doubled up and her eyes closed and a couple of chairs thrown across her. Then I would rush off to get my mother or Jessie, our London-Irish maid-of-all-work. Proudly I would point to my picture of carnage and destruction.

"Battlefield!" I would announce.

My mother, always ready to enter into the spirit of anything that came along, would raise her hands in horror, and ejaculate:

"Terrible!"

And Jessie would exclaim:

"Lord sakes alive, Thomas, what a mess you've made!"

Meanwhile, poor little Leonor had to lie quite motionless. Otherwise (I told her) the artistic effect would be ruined. Finally, I would signal her to come back to the land of the living. In a few minutes she would find herself the central figure in another sanguinary tableau. While her life was going through this phase of enforced militarism, my younger brother Alejandro was born. Leonor was allowed to see the new baby. She took one look. Then she sighed wearily:

"Another brother! Now I'll have to play soldiers all my life!"

Inside the *zaguán*, the passage leading from our outer doorway opening on the street to the inner doorway leading to the interior of our house, my father, in our military heyday, installed a sergeant—borrowed from one of the barracks—to act as a combination of porter and messenger boy. Of the various sergeants, in regulation Venezuelan uniform (but unarmed), who sat on a little stool at the end of our zaguán, I particularly remember *Sargento Primero* Félix Solórzano.

Félix, a serious owl, bestowed upon me, as a sign of his high regard, long stories about his native town of Camatagua, in the interior of Venezuela. I promptly enshrined Camatagua in my imagination as a model community, with the Solórzano family wielding patriarchal influence in all directions. Once, to my delight, the sergeant formally invited me to visit Camatagua as his guest. The underlying idea probably was that he hoped to wangle an unofficial vacation for himself, amid the Solórzano Lares and Penates. But my parents couldn't see it.

Félix had an idea, by the way, that all foreigners, no matter where they came from, were pretty much the same breed of animal. Once, while my mother was formally entertaining some guests, he strode into her presence, saluted, and announced:

"*Dos ingleses* [Two Englishmen]."

The visitors turned out to be two distinguished Belgians.

To our house between El Conde and Piñango repaired officers from the garrison who wished permission to spend the night outside their barracks. They used to be ushered into our dining room while the family was dining. After respectful greetings to my mother and a wink at me (I knew them all intimately), they would stand first on one foot and then on the other while my father placed his signature at the foot of the formal petition which they had brought along with them. It was couched in the regulation army language. Then they would receive the document from my father's hand, straighten up, salute, walk sedately through our zaguán, and then—well, they used to tell me all about it afterward, when we met at the Comandancia or at one of the barracks.

"Did you hear me tell your father how ill my aunt was and how the old girl was longing to have me sit at her bedside?" Captain X—— would ask me. "Of course you did. Did you believe me? Of course you didn't. Fifteen minutes after I had said good-bye to your mother I was at the Puente de Hierro [that was the center of the Caracas red light district]. What a night, Tom, what a night!"

In those days there were two wild youths, attached, in some way or other, to the general staff of the army, who were sons of a general who had been a leading object of my father's hero-worship in the days of his early military service. In my father's den at our house there was a big picture of this warrior, showing him with enormous mustaches and fiery eyes, with the words *El Soldado Sin Miedo* (*The Soldier Without Fear*) in big lettering underneath. My father had campaigned freely under his command until, finally, the two of them got involved in a desperate defense of Caracas against the forces of whatever party it was that had brought down upon itself their joint disapproval. Unfortunately, the forces of that party were victorious, and finally drove a batch of their foes, under my father, into the Cuartel San Carlos. There, after a spirited fusillade, they capitulated with the honors of war.

This episode (and others, equally martial) had aroused in my father such a respect for the memory of El Soldado Sin Miedo that he proceeded to act toward the latter's two graceless sons *in loco parentis*. But it was no use.

Both were young men of most distinguished appearance, but they were scamps of the first water. One or the other of them, summoned to my father's sanctum, would sit there, with downcast eyes and penitent mien, while the Comandante de Armas

MORE MILITARISM

extolled chastity, sobriety and kindred virtues. They would slink away, in their splendid uniforms—one, I remember, had a light blue tunic with thick black braid, like the cavalry uniform of the French army of those days—uttering solemn promises of reform. But very soon, one or the other or both would play a star role in some Puente de Hierro brawl and be placed under arrest, and my father had to start his sermons all over again.

Finally, in a fury, he washed his hands of the pair. Our household knew them no more. The last I remember about them is that one got into a tremendous alcoholic bout at the Puente de Hierro, and, when a comrade tried to get him home, drew a revolver.

"Oh, come now, you wouldn't shoot your best friend, would you?" protested the other.

"*Wouldn't I?*" retorted the young desperado. And he promptly blazed away at his best friend and pumped several bullets into him.

In those colorful days, my epoch of military make-believe, I even rose to the distinction of being dressed like an officer. In a letter to one of her aunts in Plymouth, my mother told about the martial splendor of my father and myself:

"The General has indulged in a Spanish cloak, wrapped in the folds of which he is very fine indeed. It seems nice to see him in uniform once more. . . . Tom, if you please, has come out in one, too, and I wish I could send him to Plymouth for you all to see. It is dark blue, with the military buttons of Venezuela, scarlet collar, cuffs and shoulder straps, and the képi (such as is used in France) is scarlet, with gold braid and embroidery. You can imagine the erect head and military swagger of Master Tom when he sails off in his uniform, with his beloved pug [that was a dog of mine, named Prince], adorned with a red bow, at his heels."

My mother failed to add that my uniform also included three gold stripes on each sleeve, the insignia of a captain, which were destined to get me into hot water.

All was well as long as I trailed along with my father and other officials of high rank. If I trotted in their wake to a military review, for instance, at which the President of Venezuela appeared, the assembled troops would present arms, an expression of respect which only the Chief Magistrate could elicit from Venezuelan soldiers. Or, when, in company of my father I passed a barracks, the guard would be turned out in a body and made to shoulder arms, for it clearly knew the deference due to the Comandante de Armas. If I attached myself to some lesser general, I would become mixed up with some lesser form of salute, in honor of that general, by soldiers mounting guard or marching past. Nobody paid any attention to me. In such august company my captain's stripes were beneath notice.

But, one day, when I was alone and in full captain's uniform, I passed the Cuartel San Mauricio. At once the corporal and private doing sentry duty at the door stood at attention—that being the salute, accorded by Spanish-Venezuelan military regulations, to an officer of the rank that I was aping.

I was delighted. What an honor for a ten-year-old boy! Spurring Don Rodrigo, I rode past the Cuartel de Carmelitas. Same performance. I found occasion next to ride past the Cuartel San Carlos. Same thing. I was beside myself with martial glee.

I took to collecting salutes. Alleging some excuse or other, I

MORE MILITARISM

would walk or ride away from military companions with insignia superior to mine on their sleeves, in order to add to my collection. There were days, I think, when I not only passed every barracks in the city, in delicious expectancy, but also managed to take in the soldiers' hospital, the prison (with its military guardians at the front door), the arsenal, and even the powder magazine, outside the city proper. Everywhere the corporals and privates on sentry duty would pay me the homage befitting a captain. It was grand.

Now and then I would take a little civilian pal past a barracks. As the salute was bestowed, his eyes would goggle and he would inquire:

"What's that for?"

"For *me*," I would answer casually.

But—alas—my father eventually heard of what was going on. He was furious. Throughout his military career he was dead against nepotism in any form. My cousin Santiago, who once acted as his aide, used to grow eloquent describing how hard he had been obliged to work simply because he had the misfortune to be General Ybarra's nephew.

I was summoned to my father's presence. He pointed sternly at my captain's stripes.

"Go back to that tailor," he commanded, "and tell him to rip those things off!"

Utterly wilted, I crept away. At the tailor's shop I was ignominiously deprived of my captain's insignia. Many a review, many a parade, I witnessed after that, in the entourage of my martial parent. Many a barracks I passed. But where was yesterday's pride and glory? Militarism had lost its sheen. The descent of the steep slope leading to drab civilianism had begun!

Chapter VI

"Yessie"

WE were in Boston. The reason was that Antonio Guzmán Blanco, dictator of Venezuela, was in Caracas. There was no room in the same city for Guzmán Blanco and my father.

So the latter had traveled northward in a hurry. Despite a fur coat of great thickness, and a fur hat with fur earpieces, the winds of Massachusetts blew right through General Ybarra and made him perfectly miserable. (I never saw anybody so catastrophically affected by wintry weather as he was. In later years, when I was perpetrating an irreverent paper in Cambridge, Mass., for home consumption, I wrote: "General Alejandro Ybarra, the noted Venezuelan resident of Waterhouse Street, is suffering from a cold, owing to the fact that a window was opened yesterday in the house next door." When my mother used to make fun of him for being so vulnerable to Massachusetts weather, he would bleat pathetically: "Laugh if joo like! Bot, som day, I die of a cheell!")

At the time of which I am writing (before my adventures in militarism narrated in the two preceding chapters), my father and mother had been married about five years. They had two children, my elder sister Elena (known as Nelita), four years old, and myself, aged two. It became necessary to hire a nurse-maid-of-all-work to take care of us. That was the signal for the

"YESSIE"

incorporation into the family of Jessie Sullivan, aged twenty or thereabouts, Cockney-Irish, fresh from London—loyal, homely, full of Cockney impudence and Irish salt, without a single specimen in her vocabulary of the eighth letter of the alphabet.

At once Jessie became an integral part of our family circle—and stayed so for some thirty-five years. She took care of four other children of my parents besides Nelita and myself, including my younger sister Leonor (nicknamed Norn or Nornie) and my younger brother, Alejandro, Jr.—also of Norn's three children after her marriage in Caracas. Nelita and I and subsequent additions to the roster of the Ybarra-Russell children accepted Jessie—along with Jack, our Dalmatian coach-dog—as in a category only slightly below our parents. In those earliest years of my life, I used to request God, every evening, to "bless Mamma and Papa and Grandma and Nornie and Jessie and baby and Jacky."

Jessie tackled life with sublime self-confidence. In the wake of her employers she moved back and forth between the United States and Venezuela, between New York and Europe, between Europe and Caracas and the Dutch West Indies. Never, at any point, did foreigners in any form make the slightest dent on her heritage from the Ireland of her forefathers and the London to which her Irish parents had migrated some years before her birth. That London centered in Sloane Street Mews, near Knightsbridge—or, as Jessie phrased it, "Sloane Street Muses, just around the corner from Nicebridge."

Throughout our childhood, Jessie lavished upon me and my sisters and my brother an unending succession of yarns about her early days in England, when her father, a bricklayer, living, apparently, in Arabian Nights prosperity, would often send her out "to fetch an 'ansom." Also, there were trips into Kent to "pick 'ops."

The England of Jessie Sullivan was invested, in my child's imagination, with tremendous pomp and circumstance. In after years I began to have my doubts, but this later doubting Thomas phase wasn't half so satisfactory as the unquestioning faith that preceded it. I remember how disappointed I was when I first saw Sloane Street—somehow I had expected a cross between the Street Called Straight and the Milky Way.

Jessie would allow no trifling with her Irish ancestry. When, emerging from childhood, I was becoming tainted with irreverence and unbelief, I would rally her about her forebears in Erin, of whom I had been hearing copiously for years.

"Jessie," I would say banteringly, "how's your family?" She would retort, with snapping eyes:

"Thomas [only when she was really annoyed did she call me Thomas], I would 'ave you know that my family was once kings of Ireland."

In Venezuela Jessie became Yessie. *Yessie Sollivahn.* Our Cockney Irishwoman looked upon the entire population of Venezuela with good-humored disdain. Always she lumped them, irrespective of sex or condition, of high, medium or low social status, as "them people."

In my brother's early childhood, Jessie Sullivan became a source of much mystification to him. I had just turned fifteen and begun an enthusiastic worship at the shrine of Gilbert and Sullivan, which still stands unshaken by the lapse of time. The names of the inimitable Savoyards, constantly on my lips, puzzled my little brother. Finally, one day, he blurted out:

"Tommy, is Jessie Gilbert-and-Sullivan's wife?"

Jessie knew how to put Spanish verbs in their place. Present,

"YESSIE"

past and future, indicative and subjunctive, were swallowed up, in the voluble conversations she conducted with Venezuelans, by one lone form of Spanish conjugation which did her bidding in every linguistic emergency as unquestioningly as a well-trained dog that of its master. At all hours, in our house, we could hear Jessie's imperious orders to Venezuelan domestics:

"Manuel! Setting the table!

"Rosarito! Making Missybarra's bed [Missybarra was Jessie's unvarying version of Mrs. Ybarra].

"Antonia! Where putting sugar bowl? Putting it here yesterday! Putting it there today! Always putting!"

And Manuel and Rosarito and Antonia would slouch away to execute Jessie's orders, quite as if she hadn't murdered one Spanish verb after another in their presence.

Once, I remember, my young brother wanted to go out for a donkey ride. So he asked Jessie to ask Manuel to saddle his donkey. While the Ybarra family sat doubled up in helpless convulsions of laughter, Jessie bawled from the patio toward the stables:

"*Manuel, encendiendo la burra!*" What she *should* have said was: "*Manuel, ensille el burro.*" What she shouted, literally rendered into English, was: "Manuel, setting fire to the female jackass!"

In Venezuela, as in all countries inhabited by members of the Spanish race, the names of God and the Virgin Mary, together with those of many saints, are constantly in people's mouths. No disrespect is meant—exclamations like *Vírgen Santísima* and *San Antonio Bendito* are the small change of conversation. (When they want cusswords, the Venezuelans go elsewhere, with appalling consequences.) Jessie Sullivan listened good-humoredly to the incessant appeals of "them people" to the Holy Trinity and to saintly individuals canonized by the Roman Catholic church. She was particularly attracted by the Spanish version of the names of Saint Peter and Saint Paul. So she decided to give them a place in her vocabulary. But, true to her inborn Cockney-Irish independence, she also decided to use them exactly as she pleased, without being hampered at any point by the rules governing the Spanish language.

One day she filled us with astonishment and delight by exclaiming to my little sister Leonor, after the latter had got her clothes spattered with mud:

"Leonor Ybarra, what 'ave you done to yourself? Why, San-Pedro-San-Pablo-come-up-and-fall-down-on-me, you've ruined your dress!"

Jessie's achievements in the language, spoken in the Caracas to which fate had led her, achieved city-wide fame—Venezuelans would gather around her, breathless with awe and wonder, while she made voluble proclamations to hypnotized storekeepers.

Despite the imperfections of her Spanish (it had no other ingredients), Jessie bossed the native domestics at our house with enormous success. They ate out of her hand. They would come to her with their troubles and she would scold and advise them in a brand of Spanish never heard on land or sea. But, by some subtle extra sense inside them, they understood her. They used to trust her with their money, begging her to keep it for them, when they were flush, and resorting to the most remarkable subterfuges to extract from her something on account, when they were broke.

I recall, particularly, the case of Raimundo. Raimundo was a soldier sent to our establishment from his barracks to act as

"YESSIE"

man-of-all-work. Whenever he was under the influence of virtue and sobriety, he would bring Jessie little sums of money—*pesos fuertes* (silver dollars) and lesser coins—and request her to hide them away for him in some safe place against a rainy day. Yessie would take the money, wrap it up in little pieces of paper, and secrete it in a remote corner of a drawer in the dresser in her room.

Then Raimundo would try to get it back. But Jessie was adamant. His reasons were not satisfactory. "*Vagabundo, yo no dando nada, tu no hablando mas*" ("You rascal, I not giving anything, thou not talking any more"), she would tell him in her private and unprecedented Spanish. So Raimundo would retire to think up another plea.

One day he appeared wearing a brand-new *cobija*, the cloak, blue on one side and red on the other, reaching from neck to ankles, which Venezuelans of Raimundo's social status prefer to all other forms of outer adornment. Seeking Jessie, he held the garment before her, stroking its sleek surface affectionately, pointing out its numerous excellences.

"Ah, Yessie!" he sighed. "What a bargain. This cobija is offered to me for—guess how much."

"Ten pesos?"

"Five, Yessie, five!"

"Well, why don't you buy it?" (What Jessie actually said was: "Well, why not buying it?")

Raimundo looked forlorn. Tears came into his eyes.

"Because, Yessie, I have no money. You have all my money. If you would let me have five pesos—*only five pesos*, Yessie—I could buy this beautiful cobija. Tomorrow it will be gone. Somebody else will snap it up."

He grew so mournful that Jessie eventually went into her

room, rummaged around in her dresser, and emerged with five pesos of Raimundo's money. He was overjoyed. All through that day and the next he strutted about, wearing his new cloak, calling on Jessie to admire it.

Then, suddenly, it disappeared.

"Where being cobija?" inquired Jessie. After a lot of stammering on Raimundo's part and intensive detective work on Jessie's, it turned out that Raimundo had merely borrowed the garment, in order to coax some of his money out of Jessie and stage a mammoth bout with wine and women. At the end of two days he had been compelled, according to contract, to return the cobija to the crony who had loaned it for the express purpose of bamboozling Jessie.

Her revenge was hideous: *she refused flatly to take care of Raimundo's money any longer.*

She returned to him every coin belonging to him that was in her possession, every copper centavo and nickel locha and silver real and bolívar and peso fuerte. She announced dramatically that she was done forevermore with being his banker. Raimundo pleaded and implored and wept.

"*Nunca mas guardando dinero!*" ("Never again keeping money.") Repeatedly we heard those words shot at Raimundo by Jessie—followed by his crestfallen retreat to the kitchen, holding listlessly in his hand the coins that Jessie had cruelly spurned.

Once, when we departed from the prevailing custom of getting servants from the Cuartel de Carmelitas or the Cuartel San Carlos, Jessie had reason to deplore the change. Instead of a soldier, a strange, brooding Spaniard named Fernando was imported into the household. Undeterred by Jessie's forbidding face and unfriendly attitude, he made violent love to her. Jessie

"YESSIE"

treated his love with scorn. Fernando, wounded to the core of his ardent Iberian soul, threatened to stick a knife into Jessie. Jessie snapped her fingers at him. Whether or not he would have made good his threat we never knew, because Fernando (possibly owing to the amorous conflagration inside him) neglected his duties and was fired by my father.

In Spanish, one addresses other persons either with the intimate *tu*, reserved for relatives and close friends, or the formal *usted*, which carries with it a note of deference and respect. But, in Jessie Sullivan's *lingua franca* toward "them people," there were no gradations of approach. For her, nothing but *tu* existed—equally applicable to the Most Illustrious and Reverend Críspulo Uzcátegui, Archbishop of Venezuela, and to Manuel, the stableboy.

Whenever my beautiful Aunt Inés would come to our house, she always made a point of going into the rear regions in search of Jessie and greeting her with cordiality—for Aunt Inés, born and brought up in the old Rivas-Ybarra house, between the corners of El Conde and Piñango, was deeply impregnated with the old semi-feudalistic attitude of the Venezuela of the middle of the nineteenth century, which considered members of the domestic staff a sort of mixture of cousin and vassal.

"Yessie!" Aunt Inés would call. And "Yessie" would come bustling out of the kitchen or the laundry, excitedly wiping her hands on her apron, her hair (done up in a tight knot at the back) somewhat tousled from her labors around the house, and exclaim affably:

"*Ah, tu aquí, Inés? Como 'ta tu, Inés?*" And Aunt Inés, far from being shocked at this burst of intimacy, built up around the second personal pronoun singular, would gravely inquire about Jessie's health and return to the front part of the house and to the rest of the family with Jessie's amiable *"Adios, Inés, tu viniendo mañana?"* ("Good-bye, Inés, thou coming tomorrow?") resounding behind her.

As Jessie advanced in age, silver hairs appeared amid the nondescript yellow of her thatch. This annoyed her exceedingly, for Jessie was vain of her appearance, an attitude justified by nothing done for her by the Creator. Jessie decided that action must be taken to remedy the hair situation. She forthwith proceeded to take it, in strict secrecy. She wrote to a firm of manufacturers of hair dye in the United States, requesting them to send her several bottles of their product, for which they claimed magical qualities.

Three or four weeks later the telephone at our house rang. A voice asked to be allowed to speak to *la señora de Ybarra*. My mother took up the receiver.

"Good morning, *señora*," said the voice respectfully, "this is the Collector of Customs at the Customs House in La Guaira. There is some duty to pay on that package of yours from New York before we can release it."

"WHAT package?" asked my mother, who hadn't ordered anything whatsoever from New York.

"The one addressed to you."

"Addressed to *me?*"

"Yes, señora."

"What's in it?"

"Hair dye."

At that, my mother hit the ceiling. An investigation was immediately started. It led straight to Jessie. Without the slightest attempt at evasion, Jessie cheerfully admitted that it was she who had imported the hair dye.

"YESSIE"

"But why did you have it addressed to *me?*" inquired my mother angrily. With great calm (all through the excitement Jessie had acted as if unable to understand what it was all about), Jessie replied:

"You are important down here, Missybarra. I am not. I thought them people in the La Guaira customs house would be much more impressed if the 'air dye was addressed to you."

Jessie was unbeatable!

In spite of our daily association with Jessie, there were times when the peculiarities of her jargon caught us napping. For instance, in the morning she would bustle up to my mother's room, when its occupant was sleeping later than usual, and inquire:

"Missybarra, shall I eat your breakfast?"

My mother, rousing herself from a doze, would answer in a mystified voice:

"Certainly not. Why should you eat my breakfast?"

"Well, it's getting late, you know. I think it's about time for me to eat your breakfast."

Then my mother would understand. What Jessie, true to her upbringing in Sloane Street Mews, meant to convey was: "Shall I *heat* your breakfast?" Again and again my mother was fooled by that matutinal query from aitchless Miss Sullivan.

At our house in El Paraíso it was Jessie who cooked breakfast for all of us. And it took all the good nature characteristic of our Cockney-Irish factotum to discharge that duty without suffering a nervous breakdown. For no two of the Ybarras were ready for breakfast at the same time, and no two wanted the same thing.

My father got up very early and demanded invariably just coffee and rolls. Next I put in my appearance—craving also coffee and rolls, but with certain frills which varied according to my gastronomic humor. Then my brother would appear and put in his order. Then my sister would call for sustenance, served to her in bed, which usually meant eggs and chocolate. And, finally, my mother would be ready for Jessie to 'eat her breakfast—consumed, as in the case of my sister, in her bedroom. All of these variegated assignments were covered by Jessie with unchanging evenness of temper.

Jessie was an admirable cook. It was good news to the household when some temporary crisis in the kitchen made it necessary for her to jump in and take charge. I have never eaten scrambled eggs like those dished up by Jessie. They looked like yellow foam, were light as air, and—literally—melted in one's mouth.

Two other great specialties of hers were bread pudding and gingerbread. Prepared by Jessie, these tasted differently from any other version of the same two delicacies encountered by me anywhere in later life. In my early childhood, the day on which Jessie was to provide bread pudding in our house was signalized by the three small Ybarras with parades through all the rooms, in which we carried big placards covered with penciled scrawls of "Delightful, delicious!" or "Delicious, delightful!" Pursuant to a law devised and promulgated by me, those two adjectives might be used separately to denote anything that pleased me or my young sister or brother, but *never together* except in praise of Jessie's bread pudding. All three of us obeyed that law for years as carefully as if it had been the joint work of the Medes and the Persians.

In our Caracas home we had no oven capable of baking anything as big as the periodical bread puddings or quotas of gingerbread which Jessie used to prepare every few months.

"YESSIE"

The unbaked mass of each would be conveyed, by some small and dusky member of our domestic staff, to the nearest bakery. From there it would come back—crisp, brown and hot—a few hours later.

Then the whole family pitched in. We ate bread pudding or gingerbread hot and lukewarm and cold. We ate it in the morning, at noon, in the afternoon, evenings, at night. We ate it in neatly cut slices or shapeless hunks, broken off at random from the main supply. We cheerfully endured stomach aches of varying intensity. I even used to go to school with a hunk of bread pudding as a pre-lunch appetizer.

Jessie admired my father. In that peculiar English of hers, as devoid of grammatical correctness as of the letter "h," she used to tell me and my sister and my brother: "None of you children ain't got your father's looks."

And she used to embarrass me by remembering incidents of my earliest childhood which, I thought, should best be forgotten.

"Thomas," she would tell me, "when you were living on 'ancock Street you used to love to sit in the coal scuttle and pour coal dust all over yourself." She also reminded me—during a period when Spanish dignity was growing up fast within me—that, in my first years in the human race, I had a passion for strange nicknames. These I would change with bewildering frequency. And I would imperiously demand that everyone around me refrain from getting mixed up on those nicknames —what had been perfectly good, in other words, on Tuesday, must, under no circumstances, be applied to me on Wednesday. Once (still according to Jessie) I was weeping bitterly (probably in the coal scuttle), and the whole household was in despair because nobody could remember my current nickname.

Finally, my little sister Nelita was summoned.

"What IS Tom's nickname today?" begged my mother. Nelita always knew.

"Why, Big-Drum-In-The-Middle-Of-The-Road," she replied instantly.

"Yes!" I sobbed. And I dried my tears. The crisis was over.

On one occasion, said Jessie, that nickname habit of mine caused most lamentable consequences. It was while we were living in Plymouth. A most particular friend of the family, whom I shall call Dr. James, a prominent medical practitioner —also directly descended from one of the original Pilgrim Fathers, which greatly enhanced his local importance—was calling on my mother. That day, unfortunately, I had chosen the visitor's name for my current appellation. In the midst of formal palaver between the descendant of the Pilgrims and my mother, Jessie Sullivan went from room to room of our house in search of me, shouting in a loud voice, perfectly audible in the parlor:

"Doctor James, Doctor James, come to sit on the pot!"

Jessie considered herself personally responsible for the health, safety and education of all the Ybarra children. My mother and father, plus school teachers—she might agree, if hard pressed—had something to do with our development and protection, but not much.

She took most particularly under her wing my young sister Leonor, who, from the age of ten, showed unmistakable signs of turning into a devastating influence on males. When Leonor was fifteen, she was already one of the belles of Caracas, with youthful Venezuelans buzzing around her like heartbroken mosquitoes. Jessie, who knew well how dissipated and unscrupulous many of the younger scions of "them people" were, felt it incumbent on her to shield Leonor from the massed ad-

Family group (including "Yessie") in front of the Ybarra home, Monte Elena

"YESSIE"

vances of admirers. All of the latter were the same to Jessie, whether prominent or humble in the community—they were just specimens of a noxious brand of insect, to be shooed away without mercy.

One youth—or insect, as Jessie classed him—belonging to the Echeverría family, which occupied a proud place in the social hierarchy of Caracas, entered the lists in Norn's girlhood as one of her most lovesick swains. When we lived in town, he would pass and re-pass our house, in the traditional Latin manner, ogling my pretty sister as she sat fanning herself at one of our front windows. When we moved to the suburb of El Paraíso, young Echeverría would mount a horse, like young Lochinvar, and come loping down to the area immediately in front of our residence, where he spent hours. At times he would gather sufficient courage to ride his steed up the road that breasted the hillock on which our house perched, to the very door, in the hope of catching a glimpse of Norn.

In the course of one audacious exploit of this sort, Lochinvar was confronted, in the garden outside our portal, by Jessie Sullivan, frowning formidably. In a panic he reined in his horse.

"Hey, Echeverría!" said Jessie coldly, "*que buscando tu aquí?*" ("What seeking thou here?")

"Hey, Echeverría!" did not answer. Whirling his horse around, he galloped back down the road. In later years, after he had placed himself (in the teeth of Jessie) on a more formal status with us, he used to delight in telling of his terror during that encounter of his boyhood with our Cockney-Irish dragon.

Then there was Ramón. He was the offspring of a rich father and a richer mother—indeed, on the latter's side, he was closely associated with the fortunes of one of the biggest import-and-export firms of Venezuela, with a full-fledged partnership awaiting him as soon as he wanted it, and millions of dollars—or so Caracas professed to believe—piled up by his fond uncles in readiness to cushion his journey through life. Ramón fell in love with Leonor. But Jessie, undazzled by his advantageous position and prospects, observed his amorous machinations with her usual fishy eye.

She professed deep contempt for Ramón—though he always treated her with apprehensive courtesy. And she took mean advantage of the fact that he was a youth of inferior muscular development, thin and weedy and wispy, by dubbing him "that 'ere snippingill"—a specimen of her aptitude for terse description which rang a bell in our family circle.

Leonor married neither "Hey, Echeverría!" nor "that 'ere snippingill." She married another swain, Bernardino Ruiz, whose family owned big cocoa plantations on the Venezuelan coast east of La Guaira. Following the birth of Leonor's first daughter, Jessie was transferred from our household to Leonor's. There she cared, in succession, for that first daughter of Leonor and two others.

While she was bringing up my sister's children according to the Sullivan formula, Jessie had occasion to visit the cocoa plantations of Norn's husband's family. There she acquired a lot more knowledge about Venezuelans, of a kind not calculated to raise her already low opinion of "them people."

For instance, there was the case of the majordomo Toribio and the cook Obdulia. This pair had been living together, in unholy wedlock, for ten years or more. They had eight children. Toribio didn't like the situation. He wanted it legalized. But Obdulia shook her head.

"YESSIE"

"Señora," she would say to my mother—while Jessie listened in shocked disapproval—"last night that man of mine again asked me to marry him. That must be the twentieth time, I reckon. But I said no. I always say no. 'Toribio,' I told him, let well enough alone. I'm one of those women who can't be happy unless she stays single. I was not born for marriage!' " Whereupon she went back to her eight children.

Jessie also heard about the baker and the butcher who, years before, used to deliver bread and meat to one of the plantations. The two met one morning.

"Butcher," said the baker, "things aren't what they used to be in old Don Casimiro's day."

"Baker," said the butcher, "you've said an earful. They are not."

"A grand old man, Don Casimiro—eh, butcher?"

"None better, baker."

"And, by the way, butcher, I'm going to tell you something. Old Don Casimiro was my father."

"Is that so, baker? Well, well. He was mine, too."

With advancing age, Jessie got eccentric. She became convinced that Norn's husband, her employer, was staging an elaborate campaign of persecution against her, based on the deep-seated prejudice of "them people" against the British Empire. This would not have been serious if Jessie had confined herself to passive resistance. The trouble was that she acted. One day my father, summoned to the telephone, found an agitated Chief of Police at the other end of the wire.

"Listen, General," said the Chief of Police, in a sad state of embarrassment and indecision. "That nursemaid at your daughter's house has just dropped into the police station on the

Plaza Bolívar, with a couple of your grandchildren in tow, and insisted on lodging a formal complaint against your son-in-law. She says he's persecuting her."

That was the last straw. With much exercise of tact and diplomacy, Jessie was eased out of the household of my brother-in-law and brought back to the United States by my mother. There, with her savings—Jessie had been most frugal all her life—she bought herself a little 'ouse in Plymouth and settled down for the rest of her days.

When I visited Plymouth some years later, I found that she had made of that 'ouse a sort of Ybarra shrine. Photographs of my father and mother and of every one of us children, in every stage of growth and costume, even as far back as Nelita (who had been dead some thirty-five years) were in places of honor everywhere. And Jessie's conversation dealt entirely with her long sojourn among the Venezuelans, and with her unshakable affection for those shining examples of immunity from "them people's" iniquity, the Ybarra-Russells.

Chapter VII

My Caracas

In my childhood, a very old Englishman used to go pigeon-toeing through the streets of Caracas, quavering praise of the city, and distributing copies of *Black Beauty* to indifferent natives, for, next to Caracas, prevention of cruelty to animals was his hobby. His name was Mr. Middleton—pronounced locally Meestair Meel-toe.

He had spent, before I knew him, more than half a century in the British diplomatic service. His many billets had caused him to stay for long periods in capitals of a number of countries—Paris, Madrid, Buenos Aires, Mexico City, etc. But Caracas, for Meestair Meel-toe, eclipsed them all.

When he got to the capital of Venezuela he was overwhelmed. As the creator of the Taj Mahal felt about his masterpiece, so this ancient Britisher felt about Caracas; he, too, could have said: "If there is a Paradise on earth, it is this, it is this." When he became ripe for retirement he elected to remain in Caracas instead of returning to England; nothing in his native land could offer him the inducements of the city which, as he kept on repeating, was "one step from Paradise."

Mr. Middleton was among the Caracas landmarks encountered by William Eleroy Curtis on his trip to Venezuela. The American writer listened to Mr. Middleton's praise of my father's native town, in which rapturous warmth vied with inordinate length. "I have been here since 1869," said the old gentleman to Curtis (as set down in the latter's book). "I have seen this country in war and peace and have experienced two earthquakes, the last of which killed three hundred people. But there is no place on earth possessing so many natural and climatic attractions. All I ask is to end my days in this eternal spring."

Mr. Middleton's wish was granted. Many years after he had settled down for good in the Venezuelan capital, the British Legation there took charge of his funeral, his nearest English kin being thousands of miles away.

Dr. Ybarra, my grandfather, also felt a deep affection for the city of his birth. To have been forced to spend his entire life there never seemed to him an unfriendly trick of fate. He used to stand in the rear upstairs corridor of his house and look at the Avila mountains for hours. With his grave savant's eyes, he contemplated them in the bright light of morning, in the heat-laden atmosphere of afternoon, in the falling shadows of the twilight, when their steep, rounded slopes lay bathed in strange hues of dappled green and brownish-purple, in anticipation of their withdrawal into the blackness of the night.

"Never," the dignified old professor used to say to his son, my father, "never, in all my life, have I seen the Avila twice alike. Never, I know, up to the day of my death, shall I see it twice alike." And he returned to his silent contemplation of the mountains that he loved.

The enchantment of Caracas also completely won over my other grandfather—Judge Russell. His letters home, written when he was United States Minister to Venezuela, abound in expressions of that enchantment. "If you could see our mountains today," he wrote to Marston Watson, "with the white streams tumbling down their sides, and with every leaf on the trees visible in this pure light, and then could see them by moonlight . . . and have June every morning and October every evening, you would not expect to see me at home in less than three years."

In another letter he said:

"We like Caracas better every day, and, now that the rains have abated, it is more beautiful than ever. Such blue skies I never saw, and the air is so soft that it is a pleasure to breathe. I wish you could have some of our weather. It would give you new life. . . .

"I should like to spend May Day in Plymouth and have a look at Hillside, but should want to return in a few days to the soft climate of Venezuela, where we think it a good thing that our house has not a pane of glass in it. I never expected to enjoy mere weather so much. And, besides, there is a quiet about the place that is delightful. . . .

"The sun is bright and a constant east wind blows freely, and it is perfumed by the trees and flowers on the mountains which it crosses. The mountain streams, too, are full, as they tumble down the sides. There are just such streams in other places, I suppose, but the wonder is to see them from the chief streets of a city. There are wonderful sunsets lately, and when the hills have grown dark the top of the Silla shines with rose-colored light."

I have quoted the foregoing tributes to Caracas because I want them to be a sort of buttressing prelude to the statement that I think Caracas one of the loveliest spots on this earth. I can well understand old Mr. Middleton's raptures. I can well understand the enthusiasm of my two grandfathers. Thousands of Caraqueños, at home and abroad, in daily enjoyment of their adored city, or in the bitterness of exile, have loved it with passionate constancy. A famous Venezuelan poet, Pérez Bonalde, was once driven from Caracas by a revolution. He ate his heart out on foreign soil. And how that heart leaped to new life at sight of the valley of Caracas is eloquently attested by his renowned *Retorno a la Patria*. That poem, from the point of view of a Venezuelan, has everything; it throbs with the feelings of a Caraqueño in whom homesickness has been swept away by the sight of sunlight on old streets, and shadows falling across mountain-walls, which, he had not known until the moment of his homecoming, were bred into the fiber of his being and the stream of his blood—

> "Caracas allí está . . . sus oscuras lomas,
> Y sus bandas de tímidas palomas. . . ."

Recite that to any native of Caracas and you will instantly learn what he really thinks of his native city; and, if a native city arouses such a response, a response measured in eyes that suddenly fill with light and tears that suddenly dim that light, it *must* have something.

Well, Caracas *has* something. To the end of its days it will find Mr. Middletons to grow lyrical about it and Dr. Ybarras and Judge Russells to stand in silent contemplation of its ever-changing yet never-changing beauty.

It lies in a valley of exuberant fertility, crossed by the little river Guaire, on its way to confluence with the big river Tuy, many miles to the eastward. On the north rises the grandiose Avila range, 7,000 feet above sea level and 4,000 feet above Caracas, dominated by the peak of La Silla (The Saddle).

MY CARACAS

The Avila cuts off the valley of Caracas from the Caribbean coast. It is bare and rugged; yet it has a certain smoothness, an undulating quality in its slopes, as they climb toward its towering pinnacles—the sort of thing that one expects in mountains which are in South America, not in Switzerland or Alaska. The Avila never reaches heights such as those in the South American Andes, far to the westward, which have to acknowledge the cold sovereignty of ice and snow.

In the valley of Caracas, spring is eternal. Neither winter nor summer ever gets a hold on its local weather. If there's rain, it's winter; if there isn't, it's summer. That's the way the Caraqueños look at the seasons. Slip down 3,000 feet to La Guaira, on the Caribbean, and you will find yourself fanning a wet brow with a wilting straw hat and cursing the blistering sunshine. Slip down 3,000 feet in the other direction—down into the valleys of Aragua, into rich coffee lands, into the midst of natives in picturesque cobijas and planters on sleek mules—and you will find your enjoyment hampered by broiling heat and flowing perspiration.

But never in Caracas. "All I ask is to end my days in this eternal spring." I can hear old Meestair Meel-toe quavering those words in the Caracas of the eighteen-nineties. May he rest in peace, in the eternal spring of another world! That should be the prayer of all who love Caracas and love others for loving it.

My Caracas, my first Caracas, the Caracas of my early boyhood, was still remote from the rest of the world. Though Richard Harding Davis called it the Paris of South America, to the joy of the natives, many of whom love Paris better than salvation, it was primitive. From under a thin surface of modernity peeped the Caracas of the Spaniards; of Simón Bolívar, Spain's Nemesis in South America; of his successors, the rough generals of unnumbered Venezuelan civil wars.

In the Caracas of my early days, most of the streets were still paved with cobblestones. *Adoquines*, big, smooth paving blocks, were just creeping into the central parts of the city. In outlying sections, the sidewalks were still made of rough slabs of stone laid horizontally, enclosed within a primitive curb of vertical slabs. But cement was rapidly driving these away. Cement became the fashion in the eighteen-eighties, after Dictator Guzmán Blanco, with his customary paternal attention to family nest-feathering, had given the monopoly of selling cement to his wife's brother-in-law, and then decreed that every sidewalk in the central parts of the city must be made of the new-fangled stuff.

Sewers were also new. A Belgian company had just installed a set of them at the behest of Guzmán. These were still functioning when I first knew Caracas. Lest the natives, rescued from primitive pre-Guzmán sanitation, should forget this gift from the dictator and the Belgians, the new sewers sometimes stank consummately. But the inhabitants of the city, with an odoriferous succession of centuries behind them, took the new stink in their stride.

Of the thousands of houses in my Caracas, roofed with red tiles and painted in a variety of colors, only a few had two stories. This was because of the fear of earthquakes. Just as the people of Venezuela's capital got to believe that earthquakes in their valley were as obsolete as Spanish captains-general, a *terremoto* would come along and give them such a shaking-up that they would camp under the trees of their plazas for days, in the belief that their roof would get into bed with them if they slept at home.

MY CARACAS

In 1812, Caracas was almost entirely destroyed by an earthquake. It came on Holy Thursday, when the churches were packed with people; of the twelve thousand who perished, a large percentage were buried under the walls of shattered temples of worship. In spite of this catastrophe and other later seismic cutting-up, the new Caracas is rapidly becoming a city of buildings with two and even more stories. Perhaps the oil companies have bought off the god of terremotos. I wonder.

In my Caracas, one often saw little donkeys, with the eyes of old philosophers, pattering along the narrow streets, with a barrel filled with rolls of *pan de trigo* (wheat bread) slung from each side of the saddle girt to their backs. On the saddle sat a youth, vigorously urging his little steed forward by digging sandaled heels into its ribs. At the door of house after house the youth stopped, strode into the zaguán with bread under each arm, and shouted loudly for somebody from inside to come and receive it.

The barrels on the donkey's back were painted bright red. On their sides were printed big letters announcing what concern had baked the bread. *Pan Marca R* was the usual inscription on such barrels in the days of my early boyhood, since the leading baking magnate of Caracas had a name which began with an R.

In later years, barrels emblazoned with *Pan Marca M* became more and more common. This was the outward sign of a terrific commercial battle between Bread Magnate R, and a newcomer, Señor M. For years the battle raged with increasing vindictiveness. Finally, *Pan Marca R* disappeared from the streets of Caracas; donkeys bearing barrels labeled *Pan Marca M* popped up everywhere; Señor M. had won a complete victory. Señor R. was driven into bankruptcy. The fury of the fight between those two was clearly shown when Señor M. appeared in court to see that his routed foe declared his every asset, even the smallest, to the tribunal about to adjudge him a bankrupt.

"Have you listed everything, Señor R.?" asked the judge.
"I have."
"Are you satisfied, Señor M.?"
"I am not."
"Why not?"
"Because he still owns something which he has not listed."
"What?"
"His burial plot in the cemetery."

One also had to dodge out of the path of the *parihueleros*. These were sandaled individuals, well-built and with good muscles, who had a monopoly in those times of the moving of furniture and other breakable articles through the streets of the little city. They got their name from the *parihuela* on which they placed the loads entrusted to them.

The Venezuelan parihuela was (or should I say *is?* I hope it still exists somewhere in Venezuela) a long-handled wooden frame, or trestle. To its handles, broad hempen ropes were attached, which were passed across the shoulders and the backs of the necks of the bearers. With the potent aid of these ropes, the brawny bearers were enabled to move along the streets, with heavy loads, in a rhythmic jog trot that practically eliminated all danger of damage to the articles carried. These included all sorts of household things—beds and dressers, chairs and tables, trunks and mirrors and pianos.

And, of course, there were the soldiers. When (aged four or five) I was out under the wing of "Yessie"—or when (aged ten or eleven) I bestrode Don Rodrigo—soldiers kept crossing

MY CARACAS

my path, in badly fitting uniforms and with caps cocked over one eye, shouldering the breech-loading Remington rifles that were still wonders of military progress to the Venezuelans. They also had big bayonets, in leather scabbards, which slapped against their thighs. How much a part of my Caracas those squads of coppery little warriors were!

One of the old two-story houses in the central part of Caracas was the one that had been occupied by Dr. Ybarra, my grandfather, and his family. It is still standing and it is now considerably over one hundred years old. It was a Rivas house.

The house, in my childhood, had a light-blue façade with white facings, and a row of small balconies on the front of the second story, facing the street. Downstairs, it had two huge iron-barred windows, with outsize *postigos*, wooden shutters, one on each side of the zaguán. This was also outsize, with an enormous door studded with iron knobs at the street end, and an inner door, painted blue like the façade. This inner door opened onto the downstairs front corridor and the big main patio, fringed upstairs by a balcony running around three sides of the house.

In the second story was a big front drawing room, covering the whole width of the front façade, usually dark and gloomy because the doors to the balconies were kept shut. Behind it were a smaller drawing room (much more cheerful and popular with the family), the big dining room, and several of the principal sleeping apartments. In one of these, my grandmother Ybarra and every one of her many children, including my father, had been born.

Behind the dining room was a big enclosed space, rather

more of a corridor than a room, with a back railing over which one could look out on a second patio downstairs and on the Avila range towering over the valley to the northward. It was on that railing that my grandfather, Dr. Ybarra, used to lean when he contemplated his beloved mountains.

In the extreme background was a little garden, filled with tropical shrubbery, with a pool of scummy water at one end. Into this I promptly tumbled, on one of my earliest visits to my grandmother, causing considerable damage to the clothes I was wearing, and bestowing upon them an ancient and fish-like smell, which, for a while, showed signs of becoming permanent.

In my grandfather's house there were thirty rooms or more, counting in everything. Yet it was not at all among the largest in the city. There were other, much bigger mansions, some dating far back into the epoch of the Spaniards. Caracas had (and still has) scores of great houses, built in the eighteenth or seventeenth century; some of them were two or three times as big as the home of my grandparents. Many of these structures eventually became such white elephants that their owners were forced to relinquish them to the Venezuelan government, for use as barracks or public offices or such-like.

The home of my grandparents was swallowed up years ago by a ravenous mortgage. After that it sheltered, for a while, a lot of Syrian peddlers sent out every morning by their chief —an Oriental with all the authority but none of the savagery of Simon Legree—with packs on their backs, to peddle cheap trinkets all over Caracas. For some occult reason, these Syrians were known as *Turcos*. Later, the house became a Protestant mission (presided over by Mr. and Mrs. Pond, from New England, of whom I shall tell more in another chapter). A Protestant mission in the mansion of the Rivas and Ybarra families! Shades of Misia Merced, my pious and crabbed Catholic grandmother! I wonder she didn't haunt that mission to death!

Several of the most elephantine mansions of Caracas belonged, or had belonged, to the Tovar family. The Tovars, when they first went out to the New World from Spain, were already a tribe of importance. Having arrived in Venezuela, they proceeded to add to their importance most considerably by getting all sorts of valuable grants from the Spanish kings. They built themselves residences in and around Caracas that dwarfed nearly all the architectural achievements of rival families.

So numerous were the Tovar houses in my Caracas that if you asked a Caraqueño to tell you about the historical background of this or that big dwelling, he was likely to answer "Oh, that's a Tovar house," on the theory that if it wasn't, it ought to be. Around the corner from where we lived, when we were dwellers in the city, stood a gigantic Tovar edifice, with a shabby and extensive two-story façade painted a dull pink. It had been reduced to the rank of a boarding-house. And, on the corner of El Conde, there was another, still bigger, covered with peeling yellow paint, which, in my childhood, housed the Ministerio de Fomento. That was a branch of the Venezuelan government that was supposed to promote immigration and national development of assorted kinds, but did nothing of the sort—at least not in any manner visible to the naked eye.

High social rank stemming from Spain had lost nearly every shred of its practical value in my Caracas. It helped hardly at all in the rough-and-ready politics of the era. In fact, too much blue blood in the veins of politicians might turn out to be a handicap in dealing with unscrupulous politicians and roughneck generals, who hadn't any at all. These gentry were endowed, instead, with an uncanny ability to push themselves onto political pinnacles which (under the Spanish king) would have been strictly reserved for *peninsulares*—Spaniards from Spain—and a small minority of the colonial upper crust.

Most of the Venezuelans of my childhood who still attached importance to Spanish blue blood belonged to the conservative party. From the standpoint of *la familia*, my Ybarras should have been conservatives; but it happened that both my grandfather and my father were enthusiastic liberals.

My father would discourse for hours about the iniquities of *los godos*, the name applied to the Venezuelan conservatives by their political enemies. *Godo*, in Spanish, means Goth. It was originally wished by the Venezuelan patriots, in their war of independence, on the Spaniards. It had the same implication that we attach to Vandal or Hun, all three appellations, of course, going back to the early centuries A. D., when Goths and Vandals and Huns were making a great reputation for themselves by sedulously pillaging and raping and assassinating in assorted parts of the crumbling Roman Empire.

My father's antipathy for los godos never left him. Northern latitudes could not cool it nor lapse of time allay it. When he was an exile in Boston, he used to spend hours gloomily orating to me (aged fourteen) about dreadful Gothic outrages in Venezuela.

The godos, he told me, were irreconcilable, doomed to remain forever steeped in wickedness. Under all circumstances, I was informed (as General Ybarra strode, a melancholy exile, along Tremont Street or through Temple Place, or across

The Plaza Bolívar in Caracas showing statue of the Liberator and the Cathedral

MY CARACAS

Scollay Square) *se les ve la hiel!* That ferocious accusation is not easy to translate. Here is a free rendering of what lay in General Ybarra's somber thoughts (there must have been an east wind blowing): No matter how charmingly *los liberales* might act toward *los godos*, the latter were sure to mix their every action with gall (*hiel*), drawn from the most poisonous purlieus of their embittered interiors.

Such monologues about how firmly original sin was imbedded in Venezuelan conservatives were common in my early years. I remember getting home one evening to Monte Elena, our home outside Caracas, and being met by my young sister Leonor with the whispered warning: "Don't go upstairs now. Papa is on the rampage. Los godos are loose!"

In addition to the Tovars, descendants of other bigwig families of Spanish days circulated in my Caracas. I recall one spare and straight individual, of whom my father—as the said individual greeted us pleasantly from across the street—used to say sepulchrally: "If that man wished, he could call himself the Marquis of Berroterán!" But that man did nothing of the sort. Instead of meditating, in solitude, on his noble Spanish ancestors, he used to drop in for lunch—Venezuelans of that epoch kept open house at meal times—and affably consume fried plantains and black beans with all and sundry. He was very Spanish, with clean-cut features and a lean jaw and sunken eyes and raven hair. Down through the years, a remark made by him at lunch, in his clipped, acrid voice, sticks in my memory: "I like women sweet and men sour."

My father, when he had nothing more important on his mind, used to pay a vague homage to the gods of genealogy. For instance, he would say that the Ascanio family (his great-grandfather's mother was an Ascanio) *"tenian una nobleza del demonio"*—which may be freely translated "were one hell of a noble bunch." But he gave no details. He disliked details.

Some of the plazas of my Caracas were adorned with the regulation South American statue, that typical bronze warrior, on a bronze horse, waving a bronze sword in the name of Regeneration or Rehabilitation, or whatever it was that history had eventually decided to call the brawl that had landed him neatly in Caracas, with the key of the presidential mansion in one hand and that of the national treasury in the other. In one plaza stood José Tadeo Monagas, veteran of fights against both Spaniards and fellow-Venezuelans. In another stood his brother, José Gregorio, whose daughter, by the way, married a noted Venezuelan writer and lived many years in New York, where some of their descendants are now one hundred per cent Americans.

On a spur of El Calvario, the Venezuelan capital's hill-made-into-a-park, one of the presidents of my childhood years placed an imposing statue of Sucre, the Chevalier Bayard of South America's wars of independence. In other plazas were more bronze figures of Venezuelans of local renown, including Falcón, hero of the war of the Federation, and Páez, the extraordinary cowboy comrade of Bolívar, whose body, after he had died in New York, was conveyed to Venezuela on an American warship. Incidentally, there was a statue of George Washington, in bronze, in the middle of a pretty little park called the Plaza Washington.

But, of course, the grandest Caracas plaza and the city's grandest equestrian statue were dedicated to the Venezuelan demigod, Simón Bolívar. The Plaza Bolívar is the heart of Venezuela's metropolis. Before my day it was just a big, open

MY CARACAS

square without adornment. In my Caracas, however, it was already a very handsome feature of the city—and it still is. The entire central part of it is covered by garden plots, rich in shade trees, and well-tended. An important event of my early days was when the broad walks between the garden plots of the Plaza Bolívar were paved with squares of bright-colored mosaics. They were of such variegated designs that my mother, in her diary, likened them to an exhibition of samples.

The big space in the center, where all the walks converged, was covered with mosaics of an especially dazzling nature, with most intricate patterns—for there rises the fine equestrian statue of Bolívar. The super-hero rides a rearing horse, with its front legs pawing the air in mettlesome acrobatics, while its rider, in flowing cloak and resplendent uniform, holds his hat in his hand in salutation to an imaginary audience of cheering fellow-citizens. I have always thought the inscription on that statue a most impressive one: *"Simón Bolívar, Liberator of Venezuela, New Granada, Ecuador, and Peru, and founder of Bolivia."* (New Granada is the old name of the land we now call Colombia.)

At one time the inscription had additional words, to the effect that Antonio Guzmán Blanco, the Illustrious American, had caused the statue to be erected. But, when the illustrious one was kicked off his dictatorial perch for good and all, those words were indignantly erased. You could still see traces of them when I lived in Caracas—just as you can decipher fragments of inscriptions, similarly treated, in the Forum at Rome. None of the statues put up in his own honor by El Ilustre Americano, and afterward wrecked by Caracas mobs, has ever been set up again. Nor have new ones replaced them.

I cannot help thinking that my Caracas, the Caracas of the

end of the nineteenth century, was more attractive than the Caracas of today—despite the turbulence of the former and the sedateness of the latter. Many who know the new Caracas, including American oil men and their wives, who now throng the upsurging, prosperous Venezuelan capital of the present, will take that remark of mine as proving that I am just another mossback—

"The idiot who praises, with enthusiastic tone,
  Every century but this, and every country but his own—"

But I don't care. There may be beauty in the new Caracas. It has modern suburbs. It has modern highways reaching out to all points of the compass—to La Guaira, to Aragua and the Tuy, to the broad Venezuelan *llanos*—that would fill the soul of Macadam, Scottish god of pavements, with the cold Caledonian substitute for bliss. It has a couple of country clubs that would fit, without alterations, into Pasadena. It has many spick-and-span, brightly painted villas, which doubtless warm the cockles of the hearts of American oil men and oil women and oil children. But, to me, its architecture—and its nature—reek of gingerbread. And, if that be treason, make the most of it, Dutch Shell! Make the most of it, Standard Oil!

Chapter VIII

El Cedral

My uncle Luis liked me. He liked to have me around. He liked to tease me. He liked to talk English with me. He, filled with Latin exuberance, liked to instill precision of speech into me—*me*, half of the reticent North! And he used to correct not my Spanish *but my English*—the nerve of him!

"Tom," he would say to me, aged nine. "Stay to dinner."

"Can't."

"Why not?"

"Oh, because——of everything."

"What do you mean?"

"Oh, because I have to see Mamma and find out if Jessie wants to see me——and everything."

"What does that mean—'and everything.' "

"Why"—here I'd shuffle my feet and twist my hands and lower my eyes—"Papa will want to see me and Leonor will want to ask me about tomorrow——and everything."

"*What do you mean by 'and everything.'* "

It was useless. I'd have to tell that pestilential gadfly of an uncle that I didn't know. Then he would smile in triumph and give me a lecture on the virtues of precise speech. And I'd run home convinced that I hated him. But, soon, he and I would be together again in amicable harmony. I called him *Deeno Weess*

—because, when very little, that's all I could make out of *Padrino* (godfather) *Luis.*

Like a small percentage of other members of the Spanish race, Uncle Luis had a blond complexion, blue eyes and yellow hair—a rare combination in Venezuela. He had studied medicine in Paris. He was there when Alejandro Ybarra and Nelly Russell arrived in France in the initial stages of their long European honeymoon. Luis, the initiated young medical student, showed them Paris in a distinctly inhibited fashion, because of the respect that he felt due to his nineteen-year-old Massachusetts sister-in-law. She resented this. Often, in later years, she would accuse Luis of having held out on her. And he would look noble, of the dominant sex, the chivalrous protector of the innocent young lass.

If she rallied him too much he would retaliate by casually putting on a slipper of hers—for he had the small feet characteristic of Spaniards and their descendants. (Antonio Guzmán Blanco, that masterful despot who ran Venezuela and all its turbulent militarists for nearly twenty years, could put on a shoe belonging to his wife, the beautiful Ana Teresa.)

Luis Ybarra once looked up his brother and his American sister-in-law in the Boston lair of the Russells. He went to the Adams House. He had my father's extremes of temper; one moment he would be smooth and charming, the next a tornado had nothing on him except size and scope. Just as he was about to unpack, he noticed one of those Bibles, placed free of charge in hotel rooms. He flew into a rage. Like many other Venezuelan Roman Catholics, he rarely if ever gave genuine thought to religion—but he hadn't come to Boston to have any blankety-blank Protestants sneak Protestant versions of the Bible into his room.

So he shouted for a bell-hop; and, when a buttony youth appeared, Uncle Luis almost blew him across the hall with the cyclonic command:

"Take that book away!"

He dined that evening with his brother and sister-in-law and gave an account of the incident. My father, I feel sure, nodded his head in complete Latin comprehension and sympathy. And my mother, I feel equally sure, almost exploded trying to keep a straight face.

After Uncle Luis, having finished his medical studies in Paris, was free to return to Venezuela, in the early eighteen-eighties, he showed common sense rare in a young man; or, for that matter (honesty compels me to confess), in any member of the Ybarra clan. He did not start to practice in Caracas, as a competitor of many other older and firmly established doctors. Instead, he went to the gold mines of the Yuruari, deep in the jungles south of the Orinoco. There surgeon-doctors were as rare as broken legs and burning fevers were common. From the moment of his arrival, the student fresh from Paris had as much of the two—and of other assorted fractured limbs and tropical ailments—as he could possibly handle.

He turned up after a while in Caracas with a money belt buckled around his middle, into which he had stuffed over $30,000 in gold. He used part of his Yuruari nest egg to set himself up in practice in Caracas, and another part to get married. He took as his wife Columba Delfino. Her father, an Italian, had made a fortune years before operating the diligences on the carriage road between Caracas and La Guaira, before the railroad was built. She returned from a trip to Europe with a Paris trousseau that knocked the Caraqueños cold.

After his marriage, Uncle Luis started buying coffee plantations. In the long run, that habit did him no good; but, when he was new at it and the money was holding out valiantly, it brought to him a little profit and a lot of hope, and, to me some of the keenest pleasure and most vivid memories of my whole life.

His first purchase was El Cedral, a plantation in the rich coffee area of *la fila de Turgua*. El Cedral was not far from La Envidia, a bunch of tumbledown shacks, enjoying, for the time being, the honor of being the terminus of the *Ferrocarril Central de Venezuela*. That English-owned railway of the magnificent name was trying desperately to push itself into the rich valleys of the Tuy and thus exorcise the specter of financial crisis constantly gibbering at it.

Shortly after he had gone to his new plantation, with Aunt Columba and their little daughter, I got an invitation from Uncle Luis to join them there. I was overwhelmed with joy. I was entrusted to the care of Sergeant Félix Solórzano, then on duty as the guardian of our front portal. Félix got me aboard the diminutive train that ran daily to La Envidia. He watched over me solemnly while it puffed around sharp curves and took steep grades and buzzed over high viaducts.

All around us were green-covered mountain spurs and rushing rivulets. Little shacks hugged the steep mountainsides. They were roofed with big yellowing leaves and walled with sheets of tin, beaten out flat, which had begun life as American kerosene cans. I absorbed everything—always I have been a

EL CEDRAL

born traveler. Every stop was an adventure. Ragged little boys and girls, colored brown by nature and browner by dirt, crowded around the train. They carried on their heads greasy trays filed with *empanadas*, a national meat pie of Venezuela. It is reddish-brown, with a crust of sweetened corn pulp; and (when hot) it exhales a most alluring aroma.

"*Empanadas de pollo!*" shouted the dirty little boys and girls, holding their wares under my nose as I sat in the train.

"I'd like to eat one," I hinted to Félix Solórzano, who was the treasurer of the expedition.

"Better not."

"But they're made of chicken, aren't they?"

"No."

"What are they made of?"

"Cat."

At La Envidia, Uncle Luis was waiting for me, on horseback. Beside him, a peón held another horse, the one I was to ride. Sergeant Félix Solórzano bade us good-bye and installed himself in the down-at-heel little station of La Envidia, stolidly patient, until such time as the Ferrocarril Central de Venezuela should be ready to take him back to Caracas.

Uncle Luis climbed on his horse and I climbed on mine and the peón climbed on his. We started up the steep trail leading toward El Cedral. The hamlet of La Envidia, with its thatched huts (where ragged women were probably baking empanadas in the hope of tempting Félix Solórzano before train time) got smaller and smaller. The shack that served as station slept in the sunshine, at the end of the glistening narrow-gauge track of the railway.

As our horses stumbled up the stony trail, birds sang in the thickets. Above our heads rose verdure-covered ridges. Small snakes zigzagged across the pathway ahead of us. Wild pigs crashed through the bushes. Young deer, with spotted coats and frightened eyes, scuttled into the shadows of the forest. And the warm air that we breathed, as we scrabbled and slipped over pebbles and deep ruts, was steeped in the fragrant odor of Venezuela—the odor of coffee. That odor, suddenly blown into my nostrils as I stand on a wharf in Brooklyn, where steamers from South America tie up and unload, awakens inside me even now many years later, sharp longing for *la fila de Turgua.*

Coffee groves came right down to the edge of our trail. Coffee plants, no higher than a man, clustered in the shade of huge trees—without such protection, every one of those plants would have shriveled and died. Birds darted in and out, among plants and trees, birds of gorgeous trappings and strange names —tipped with red, fringed with blue and purple, splashed with gold.

Just as the sun was getting really hot, and our horses were panting, and we ourselves were beginning to glisten with sweat and think affectionately of lunch, we suddenly emerged from a girdle of coffee thickets into a big clearing.

In front of us stood a rambling one-story adobe house. It had a wide veranda along its façade. Red tiles covered its roof. Behind it, and at its sides, I caught glimpses of enormous patios, on which millions of coffee berries were drying. Inhabitants of the neighborhood, transformed into employes and feudal retainers of Uncle Luis by the fact that the coffee-picking season was on, stood about, in attitudes of lazy comfort. They touched their hats to my uncle—with a curious fusing of respect and familiarity. He turned to me:

"El Cedral," he said.

EL CEDRAL

On that day, at that moment, an interlude of enchantment began in my life.

I did not know until I started writing this chapter how deeply El Cedral had bitten into my memory. I did not know how vividly the time I spent there had etched itself into my consciousness. But as I began trying to set down words of description, to recall lineaments of happiness and scents of joy—then I knew. Coffee groves lived again. The fragrance of coffee berries blew from a past that was fair and fresh, across a present interwoven with disillusion and touched with tears.

Brown workers from Francisco de Yare, down in the valley of the Tuy, looked out of yesterday. They held dirty fingers to frayed straw hats.

"*Buenos dias, Don Luis.*"

"*Que hay, Feliciano? Que tal, Gumersindo?*"

"*Bien, Don Luis.*"

Smoke came from the kitchen, where big chunks of fresh-killed beef were cooking. Eliodoro, the majordomo, in clean white jacket and trousers, walked forward, a broad-brimmed straw hat in his hand, spurs on his high riding-boots.

"This is my nephew Tom, Eliodoro."

"*Buenos dias*, Señor Tom."

A servant held my stirrup. My aunt Columba—not wearing Paris clothes, but in rough-and-ready country garb, smiled from the doorstep.

"*Como estás, Tía Columba?*"

"*Cuanto gusto, Tom!*"

It took a long, long look at the segment of New York visible outside my window to make me remember where I really was. I shook myself. I straightened up. I went back to pounding the keys of my typewriter. "Chapter VIII. El Cedral." For a moment I could not see those keys.

I had a regular job at El Cedral. Eliodoro set me to helping him keep tally. I used to sit beside him, with a pencil in my hand and a soiled sheet of thick paper on my knee.

One by one, the members of the transplanted population of San Francisco de Yare would come up to where we sat, and empty, out of square wooden boxes, the coffee berries they had picked that day. At dawn they had roused themselves and gone into the cool groves; at noon, hot and tired, they had knocked off for lunch; and now, with the afternoon shadows falling across the big drying-floor, they had come for the reward of their hard work.

"*Uno, dos, tres*——" Eliodoro would chant, as the contents of box after box were poured on the drying-floor in front of him.

"*Uno*——"

I would make a mark on my soiled sheet of paper.

"*Dos.*"

A second mark—and a lick of my tongue on my grubby pencil.

"*Tres.*"

A third mark. Another lick.

"*Uno, dos, tres, cuatro*——" Over and over again, through the warm afternoon. After each picker, man or woman or child, had dumped all the berries that he or she had picked since dawn, Eliodoro would hand over dirty squares of thick cardboard, with numerals printed on them. Some were inscribed "1 centavo," some "5 centavos," some "1 real" (ten centavos). Each piece of cardboard had "El Cedral" printed on it, and my

EL CEDRAL

uncle's name. After a good piece of the big drying-floor was ankle deep in greenish-brown coffee berries, Eliodoro and I would call it a day. He would take from me the tally sheet that I had been diligently marking. The population of San Francisco de Yare would straggle off to the shanties where they lived. Amid the scent of coffee groves and the chirping of birds, the sun would set in glorious coloring.

In the early hours of the morning, my Uncle Luis would take me out riding with him. Sometimes we would merely visit the various sections of El Cedral—each of which had a special name. The hoofs of our horses sank deep into the squashy turf of the coffee groves. Wild parrots screamed in the branches overhead. Coffee pickers, swinging machetes as they strode, popped out of the underbrush.

"*Buenos días, Don Luis.*"

"*Que tal, Epifanio?* What place has been chosen for the picking today?"

"The brook of the Holy Virgin."

"And for tomorrow?"

"The gully of Jesus Christ."

Sometimes we would ride beyond the boundaries of El Cedral to visit neighboring coffee planters. At La Fundación we would be made welcome by Señor Muro, a handsome Caraqueño, who, having gone native for a few weeks, wore riding breeches and muddy gaiters and rusty spurs to prove it. At Cedral Bello, Señor Bello, the proprietor, would discuss wisely with my uncle the merits of the old and the new. They would compare primitive methods of grinding and cleaning the coffee berry with the achievements of new-fangled machines, made in the United States or Europe. After arrival in Venezuela, these had had wished on them exotic names, such as *descerezadora* and *trilladora*. (My uncle, by the way, was going in for modernity. On El Cedral we had a specimen of each of those machines.)

We would ride homeward, through the heavily-shaded, heavily-scented groves.

"Tom, are you enjoying yourself?"

"Yes, Uncle Luis."

"What pleases you especially?"

"Oh, the tally-keeping, and riding with you through the *cafetales*, and everything."

"What do you mean by 'and everything?'"

Adjoining one of the big patios behind the house at El Cedral was the general store of the plantation. The storekeeper—from San Francisco de Yare—paid regular rent, at a rate agreed upon with Eliodoro before the start of the coffee-picking season. He kept on hand a variegated stock—brown sugar and white sugar and black beans, cheap crockery and straw hats and alpargatas, kerosene and brushes and *aguardiente*.

Nobody ever gave him cash. The pickers, male and female, would simply pay him with those greasy squares of cardboard that they had received from Eliodoro in payment for the coffee they had picked—the coffee on which I had kept tally, with my dirty sheet of paper and spit-moistened pencil.

One evening, at the end of the season, I sat beside Eliodoro when the storekeeper came to him to square accounts. The storekeeper dumped out on a table a big heap of thumb-marked cardboard squares. He separated them into piles according to color and value—green, 1 centavo, blue, 5 centavos, red, 1 real.

The total to which it all added up amazed me—in my child's

EL CEDRAL

mind I hadn't realized the length of the season, nor the size of the population of San Francisco de Yare, nor its prowess in coffee-picking. But when Eliodoro saw the total—laboriously added up with much grunting and pencil-wetting by the storekeeper—he took it quite casually. He just nodded. Then he unlocked a safe in a corner of the room. Out of its insides he took gold coins and banknotes and silver pieces. For a while there was no sound but the stacking of specie and the imprisonment of bunches of paper money in elastic bands. Then, from Eliodoro—

"*Conforme?*"

"*Conforme, Eliodoro—y muchas gracias.*"

In the Massachusetts of my early childhood, I used to play in the snow. With little cronies, boys and girls of Roxbury and Plymouth and the Back Bay, I used to plunge into deep snow drifts. I used to go home dripping wet and shivering with cold, to be met by angry denunciation from my mother.

At El Cedral my little cousin Columbita and I played a similar game—in the company of the small fry of San Francisco de Yare. Like the children of faraway North America, we took dives, amid shrieks of laughter, into drifts. We threw ourselves head first into banked-up masses.

But those drifts weren't white. They were greenish. Those banked-up masses weren't snow. They were coffee—millions of coffee berries. Presently Aunt Columba would chase us away from that wonderful game, with sharp protests. It wasn't because we were wet. It wasn't because we were shivering, as those cronies and I had been in Plymouth and Boston. It was because she didn't want us to acquire *niguas* or *garapatas*. Niguas are nasty little insects, which burrow in between your toes, and, having installed themselves there in comfort, thumb their noses at punitive expeditions. Garapatas are the same thing, only more so.

Sometimes I feel that I have wasted much time in my life. Sometimes I look with envy on American friends who sit on boards of directors, and clip coupons, and talk, as man to man, with liveried chauffeurs. But, when I get too glum from such thoughts, I say to myself:

"Ha! Not one of them ever made a dive into a pile of coffee berries. Not one of them ever took a header into a coffee drift. Not one!" And I get so bumptious that I think sneeringly of boards of directors. And of coupons. Once, after such a train of thought, I even snapped my fingers at a liveried chauffeur.

The population of San Francisco de Yare is getting together for a *joropo*. It troops into an inner patio of the El Cedral house. Dozens and dozens of men and women. Among them are the town's most proficient guitar players, also experts with the *maracas*, hollow gourds filled with little pebbles. Everybody squats in a circle around a big space in the middle, carefully kept clear. The stars are bright. Evening breezes sigh across the patio.

Suspense quivers in the air. The guitarists strum. The men with the maracas give their gourds a few preliminary shakes. But the party can't begin yet. There's a protocol in such matters —an unbreakable etiquette.

A big, dusky coffee-picker stands up. He crosses the brick-paved floor to where my uncle and aunt are sitting. They are flanked by squatting men in rough white jackets and shirts open at the neck, or no shirts at all; by women in scant calico, with sandals on their feet and flowers in their hair.

EL CEDRAL

The big coffee-picker bows low.

"Will Don Luis and Doña Columba honor us by opening the dance?"

Luis Ybarra, formerly of the École de Médécine in Paris, and Columba Delfino de Ybarra, who came back from France with the latest thing in French trousseaux, walk to the middle of the cleared space. The grimy population of San Francisco de Yare applaud politely. Guitars sweep into rhythmic melody. Maracas rattle. Off go my uncle and aunt into the measures of the joropo, the typical dance of the Venezuelan countryside. Through its simple measures they tread—far, very far, tonight, from the Sorbonne and the Rue de la Paix. Nobody else dances.

They sit down. More applause, suggestive rather of politeness than enthusiasm.

Then the real joropo begins. There's no getting around the fact that, so far, my uncle and aunt have been rather a clog on the free expression of the soul of San Francisco de Yare.

Twenty couples leap to the cleared space. Fire sparkles in black eyes. Lithe limbs bend. Alpargatas shuffle through the dust of the floor. With an authority of sweep and rhythm that was not there before, the guitarists swing into a joropo tune. And, now, for the first time of his life, the ears of a little boy born in Boston absorb the notes of the dance of Venezuela peóns, the measure invented long ago and faithfully cherished ever since by the Venezuelans who pick coffee, who load and unload donkeys, who till patches of corn on steep mountainsides, who bake empanadas, who carry rifles in revolutions that mean nothing to them, and die on bloody battlefields or in reeking hospitals. The joropo—how zestfully guitarists twang it and men with maracas rattle it and dancers shuffle it!

Out of that twang and rattle and shuffle leaps the spirit of Venezuela; the joropo is as unmistakably that spirit as the tango is the soul of the pampas of Argentina and the rumba the voice of Cuba. The joropo is the distilled gaiety of Venezuela; Venezuela's farce and tragedy; her melancholy; the languor of her siestas; the passion of her loving; the sharpness of her wit and the fury of her temper.

While the dancers sway, and teeth gleam, and sweat pours from men and women, a prominent humorist of San Francisco de Yare installs himself beside the musicians. To the tune being played he improvises verse after verse—greeted with shouts of enjoyment from all over the patio. He pokes fun at budding love affairs; at cases of laziness and avarice and double-dealing. Nobody is safe. Even my uncle and aunt get a share—sung with a respectful touch, but with a barb on it just the same. Every verse ends in a refrain praising the native town of the coffee-pickers—tumble-down and badly roofed, dusty or muddy, broiled by the sun or flooded by the rain—but their home town just the same, beloved and unforgettable—

> *"Donde están las muchachas bonitas?*
> *En San Francisco de Yare!"*

After a couple of hours, my uncle and aunt leave quietly. And I toddle along behind them. Nine-year-old eyelids grow heavy early. But that joropo will keep going far into the first morning hours. For tomorrow will be Sunday, and there won't be any coffee-picking, and the dancers can lie abed late. A sleepy little Bostonian closes his eyes. . . .

> *"Donde están las muchachas bonitas?*
> *En San Francisco de Yare!"*

EL CEDRAL

Guitars whir. Maracas rattle. The stars grow dim. . . .

A morning comes when Uncle Luis and I ride back, down the mountain slopes, through the scented groves and the bird-haunted thickets, to La Envidia. There he hands me over to *Sargento* Félix Solórzano—dispatched on the train that had left Caracas shortly after dawn, to fetch me home.

The little engine puffs over the siding. It gets itself coupled to the other end of the train. It snorts to make passengers take their places. It whistles importantly: "Let's go!"

My uncle gives me a slap on the shoulder. Félix Solórzano salutes.

"*Adios*, Tom."

"*Adios, Dino Weess.*"

My uncle waves from the station platform. I wave back until he is out of sight. Again we creak around sharp curves and shriek over high viaducts. In my mind the impressions left by my visit to El Cedral are jumbled in delightful confusion. I sit in silence, sorting them.

The train groans to a stop.

"*Empanadas! Empanadas de pollo!*"

The savory smell of the burnt corn enclosing those hot empanadas makes my mouth water.

"I'd like to eat one, sargento."

"Better not."

Chapter IX

Revolution

AFTER my father had been Military Governor of the Federal District for a year or thereabouts, he became Minister of War (as my mother had prophesied in her diary). He had offices in a wing of the big building officially known as the Capitolio. This edifice, pretentious and stucco-ridden, but beautiful to the eyes of my boyhood, also contained a couple of other ministries, the legislative halls reserved for Venezuela's Congress (on the rare occasions when it was allowed to function), and the *Salón Elíptico*.

The latter was a sort of Hall of Fame, with ceilings and walls covered with stirring episodes in Venezuela's war of independence against Spain. Once I was raised to a pinnacle of boyish elation when certain repairs being made in the painting of one of Venezuela's most famous battles were shown and explained to my father and me by the artist in person, Martin Tovar y Tovar—dolled up in a dingy smock, bedaubed with paint, reminiscent of the Latin Quarter.

After some months of the War Ministry, my father was appointed Governor of the State of Carabobo. While he was running that region, General Joaquin Crespo, in revolt against President Andueza Palacio, marched on Valencia, Carabobo's capital. That was back in 1892.

REVOLUTION

After directing some hot fighting, my father brought an army of several thousands to Caracas. I promptly started hobnobbing with that army, according to my militaristic wont. But I remember clearly only one member of it, a swarthy and valiant general with the extraordinary name of Braulio Yaguaracuto.

My father's army joined up with the other governmental forces preparing to engage Crespo in decisive battle. And that's where I came briefly into the foreground of the picture.

General Ybarra, a martial gleam in his eye, rode up to the front of our house to bid farewell to his family. Behind him, I remember, rode an orderly with saddlebags filled with dozens of succulent roast beef sandwiches supplied by my mother. My father fully intended to include me in the general outburst of farewell. But I had other plans. Mounted on Don Rodrigo, I suddenly bobbed up in the midst of aides and orderlies. I put on a suitably appealing expression. Couldn't I ride out with the army? Just a few miles? Please!

"All right," said my father, always an indulgent parent when not in a temper.

"Remember now, only a few miles," my mother chimed in.

And off I went with the cavalcade, fully determined to participate in the imminent battle against the revolutionists. For was I not a mature warrior, eleven and a half years old?

Flanked by long lines of sandaled infantry, by the cannon of my father's pet half-battalion of artillery, by horsemen armed with carbines and lances and wicked little Winchester rifles, who kicked up a great yellow dust-cloud, Don Rodrigo and I covered some three miles of the march toward the battlefield. I kept myself as unobtrusive as possible—the less my father had me on his mind, I reflected, the better chance I had of not being arbitrarily eliminated from the martial procession. But, at a little place called El Rincón del Valle, just outside Caracas, my parent suddenly fixed a cold eye on me.

"Go home," he ordered. "Nelly will be getting worried about you."

"But, Papa——"

"Go home, I tell you."

This time he spoke in a tone that I knew well, a tone of doom. My campaign was over. I put Don Rodrigo to the right-about. We trotted dejectedly back along the road to Caracas where I had just been dreaming dreams of high military adventure.

The army, meanwhile, trudged onward. Within a few days it encountered Crespo's forces and beat them (though Crespo eventually won the war) at a place called El Guayabo. In that battle my father's pet artillerists distinguished themselves; and they became the heroes of an anecdote that afterwards he never tired of telling to auditors in South and North America.

One of the enemy's principal leaders was a fiery Corsican-Venezuelan, with a flowing beard and a flashing eye, named Juan Pietri, who was both a doctor and a general. Pietri had incorporated into the rebel army an Italian adventurer called Montecatini, who had proclaimed himself the inventor and sole successful operator of a terrible form of bombardment by dynamite which (he assured Pietri) would blast the government army off the map. When the battle of El Guayabo was in full swing, Pietri heard a series of tremendous detonations.

"Ha!" he exclaimed, fingering the foliage on his face. "That's Montecatini with his dynamite!"

"Fiddlesticks!" sneered another rebel general, in closer touch with reality. "That's Alejandro Ybarra with his cannon!"

REVOLUTION

Soon after my abrupt return home from my abbreviated El Guayabo campaign, my mother got a message from my father that he would be back on a certain day. At once she began elaborate preparations for welcoming the hero. She made plans for a sumptuous feast, of which, she decided, a large turkey—at the time a leading ornament of our backyard—should be the central feature. In accordance with Venezuelan custom, some red wine was fed to that turkey on the night before his doomsday—a treatment supposed by Venezuelans to make the meat tender. Before the fascinated eyes of my sister, my brother and myself, the big bird reeled around our yard, dead drunk, amid an extraordinary succession of hiccuping noises. Then a telegram arrived from my father—"unavoidably delayed."

The dinner of welcome was postponed. The turkey sobered up. Another telegram arrived "Reach Caracas Thursday." Again the turkey staggered about the yard with a superb jag. Again he was reprieved—my father's arrival was postponed a third time.

Finally—after another colossal bun—the turkey was duly slaughtered and served at the dinner to the conquering warrior, which came off at last, with a choice assortment of relatives and friends present. If that turkey's meat wasn't of superlative tenderness, he was the toughest bird in the entire range of ornithological history!

With President Raimundo Andueza Palacio, I came into frequent contact. One reason was that my father rose to high local eminence during the Andueza Palacio administration, an eminence from which he fell later, with a terrific thud and far-reaching consequences to the Ybarra tribe.

meant to lock us up. A typical Venezuelan talk, all flowers and compliments, with the meaning left to anybody's guess.

After arrival at La Guaira, my father decided that the best thing for him would be to spend the night at the United States Consulate, which, he surmised, Eduardo Pepper would consider beyond his jurisdiction in case he was seized during the night with a yearning to put the Ybarras in jail. As usual, my father knew the American Consul—his acquaintanceship with Americans in Venezuela was always wide and varied.

The Consul welcomed us heartily. He spent the evening giving us heated descriptions of his troubles with Eduardo Pepper's ruffianly soldiery. The main source of friction was that the Consul was deaf, and Eduardo's sentries persisted in challenging him, when he walked abroad at night, and firing at him when, because of his deafness he neglected to answer them. So far, they had failed to hit him (an old Venezuelan custom). But, if they had punctured him like a Swiss cheese he could hardly have been more angry.

Next morning, my father and I awoke to the peaceful chirping of birds, in warm sunlight. Eduardo Pepper hadn't sent around to nab us. But the more my parent thought things over the less confident he felt of the continued placidity of Eduardo. While we were pacing the waterfront, General Ybarra abruptly turned into a man of action. He hailed a man in a rowboat.

"Take us to the American steamer," he ordered. The Red D liner *Venezuela* was lying just offshore, between two foreign gunboats—I forget to what two European nations they belonged.

The boatman nodded. We stepped into his dory. In a few minutes we were aboard the *Venezuela*, with the American captain, another old friend of my father, greeting us effu-

REVOLUTION

sively. We were out of danger. What could Eduardo Pepper, even at his pepperiest, do to persons of whom he disapproved if they were on an American ship flanked by the warships of two European Powers?

That same day the *Venezuela* raised her anchor and steamed away for New York. The simplicity and shining success of the method chosen by my father in leaving his native country reminds me of the yarn by Artemus Ward about the man who had languished for thirty-seven years in a dungeon cell—"Suddenly he had a brilliant inspiration. He opened the window and got out."

A few miles down the coast, our navigating officer noticed a rowboat bobbing up and down in the choppy water alongside, with two men aboard making excited signals. The *Venezuela* stopped. A rope ladder was let down her side. Up clambered the highly respectable forms of Don Juan Estéban Linares and Don Pascual Casanova, two of Venezuela's leading capitalists. They had practically no baggage worth mentioning except money belts stuffed with gold pieces; and they were on the broad grin at the thought that they also had outwitted Eduardo Pepper.

Don Juan Estéban and Don Pascual had decided some days before, in Caracas, that the transition government there would come down on them in all probability for an *empréstito forzoso*, one of those forced loans that had in the past frequently financed Venezuelan régimes. So the two capitalists had quietly slipped away to the diminutive sea-bathing resort of Macuto—the "Venezuelan Newport," as local purveyors of rhetoric sometimes called it. And they had put out to sea in that rowboat of theirs just as soon as they had sighted the *Venezuela* steaming toward them.

YOUNG MAN OF CARACAS

How ordinary a thing excitement was, as an ingredient of my mother's daily life, at times when the ingrained turbulence of Venezuela was in the ascendancy, leaps constantly to the eye when I peruse her diaries. (These, by the way, she kept constantly from her early girlhood until just before her death, a span of nearly half a century. I have stacks of them, some stained and yellowed by the years, some ravaged by book-devouring tropical insects.) Once she wrote:

"We are in a military camp, passports required to leave the city, all cattle being confiscated for rations, beef 40 cents a pound."

On another occasion, when she was ill and my father in high political position, she casually recorded: "There was a meeting of the Committee of Ways and Means over my bed." And again:

"Julio Sarría and many more came to the house and we had a political crisis in the corridor."

When matters became acute (in 1892), and the government backed by my father was about to fall, and he himself was en route for the United States, she noted in her diary:

"Two men stopped under my window (her room was on the ground floor and fronted on the street) at 2. A.M., and one began to insult Alito. 'Poor woman, let her sleep,' said the other. 'No, now that he is gone, let *her* suffer!' . . . It was horrid . . . all alone there at night. . . ."

But, to give a real idea of what Venezuelan revolutions could do to turn Nelly Russell's married life upside down, I must go back to its earliest years, when she was still a young bride. Rummaging, a short time ago, among a lot of old papers in Caracas, my sister Leonor found and sent to me a long letter,

REVOLUTION

written by my mother, shortly after the end of her honeymoon, to her sister Minnie, in Boston.

At the time, Nelly was living in the old Rivas-Ybarra house in Caracas. The government of the day, of which her husband was a leading adherent, had declared against Dictator Guzmán Blanco, who was in Paris. Against this government, pro-Guzmán elements, under General Cedeño and others, had risen in revolt.

Discord divided the Ybarras. Alejandro's father, Dr. Ybarra, sided with his son against the absentee dictator. But the young general's sister Inés was the wife of Roberto Ybarra, Guzmán's brother-in-law, which made her pro-Guzmán. Most of the rest of the family also favored El Ilustre Americano, including three aunts of young Alejandro, who lived in the old house, as did Inés and her sister Mercedita.

I can imagine the shock caused by that letter from my mother, when Minnie Russell showed it to relatives and friends in calm Boston and peaceful Plymouth. It must have sounded like echoes from the life of mad people on a planet of insanity. Under date of February 4th, 1879, my mother wrote:

"In rushed Alito, much excited, to say that the enemy had made a furious attack on La Victoria . . . and had finally retreated, leaving 600 men dead on the field. This might mean the triumph of the government, so you can imagine the delight of the Dr. . . . But things strike people differently . . . how it appeared to Soledad (one of the aunts) was to make her run as fast as possible to the balconies and shut up windows and *postigos* tight, precisely as if we were in mourning, and Mercedita began to give despairing shrieks of 'Roberto, Roberto, where do you suppose he is?'—which was, of course, consoling for Inés. Inés, however, said nothing, only looked imploringly at Alito, who explained that Roberto was in no danger at all, as he was in the Estado Mayor [staff]. . . . If Inés were like Mercedita, she'd die. . . .

"Well, that was night before last, and, since then, the enemy had begun to fight again. So imagine the suspense here. . . . Oh, you can't imagine the joy that rockets give! Today, when we heard them bang-bang-banging, and smelt the powder, we knew it must be some great news . . . and, when the Dr. hove in sight, we pounced on him. '*Qué noticias?*' He was beaming and shouted 'Colina is in La Guaira' [Colina was a sort of Grand Old Man of Venezuelan revolutions, bitterly opposed to Guzmán]. Min, if you knew what harm the non-arrival of Colina has done the government, how anxiously every one has been waiting to hear where he was, how much it was feared he had been captured, and what a blow his arrival will be for the Guzmancistas, you'd understand. . . .

"So many young men present themselves as common soldiers that Alito has formed them into a separate corps, called La Descubierta [the Unprotected]. They are to lead the way always into battle and be with him wherever it's most dangerous. . . ."

"I have just come from watching the departure of Alito, who went in command of the troops to La Victoria, with Colina and Urdaneta. Not that I went out of the house, but I've been perched so long in the window seat with an opera glass, watching the troops and Alito at the corner, that to come to my writing desk seems like returning from somewhere. . . . He spent the night at the cuartel and came back this morning at 7 in his campaigning costume. Such a beauty as he was! It's the same

REVOLUTION

one he had that photograph taken in, only, as he's slenderer and his complexion very clear and fair, he's handsomer than ever. I wish they could have seen him at home. You remember the little round dark blue hat? Well, over that he had a huge straw one, like those Dora and I had in Sabána Grande, only with the brim three times as large, and this was tipped on one side. . . .

"Mercedita lies on the bed and watches me write, and converses. It makes me nervous and fidgety. The aunts are bricks—they leave me alone. . . .

"Poor Inés, she broke down this morning for the first time. She made me feel awfully, as she never goes about sniveling. Today is the first time I've seen her cry, and she suffers awfully. Poor thing, she clung to Alito and begged him to look out for Roberto, if he could.

"I saw Alito off with much calm. I know they think me horribly hardhearted, but none of them know what it is to feel as desolate as I did last night, when Alito said good-bye to me before going to the cuartel. That was, for me, when he really left. I'm bad, I think—for the way they sort of gloat over their grief makes me cross instead of sad. What's the use of hoping nothing will happen, in a doleful tone, or of saying, '*Ay, cuando acabará esta campaña?*' ('when will this campaign end?') and everything that can most sadden a person. . . .

"Alito was certainly made for a soldier—you never saw anyone so elated as he was this morning, setting off with the *muchachos*. . . ."

"February 8th. Last night I turned in as usual, and, about one o'clock, was waked by horse's footsteps in the patio. Then I heard Alito's voice. Imagine how I flew to open the door . . .

Poor Tico—couldn't speak at all, and then said: '*Se entregó La Victoria*' ('La Victoria has surrendered.'). . .

"Oh, Min, all this treachery makes one wild. I am boiling over with indignation . . . and the old doctor is a consolation. The others, of course, snivel and sniff and weep, but they can't make me break down, do what they will. . . . It would have been the complete finish of the revolution if only Colina, Urdaneta and Alito had reached La Victoria some days before! . . .

"Of course, it was turnabout and back to Caracas. . . . What a contrast to the enthusiastic setting out day before yesterday. . . . What's to be done? León Colina will not surrender. Urdaneta says the same. . . . Colina threw his arms around Alito. 'You have raised a banner high in this country,' he said. 'I should like to see Venezuela governed by you. You are young and I am old, but remember—whenever you need me for anything, call on León Colina.' . . . On one thing, all agree: Colina is a hero. . . .

"I've adopted Mr. Micawber's motto and am always in hope of something turning up. . . ."

"Well, Minkie, it's all over and I am preparing myself for the triumphant entrance and the pitying visits. Oh, it's so hard, to have to surrender to treachery only. And now they will come in, triumphant, to take possession of Caracas and patronize poor Alito. . . . I must say I regard all these cousins and brothers with very un-Christian feelings. . . .

"The Herreras [pro-Guzmán cousins] said to Inés: 'How happy you must be at our triumph.' And she answered: 'I am happy because my husband is coming back—for that reason and no other.' . . .

REVOLUTION

"Of course, we shall sell Guachafita, our horse, and my dear little carriage, and Alito's large one. His diamonds, too, which I don't mind a bit, but I confess that Guachafita and the *cochecito* break my heart. The most heartbreaking thing of all is Alito's sad face. . . . I hope something will turn up for the poor boy. I dread so the days when he will have to be idle, just lounging around here, and being pitied by the Herreras, etc. He'll kill them if they dare say a word to him.

"I shall go mad if this doesn't end soon. . . . Imagine, Min, the city waiting to be taken possession of by Cedeño . . . and the only person to keep order is Alito, with his 200 soldiers—who, of course, don't want to sacrifice themselves to be surrendered afterwards. There are some bandits, on the road to La Guaira and Antímano, who only want plunder—and, as the troops of Cedeño are in Los Teques, there's danger that these bandits may enter, do a little sacking, and depart. . . .

"Oh, Min, El Berraco [a bandit chief] is on the Calvario and is entering the city, and they will send Alito to die perhaps, to preserve the city for Cedeño!"

"10th. Such an hour or two as I passed yesterday . . . for El Berraco and his troops were firing on the Calvario, and we could distinctly hear their cries and shouts, and expected them every moment to enter the city. Salvador Rivas came, and we looked at them through opera glasses—he was much excited and said that the only hope Caracas had was Alito.

"I went to lie down, and Soledad came and tore about the room like a mad woman, and begged me not to frighten myself, and made me so nervous and miserable. . . . Inés begged her to let me alone and finally she did.

"Alito stationed soldiers on the corners of the streets. Then the Dr. came with the news that Colina had ridden out and that his horse had returned without him. It was all very exciting, and I should not mind if the family didn't excite me so by their '*Ave María! Jesús!* What will become of Alejandro?' etc, etc. . . .

"Mr. Baker [the American Minister] has behaved very well. He came last night—offering me the Legation, if we should need the protection of the flag. . . . Caracas is sad. It's frightened by the fulfillment of what it has been longing for. . . . Colina has said publicly that the only hope he sees for the future is Alito. . . ."

In the midst of all these alarums and excursions, young General Ybarra was persuaded to play the old Venezuelan game of going into hiding. But he obstinately refused to abide by the rules—as is clearly shown by the next part of the letter of his young American wife to her sister in Massachusetts:

"Monday 11th. Minkie, my dear, such a rumpus, and anything so exasperating as Tico you never saw. . . . He was at home here when, about 4 A.M., we were awakened by rockets and cheers and howling of all kinds. Those bandits had entered the city. . . . Finally, I persuaded Tico to go where he had a house offered him, for no one could tell what would happen, and those rascals are more to be feared than the real army. As it was dark, no one saw him go. . . .

"Since then he has been back twice! I told him the last time he would kill me if he came any more. The first time they came rushing to tell us that there were soldiers at the *solar* in front, and he had to hurry off. . . . In an hour he was back again, as lively as you please, hollering 'Nelkie!' He had come for breakfast with me. . . .

REVOLUTION

"Oh, dear, if only these next three or four days would pass. . . . If only Alito weren't so irrepressible. I expect him dodging in at any moment. . . .

"12th. Oh, Min, such a mess as there was yesterday. El Berraco and some other chiefs of the same kind took it into their heads to enter Caracas before Cedeño and establish themselves here. Well, Mercedita, Inés and I were in the room, playing with Inesita . . . and everything as quiet as you please, when suddenly the whole street was full of people running from the Plaza Bolívar, and round the farther corner came people running toward the plaza, and the street got blocked up with a carriage and some cattle, and firing was heard in the plaza, and soldiers were seen loading their guns on the Esquina del Conde.

"In the midst of all this came a man on horseback to demand the key of the artillery barracks, and he insisted I must know where it was. Then someone cried out in the street: 'They are fighting with the government troops on the plaza and the General is there!'

"That finished me. If that dreadful Alito had gone out and got mixed up in that rumpus! To make matters worse, a man on the corner of the street shouted 'Viva Guzmán!' . . . He brandished his sword and began to threaten. Seeing the man raving so, Inés was afraid he might direct his wrath toward this house, so she seized the flag, dropped Inesita in the middle of the room, rushed onto the balcony, and let the flag float out!"

Just a few days in the life of a young girl from Boston who had chosen to marry a native of the Venezuela of the eighteen-seventies!

Chapter X

Under the Surface

Soon after my arrival in Caracas from Boston, when I was a very little boy, I went for a walk with Jessie Sullivan. Our way was suddenly blocked by long lines of men in rags. They were black with dirt. Dirty ropes tied them together, two by two. They were escorted by officers with drawn swords or machetes, and soldiers with muskets. The faces of the roped men were gray with fatigue. Their cheeks were hollow, their eyes sunken, their gait stumbling. Many of them were listlessly sucking oranges. Orange peels littered the cobblestones around them.

On my return home I described what I had seen, with much animation, to my father and mother.

"Who were those men?" I asked. "Why were they tied together?"

My mother didn't answer. My father was evasive at first. But I insisted eagerly.

"Oh, they were prisoners," he said finally.

"Why?"

"Probably rebels against the government."

Small though I was, I knew that there was no civil war on. But I had to be satisfied with that unsatisfying answer. Later I found out all about what I had seen that day.

Those dirty and unhappy men, bound together like criminals and driven like cattle, were just a batch of recruits for the Venezuelan army. They had been rounded up in the interior

UNDER THE SURFACE

by merciless press gangs. They had been seized in marketplaces and on solitary mountain trails. They had been snatched out of the shanties that were their homes, while their women screamed and their children clung, whimpering, to their knees. Clubbed by rifle butts, hit over the shoulders by the flats of machete blades, they had been roughly herded into barracks in nearby towns. From there, when enough of them had been collected, they were forwarded, like sacks of coffee, to Caracas. Before them lay years of slavery, euphemistically called "military service." If they did not perish in battle, or rot from disease, they could hope to go home after two or three years—unless their officers were too busy to bother about the trifling fact that they had served their time.

In my tales about Venezuelan barracks and revolutions, I realize that I have scarcely touched at all upon the underlying cruelty of militarism as it existed in the Venezuela of my childhood. For this omission, it seems to me, I have a perfectly valid reason.

In looking back on the Venezuela of my other life, I am depicting it almost entirely from the point of view and through the eyes of the child that I then was. I am seeing it, first and foremost, as it was seen by a little boy suddenly projected into warlike surroundings from peaceful Massachusetts. As a lad, receptive and impressionable and imbued with a child's sense of romance, what I saw mainly was military glamour and the fascination of the daily military round. Having decided, inside my child's mind, that my father's calling was admirable and beautiful, I tried to shut my eye to the seamy side of it, or simply didn't see it at all. All was for the best in the best of all possible martial worlds.

Later on, bit by bit, the glamorous milieu of my earlier years began to take on quite another hue. It exuded injustice and heartlessness and suffering. Out of memories from which had shone nothing but the pride, pomp and circumstance of glorious war—or, rather, near-war—leered terrors and horrors and miseries which, before, I had ignored.

As a matter of fact, there was never a time, even as far back as my tenth year, when I first met militarism, that I was not uncomfortably conscious of the stench that lay behind the glittering façade. Nobody, even a little romantic lad, could enter a Venezuelan barracks and not sense the ugliness underneath the color and glitter. Nobody could go into the prison of Caracas—the place, for the Tom Ybarra of my boyhood, where the *guardia de cárcel* stationed its sentries and gave passing officers salutes—without retching at the air from stinking dungeons and averting eyes from the sunken cheeks and clanking shackles and dying gaze of ragged prisoners, as they went shuffling past or peered out listlessly from behind greasy iron bars.

Nobody could remain susceptible only to the dazzling side of militarism after a visit to the Caracas military hospital—where unhappy Venezuelans of the lower class, torn from their homes in interior villages, lay on dirty cots, covered with sores, weakly calling for water—or howling in delirium—or coughing out the last breaths of life from emaciated throats. There was no martial glamour either at the cárcel or the military hospital, if one looked under the surface. And there was little competent care or conscience or human kindness.

At the hospital, inadequate medical work was eked out by French and Venezuelan nuns. God bless them, one and all! I can still see their pale faces and humble walk. If there is salvation for anybody born into this sinful world, there is for women

UNDER THE SURFACE

like la Mère Saint-Simon. She went to Venezuela from France more than fifty years ago, simply and solely to help comfort the suffering and pray for the dying of an alien, distant and pitiless land. And there must be salvation, with rest and celestial glory, for all those other nuns, nameless in my memory, who stood beside foul bedding, holding water to fevered lips and wiping the sweat of death from burning brows.

Cruelty grimaced everywhere from behind the tinsel of my martial childhood. It grimaced from among my father's innumerable yarns of his warrior's youth. One day, on the street, when I was a small boy, he introduced me to a veteran general.

"The cruelest man in Venezuela," he said, when we were out of hearing. And he told how the man whose hand I had just grasped had walked into the house of a political foe years before, at lunch time, while a civil war was raging.

"Will you honor me by staying to lunch?" the owner of the house had asked.

"Certainly, delighted to do so," replied the visitor. They lunched together. They talked pleasantly about mutual friends. They drank each other's health. At the end of the meal, the visitor pushed back his chair and stood up.

"I came here," he said, "to shoot you."

He beckoned to half a dozen soldiers who had come with him and were standing outside. They took the man whose guest their commander had just been to the back yard. A volley sounded. The soldiers returned—saluted—reported. Their general, with a nod of satisfaction, mounted his horse and rode back to his headquarters.

At one time, my father, in his early career, served under that man. Fortunately, he exerted an influence over his chief which, at least on one occasion, was providential.

151

all about a trifle. But he flew into one of his diabolical rages, shook his fist in my face, and roared:

" 'I'm going to shoot you, Mancera! I'm going to shoot you, right here and now!'

"He started to summon a firing-squad. But your husband suddenly stood in front of him.

" 'General,' he said, very calmly. 'You are not going to shoot Mancera.'

" 'What!' howled the cruelest man in Venezuela. 'How dare you . . .'

" 'You are not going to shoot Mancera.'

"Our chief, livid from fury, shouted to another officer to bring some soldiers to take me away. Alejandro—still perfectly calm—walked to where his artillerymen were quartered. He quietly ordered them to line up behind him.

" 'General,' he said, to his chief, 'if you shoot Mancera, you won't do it until you've shot me and every one of my soldiers.'

"The cruelest man in Venezuela strode up and down, fire flashed from his eyes, his nails dug deep into the flesh of his hands. Then, after ripping out one last terrific oath, he dashed into his room, slamming the door violently behind him.

"Señora, I am sure Alejandro never told you that story."

"General Mancera, he never did."

"Well, now you know it. Goodnight, señora. Goodnight, Alejandro."

Then there was the man known as *El Tigre*—the Tiger. He was a cruel leader of the forces of the government during the ascendancy of the conservatives, my father's pet aversions, some eighty years ago.

UNDER THE SURFACE

My father, then a little boy, went with my grandfather, Dr. Ybarra, into a shoe shop. As became a professor, Dr. Ybarra had no truck with militarism. His thoughts were for the classics and mathematics and philosophy. He wandered in and out of political complications—and bouts of street fighting in Caracas—with his head in the air and his mind in the clouds.

Acting in that Olympian fashion, he called the shoe clerk and asked for a pair of shoes that he had ordered a short while before. While the clerk was in the back regions, looking for the shoes in order to wrap them up, a ferocious individual, with a sword on one hip and a pistol on the other, strode truculently into the shop.

"Measure me for a pair of shoes!" he shouted.

"What kind?"

"Tiger skin! I want people to recognize me even by my shoes!"

My grandfather came out of the clouds.

"El Tigre!" he whispered. "My boy, this is no place for us." And, pulling his little son along, he moved unobtrusively to the door and out on the street, without bothering to wait for his parcel. That was the effect that a genuine *machetero* of the old Venezuela had on peaceable persons.

One of my father's countless yarns of the past that made a particularly deep impression on me, in my childhood, was about a guerrilla chieftain of merciless habits known all over Venezuela as *Se Llamaba*. He got that nickname because of his endearing custom of taking a loaded pistol in his hand, going up to a prisoner just captured, and demanding:

"*Como se llama?*" ("What is your name?")

"Antonio López."

YOUNG MAN OF CARACAS

After my father's return from the Guayabo campaign, there is this entry in her diary:

"Alito is horrified with Crespo's cruelty. . . . They found prisoners tied hands and feet, and killed with blows from machetes, because their feet were too bad for them to follow."

In President Andrade's campaign against rebellious Cipriano Castro in 1899, my father went along at first without any definite military appointment. Somewhere, between Caracas and the front, Andrade appointed him Chief of Operations in Aragua, the fertile region southwest of the Venezuelan capital, through which the government forces were marching.

The appointment filled my parent with martial fervor. He began to issue crisp, sharp orders.

"Captain!" he snapped at an officer whom he had just annexed as an aide, "we must raise troops. Send recruiting squads into every part of Aragua. *Y que no se me escape ni el gato!* [And see that not even the cat escapes me]." That remark sank deep into my consciousness. Today, many years after it was uttered, as I look back on it, it seems to me that it was the farthest point from Massachusetts that I ever reached.

All these happenings of my boyhood lent cruel point to a story, famous all over the Venezuela of those days. It was about a recruiting officer who dispatched to his commanding general three hundred men bound together with ropes.

"I'm sending you herewith three hundred volunteers," ran his accompanying message. "Return me the ropes and I'll send you three hundred more."

But sometimes the worm would turn. Sometimes the underdogs of Venezuela, driven to sudden fury, would snarl and bite and kill.

UNDER THE SURFACE

When I was eleven years old, there was a terrible example of this. It happened right on the threshold, so to speak, of Caracas —in the little town of Los Teques, on the railroad that a German company was building from the capital to Valencia. Los Teques is perched high in the uplands that lie between Caracas and the valleys of Aragua. The Caraqueños of my boyhood liked to go there to breathe mountain air for a few weeks, when home had become stuffy and rainy. I knew Los Teques well.

When Guzmán Blanco was dictator of Venezuela, back in the eighties of last century, he appointed one of his roughneck generals governor of the Los Teques district. In those days, plenty of injustice was visited by government officials on the lowly folk in their jurisdiction; extortion and high-handed assertion of authority, as well as downright cruelty, were commonplaces. But Guzmán's appointee at Los Teques went nearly all his corrupt and heartless contemporaries one better.

He rode callously over the susceptibilities of the little town's inhabitants. He robbed them of their property. He imprisoned them without reason. He stole their women for himself and his mercenaries. And he spiced the whole brutal catalogue of crime with savage assaults and outrageous murders. The unhappy Tequeños endured in impotent anger. They could do nothing about it. They suffered in silence; but, in their silence, they brooded; and, brooding, they made vows.

Years went by. The merciless governor of Los Teques had left that town for other posts and other orgies of cruelty. Never had he shown his face in the district where he had governed so cruelly as to make himself detested as no man had ever been detested there.

Then, one day, he returned—about ten years after he had

Chapter XI

"Dips" and Others

An old Caracas house. 1890. One corner of the rectangular front parlor is cut off from the rest of the room by a big sofa, placed transversely from wall to wall, like the hypotenuse of a right triangle.

The walls forming the other two sides of the triangle are lined with book shelves filled with many books, of many sizes on many subjects. Part of a rug, sticking out from under the sofa, covers about one-half of the floor space enclosed between the walls and the sofa.

Stretched across that rug, on the floor, completely concealed from the view of anyone in the room, a little boy of solemn countenance lies flat on his tummy. Propped in front of him is a book. He is reading it in a trance of absorption so profound as to cut him off effectively, for the time being, from everything else in the world.

Visitors come and go. They drink tea with the ladies of the house, four old English spinsters. They eat cookies. They make polite social conversation. Not one of them suspects that, behind that hypotenuse-sofa, a little boy is hidden. Not one of them disturbs him. He makes no sound.

Page after page he reads. The book before him may be a tale of exciting naval adventure, by Captain Marryatt; or a volume of travels in distant and dangerous regions, by Sir

"DIPS" AND OTHERS

Francis Burton; or a novel, by some forgotten writer of the early nineteenth century, about life in Venezuela at the time of Bolívar's struggle to make it independent of the Spanish King. All of these—and other tomes on other topics—hold magic for that little bookworm. He devours them, one and all, with the same eager appetite. And he turns each page so noiselessly that not a tea-guzzler nor a cookie-swallower ever hears the rustle of it.

After the last visitors have gone, one of the old Englishwomen crosses the room to the sofa and peers behind it.

"All right, Tom?"

"Yes, thank you."

"Found an interesting book?"

"Yes, Miss Eleanor."

"Isn't it too dark to read any more?"

"Oh, not yet, Miss Eleanor—just a few minutes more, please."

She leaves him to his reading. And back to the book before him go the eyes of that little boy—until Miss Eleanor or Miss Isabella, Miss Alice or Miss Eliza, firmly tells him that he simply must not hurt his eyes any more by reading in such a bad light. Besides, they say, it is time for him to go home, or his mother will get worried. With a sigh of reluctance he puts the book back on the shelf. He makes his farewells to the old ladies and starts for home.

I was that little boy. With the four old Englishwomen I had made a solemn compact. I was to be free to read their books at all hours of the day, in any part of their parlor, or curled up on a chair in the corridor beside their patio. But, just as soon as visitors put in an appearance, I was to be allowed to crawl silently into that little space behind the sofa, and remain there, unseen and unmolested, until the coast was clear. The old ladies observed faithfully the stipulations of our compact. Never did they fetch me out to shake hands with Doña Fulana, or say a few nice words to my mother's dear friend, Doña Zutana.

Their name was Alderson. In the early years of the nineteenth century they had left their home, the ancient English town of Chester, with their father and brother. The male Aldersons wanted to try their luck as plantation-owners in the strange land of Venezuela, just liberated from the rule of Spain. On the way out to their new home they had passed through the United States.

In Caracas, the English family were welcomed cordially by the hospitable Venezuelans. Mr. Alderson bought plantations. Alfred, his young son, helped him to run them. They prospered. They met everybody. Simón Bolívar, then in the full tide of his glory, became greatly attached to the head of the family, a grave Briton utterly unlike the explosive Liberator. So deep was the respect and affection of the ardent Venezuelan hero for his serene Britannic friend that, one day, he asked Mr. Alderson to grant him a special favor. A traveling foreign artist had just come to Caracas. He was painting a portrait of Bolívar. Would Mr. Alderson honor his Venezuelan friend and admirer by having his own portrait painted by the visiting artist and allowing the two portraits to hang side by side in his home?

The Englishman granted the request. When the two paintings were finished, they were placed side by side on the wall of the parlor of the Alderson house—the Britisher in quiet garb, breathing coolness and poise, Bolívar, wearing a grand blue-and-red-and-gold uniform, with brightness in his smoldering dark eyes and electricity in his nervous body. I could see those two portraits plainly from where I used to lie behind the Aldersons' sofa.

The Alderson sisters lived practically all their lives thousands of miles away from their native Cheshire. They lived in the midst of alien people and alien customs. At every hour of the day, for decade after decade, they had the closest sort of contact with un-English influences that might have been expected to shape and mold them. Yet they remained to the end of their long lives completely and uncompromisingly English.

When they first reached Caracas, back in the eighteen-twenties, they brought England with them. Into every house they occupied in the city, until the last of the four had died ripe in years, they imported England. Everything in every one of these houses breathed the soul of England. The last survivor of the sisters, Miss Alice, died when she was well over eighty. She had been a resident of Caracas for something like three-quarters of a century. Yet I can truly say that Miss Alice never left Chester. Neither did any one of her three sisters. They carried England with them wherever they went and in whatever they did; and, when the last of them was laid in her grave, a piece of England went out of Caracas.

They were well-liked. Venezuelans constantly paid calls on them, in that front parlor where I used to lie hidden. The old spinsters were the incarnation of respectability and tradition, two things to which Latin Americans instinctively pay homage. As for the foreign colony of Caracas, it looked upon the Alderson home as a sort of rallying-point. Foreign diplomats came and departed, but the Aldersons went on forever. My mother met the four sisters soon after her arrival in Caracas at the age of sixteen; always, after that, until the last of them was dead, they were admired and respected and beloved friends of hers.

Her diaries abound in entries about the four old English ladies. After making one of her innumerable calls at their house, she wrote: "I don't know what I should do without them." Here is another note: "Went to the Aldersons'—Miss Isabella's birthday. She was very low and begged me to promise to have her veins cut when she died, and make sure she was not buried alive. So I did."

All through her sojourns in Caracas, my mother derived unceasing amusement and stimulation from foreigners and showed unflagging interest in association with them. This was especially true of Americans and Britons. Her attitude proved the tenacity of her New Englandism.

It was a stern and rockbound New Englandism—tempered, though, in her case, by brightness and joy and humor and a tireless quest for romance. She opposed to the storms of life a wall of unbreakable strength; and she remained always illumined from within by steady and constant rays, like one of the lighthouses on the coast of her native New England.

For staying a New Englander through thick and thin, she had the necessary background. On her father's side she counted not only Myles Standish as an ancestor—that tough English warrior who drilled his Pilgrim comrades for Indian fighting—but other forefathers of the Old Colony, in each of whom steadfastness and stamina and piety united to make a man. Far away from Plymouth, she saw, in her reveries, the white church steeples of Massachusetts, and Massachusetts hill-slopes, radiant in the green garment of spring or the golden apparel of autumn. She saw the brooding face of Emerson and the

"DIPS" AND OTHERS

rugged beauty of his friend, her Uncle Marston Watson ("the handsomest man I ever saw," she used to tell her children).

She heard the songs of birds of northern climes, whirring through the treetops of Uncle Marston's Hillside; she breathed the scent of the sea, swept landward by the breezes that ruffle Plymouth harbor. She was conscious always, long after his death, of the presence of Thomas Russell—in whom, as in herself, the granite of New England was bathed in the flashing light of laughter. She felt the presence, likewise, of his brother, her Uncle William, also a man of granite. He had that Ancient Roman quality (he looked to me always as I imagined Cicero), which was the stamp of the most typical New Englanders of the nineteenth century.

On her mother's side, Thomas Russell's daughter could (and did) point proudly to her grandfather—"Father Taylor." That renowned apostle to seafarers grew to be an integral part of Boston, of Boston flintiness, with his furrowed brow and severe features—yet he came from Virginia. He ran away to sea when he was seven. For years he served as cabin boy and as a sailor before the mast and as a mate of sailing vessels. He landed in Boston to devote the rest of his life to saving the souls of mariners; and Boston still remembers the eloquence of his word-pictures of salvation and the ferocity of his denunciations of sin. From Father Taylor my mother got part of her love of salt water, of stinging spray, of decks tilted by tempest, and the screams of the birds of the sea. Also from him came part of her courage, of her capacity to look peril in the eye, of her steel.

At her father's house in Boston she saw John Brown. He was hiding there, before the Civil War, when my mother was two years old. A bodyguard of Massachusetts abolitionists had sworn to shield him with their lives. But John Brown believed —and often told Thomas Russell, one of his protectors—that by his death alone could he give the cause to which he was vowed the impetus that he wished to give it.

One day he took little Nelly Russell on his knee.

"After I have been hanged," he told her, "you can say that you sat on John Brown's lap." Soon afterward, his body was dangling at the end of a rope in Virginia.

All that went into Nelly Russell's make-up. All that stiffened her in the long years of her residence among aliens in an alien land, encompassed by alien traditions and lighted by alien ideals. All that buoyed her up when alien floods threatened to engulf her.

In Venezuela, far from her Massachusetts, New England granite always hardened her, New England steel always gave her fortitude. At one of the times (painfully frequent in her Venezuelan era) when political strife was seething, and militarism running rampant in Caracas, she wrote in her diary, apropos of the fact that one of her sisters-in-law was afraid to go out at night: "I am so glad I have no nerves."

In a land where tea was practically unknown, Nelly Russell had it served at her house every afternoon, though revolution and earthquake might be raging outside. My cousin, Santiago Ybarra, who was very fond of his Massachusetts aunt, used to tell how, when he was suffering from a serious case of man-about-town, he would interrupt roistering parties with gay cronies by suddenly announcing; "Good-bye—I must go to tea at my Aunt Nelly's." And when my brother, Alejandro, Jr., was a baby, he toddled into the room where my mother and several other ladies, Venezuelan and foreign, were assembled, gazed about in a surprised way, and queried: "Tea?"

"DIPS" AND OTHERS

"He thinks," noted my mother in her diary, "that we must *always* drink it when we are together."

Her two best friends in Caracas were an American woman and an Englishwoman—married, like herself, to Venezuelans who had preferred the exoticism of a foreign wife to the humdrum normality of the home-grown product. She delighted in cultivating the members of the ever-changing diplomatic corps—the "dips" as she called them. In the midst of dozens of Venezuelan in-laws and other acquaintances among the Caraqueños she always remained essentially foreign; only with Americans (and, to a considerable extent, with Britishers) did she seem entirely at home.

In our household the report of an inpending change at the American or British Legation was a matter of tremendous importance. We used to get all excited as soon as the report arrived. What sort of man, we expectantly wondered, would the new United States Minister be?—or the new British Secretary of Legation.

Eventually, he would arrive—to be copiously gossiped about over the telephone and minutely observed out at the tennis club, a one-court affair near the station of the Ferrocarril Central, founded and faithfully maintained for years by Mr. Cherry, the railway's manager, as English as the Aldersons. I remember the sensation caused by Monsieur Jaurett, a French resident of Caracas, usually first with tidbits of news about the "dips," when he declared, in the midst of a tennis match, that he knew the name of the new British Minister just appointed by Downing Street.

"What is it?" eagerly asked the ladies of the Caracas foreign colony.

"Iron Backsides!"

As a matter of fact, it was Bax-Ironsides. Monsieur Jaurett professed, at times, to have more difficulty in speaking the English language than he actually encountered. And he liked a joke, the more Gallic the better.

Caracas was unimportant as a diplomatic post. Nevertheless, the "dips" accredited to the Venezuelan government hedged themselves about with all the pomp of protocol and etiquette. Everything they did officially had to be done just so—though, in off hours, some of them were, to say the least, untrammeled.

On Bolívar's birthday, and on other days of impressive ceremonial, they put on high hats and tail coats and boiled shirts (with wide red ribbons bespangling their bosoms), and toddled off, dignified and stately, to greet the President. At dinners, they were awfully formal. Once, that Englishwoman who was my mother's particular friend, got fed up with diplomatic formality, in which she had been immersed all her life, since her father had been British Minister to a number of countries. Tradition was all very well, she told herself rebelliously, but it had its limits. She liked the German Minister of the moment, and she wished to do him honor. So, when the time came for going in to dinner at her house, she asked him to give her his arm and lead the way to the table.

He shook his head in solemn dissent.

"I cannot do as you wish," he told her.

"But I insist."

"I am honored, madame—but I cannot do as you wish."

"Why not?"

"I am not the dean of the diplomatic corps of Caracas. The dean is the American Minister. He is present here tonight. It is to him that the honor belongs of escorting you to the table."

"DIPS" AND OTHERS

She had to ask the American Minister to give her his arm. Somewhere in her wake, in the exact place assigned to him by etiquette, followed that formal Teuton.

Speaking of Germans, there was once a German Minister in Caracas who looked upon the beautiful Avila range of mountains with feelings utterly different from those which it inspired in my two grandfathers, in old Mr. Middleton, and in most other people who saw it. The heart of that German was all in the highlands of his native Germany. Mountains, as supplied by the Creator to Venezuela, were not for him. They violated, in some unexplained fashion, the canons of his taste; they would, he implied, have been *verboten* in Germany. So he didn't like them. He used to drop around to take tea at our house; and, as my mother was pouring him a cup, she would rally him about his anti-Avila attitude.

"Come, come now, Herr von Glumm," she would protest, "you have to admit that the mountains here are beautiful."

"Perhaps, madame, they are," he would assent, in a most lugubrious Teutonic grunt, "but—*they say me nothing!*"

Social amenities of a most attractive sort were cultivated by the Ybarra clan with an English diplomat, who, in my boyhood, served Queen Victoria as British Minister to Venezuela. He was a typical Englishman of his class and day—he seemed to have been built up around his monocle. He admired my mother's humor and knowledge of people. And he pumped her, on occasion, when he was in quest of background for his official communications to Downing Street. One day he told her, in a voice that would have well become Elijah or somebody like that:

"Do you know what I did this morning?"

My mother shook her head.

171

"I mentioned you in dispatches to the Foreign Office."

He drew back a step, to await her reaction—which (he doubtless thought) would be similar to that of a woman suddenly apprised of canonization.

My mother's comment, I am afraid, disappointed him. Undoubtedly, it was something like, "Be sure to tell me what Queen Victoria said." But it probably also amused him. Her comments usually did.

Once, while the Boer war was on, I met that same British Minister on the street in a high state of agitation.

"Tom," he said, losing and retrieving and losing his monocle, "I understand that the military band at the concert tonight in the Plaza Bolívar is going to play the Boer national hymn. If it does, that will be an unfriendly act toward Great Britain, with which Venezuela is maintaining normal and amicable relations. Will you do me a favor? Under the circumstances, I cannot go myself to the concert to find out whether the band is going to take such an undiplomatic line of action. Therefore, will you please go in my stead and let me know if it does?"

That put me in a tight place. I didn't want the job of snooper for Queen Victoria. I groused and growled at dinner. Eventually I made my decision—which, I cannot help thinking, showed that constant association with assorted diplomats had not been without effect on me.

Next morning our telephone rang. It was the British Minister. In a voice quivering with excitement, he inquired:

"Tom, was the Boer national hymn played at the concert last night?"

"I don't know," I replied, "I wasn't there."

"DIPS" AND OTHERS

Among the members of the foreign consular corps functioning in Venezuela in those days there was far less gravity than among the ministers and secretaries of legation who came and went in my Caracas. Some of these gentry were of homespun character, with incisive methods of expressing themselves. There was one whose name was Bird. While he was serving as United States Consul at La Guaira, his wife died. Meeting him soon afterward, my mother told him how sorry she was. He grabbed her impulsively by the sleeve with his left hand, and, shaking his other hand impressively in her face, he told her:

"In this right arm she died. She was lying there quite peaceful when, all of a sudden, she sat bolt upright and started to recite the Lord's Prayer. She'd got as far as 'give us this day our daily bread' when she sez: 'Winfield Scott Bird, I'm a-goin' —*and, by God, she did!*"

In addition to the diplomatic and consular corps, there were rich sources of foreigners in the two English railroad companies, the German railroad company, the English telephone company, the French cable company, and other similar local enterprises run by men from abroad. Britishers often came out to do engineering or office work on the Ferrocarril Central or the Ferrocarril de Caracas a La Guaira—both owned in London. Similarly, the German Gran Ferrocarril de Venezuela, at that time pushing its rails steadily nearer Valencia, lured Germans from the Fatherland for long or short stays in Venezuela. And a new Frenchman bobbed up at irregular intervals to take charge of cables to Europe.

I don't know which stayed longest in Caracas, Mr. Wallis of the English telephone company, or Mr. Cherry, who ran the

Ferrocarril Central. Anyhow, both of them eventually became a part of the scenery. At one time, while Mr. Cherry was in residence, the La Guaira railroad came under the charge of Mr. Almond, and a third Englishman, Mr. Orange, arrived from England on some job or other. Cherry, Almond and Orange made an appetizing trio.

Caracas, by the way, back in the eighteen-nineties, was telephone-minded. Telephones were far commoner there at that time than in Boston. A high percentage of the city's homes had them—and what channels of gossip they were!

Further evidence of how strong Massachusetts always remained in my mother was her friendship for the Reverend Mr. Pond and his wife, who ran the Protestant Mission installed in the old house of my father's family, after the said family had let a mortgage devour the place.

Mr. and Mrs. Pond were one hundred per cent New England. They had been all over the world. Out of their talk would come casual references to adventures in converting Chinese on the Yangtze or in housekeeping on the slopes of Mount Lebanon. Mr. Pond was mild and gray and saintly. He had deacon written all over him. He and his wife carried New England around with them just as the Aldersons carried Old England.

My father always called Mr. Pond *el reverendo*.

"Tom," he would whisper to me, while the missionary couple were drinking tea with my mother at the other end of the room, "I don't like el reverendo." He didn't really mean that, for it was hardly possible for anybody to feel anything as active as dislike for a man of such mildness and goodness as Mr. Pond. Nevertheless, the saintly missionary didn't appeal to General Alejandro Ybarra. The latter, I suppose, could hardly have analyzed himself what the basis of his objections was. Maybe, he had an uneasy feeling that el reverendo might try to convert him.

One by one, the Alderson sisters dropped off. At the funerals of Miss Eliza, Miss Isabella and Miss Eleanor, the diplomatic corps came out in force. The British Minister and his staff appeared, in the long coats and somber hats and black neckties prescribed by funereal etiquette.

The burial service, of course, was Protestant, exactly like every such service in orthodox Cheshire. If no Protestant clergyman was available, one of the British diplomats read the service. Flowers from the numerous friends of the old ladies, foreign and Venezuelan, were banked high around each coffin. And thus, one after another, three of the sisters who had come to the land of Bolívar, never to return home, were carried to their graves, thousands of miles from England—which, though their eyes had not seen it for more than half a century, their souls had never abandoned.

Finally, only Miss Alice remained—tall, wrinkled and gaunt. She lived far on into old age, with no sisters around her; attended by only one servant girl instead of the half dozen of happy years; staring into the shadows of the other world from a little house on a side street, instead of a big house on a main thoroughfare, such as the Aldersons had occupied in childhood and girlhood, middle age and early old age.

One day, Miss Alice said to my mother, as the two sat drinking tea in the old Englishwoman's little parlor:

"Nelly, I feel that my end is not far away."

Then she pointed to the two portraits, of her father and

Simón Bolívar, hanging side by side, as they had hung for some seventy years.

"Nelly, you know the history of those two paintings?"

"Of course I do, Miss Alice."

"Well, I want you and your husband to have them. Will you promise to see that they continue to hang side by side wherever they may be, as General Bolívar wished."

"Of course I will, Miss Alice."

A few days later the two portraits were moved to our house, Monte Elena, in the suburb of El Paraíso.

Soon the British Minister and other members of the Caracas diplomatic corps—together with a few foreigners and Venezuelans whose memories ran far back into the past—gathered at that little house on its side street. One wall of the parlor showed two big, bare spaces, where two paintings had hung. In the middle of the room stood a coffin heaped with flowers. Miss Alice Alderson was dead. For the first time in nearly three-quarters of a century, since before Simón Bolívar's death in 1830, there were no Aldersons living in Caracas.

Side by side, as Bolívar had wished, those two portraits, which Miss Alice Alderson had given to my mother and father, hung for years in our house. Shortly before my father died, he reminded my mother of the Liberator's wish and asked her to see that it was fulfilled in future years.

After my mother's death, in strict fulfillment of explicit instructions from her, the portraits of Simón Bolívar and Mr. Alderson were presented by myself and my sister and brother to the Bolívar Museum, which now occupies the house in Caracas where the Liberator was born. In making the gift, we stipulated that the paintings should remain together. Now,

"DIPS" AND OTHERS

more than a century after Bolívar expressed his wish, the two portraits of those two strikingly dissimilar friends—the calm Englishman and the fiery Venezuelan—hang side by side, exactly as Simón Bolívar desired.

Chapter XII

The Language of the Tribe

My French has improved decidedly since the time when I thought that "le médécin malgré lui" meant "the medicine disagreed with Louis." Nor do I believe any longer that *ris de veau à la bonne femme* means "laugh of the calf at the good woman." Nevertheless, my French is still strikingly unlike the language spoken in France. But let that pass. We'll consider my German. That's good—even Germans admit it—thanks to two years in Munich, plus almost as long in Berlin, plus sojourns of varying duration in Germany or Austria, on my lawful occasions as a journalist working for New York publications. I also have a smattering of hotel, railroad, restaurant and customs-house Italian.

As for my Spanish, it practically runs neck and neck with my English when I'm in top bilingual form. To this day, it shows a slight rustiness only when I am not thrown for a stretch of months with Spanish-speakers. But, just as soon as I fall among them again, the language of my father's forebears bursts forth from my interior like a freshet in the spring, and I become one hundred per cent bilingual.

This linguistic prowess has stood me in good stead in verbal dealings with the Ybarra family. In the early part of my life, down in Venezuela, Spanish and English—seasoned with stray bits of French and Italian—and even German—were bandied

THE LANGUAGE OF THE TRIBE

about around the Ybarra table with amazing impartiality. It was nothing, at lunch or dinner, for me or my sister Leonor or my brother Alejandro, Jr., to shoot a sentence in Spanish at my father, interpolate an aside in English to my mother, recall an incident of bygone days in Munich, spit out a salvo of German, hum a snatch, with the original Italian words, from the preceding night's opera at the Caracas Opera House, and then scramble back to English or Spanish—according as to whether we had decided to bestow the remainder of the sentence on Jessie Sullivan or on some Venezuelan cousin who had casually dropped in to sample the Ybarra cuisine of the moment.

That cuisine—like our conversation—had an international variety that was highly esteemed in Caracas. My mother believed in hiring good cooks (statuesque French-speaking Negresses from Martinique, when we were flush, slatternly native Venezuelans when we were broke) and letting them go their dusky way, within reason.

But she was adamant about garlic. Black beans in exotic messes, yes—and firm fried plantains, or squashy boiled ones, and *carne frita*, greasy but alluring, and *mondongo*, Venezuelan tripe soup of succulent tripiness—but unrestrained garlic, never—or hardly ever.

Just as soon as the current cook showed a tendency to drop mountains of garlic on molehills of victuals, my mother would go one hundred per cent New England. Sweetness and light would move out of her and granite move in.

In battle formation, she would stride kitchenward to confront the cook—not for nothing was my mother a descendant of those purposeful Pilgrims who had landed on Plymouth Rock. (At such times of crisis, my father, who privately liked garlic in bulk, undoubtedly wished that Plymouth Rock had landed on the Pilgrims.) But he couldn't do anything about it.

In the kitchen, my mother's Spanish, or French, would rise to torrential fluency. The cook's rebuttals would wilt—and wither—and collapse. My mother would return to the front part of the house with a mien reflecting victory. Jessie Sullivan, after glaring at the cook, would mutter something—quaintly supposed by Jessie to be in Spanish—about cooks in general and the current specimen in particular, winding up (in Cockney-Irish) with "Missybarra you always 'ave to keep your eye on them people." Thereafter, until the next signs of kitchen revolt, garlic worked its way into our food only in the smallest quantities and solely under an official laissez-passer from my mother.

In spite of the many years that she spent in Venezuela, my mother never really got accustomed to the Venezuelans nor they to her. When she first knew my father and his brothers and cousins and nephews, they used to terrify her with their violence of speech and ferocity of gesticulation. Once my father and his two brothers trooped into the next room from where she was and engaged in a most furious argument. Each talked at the top of his lungs and hurled at the others the most dreadful insults. My mother, cowering in the next room, felt that bloodshed must surely ensue. The crack of a pistol would not have surprised her at all.

Suddenly the uproar stopped. From the next room my father emerged between his two brethren. One of his arms was around his brother Francisco, the other around the neck of his brother Luis. All three were on the broad grin. When my mother recovered from her astonishment, she asked what all the rumpus had been about.

"Oh, jost a leetle discossion," said my father airily.

THE LANGUAGE OF THE TRIBE

There were certain goatlike jumps of Venezuelan minds, from one promontory of thought to another, quite unrelated to the subject in hand, which sometimes took my mother by surprise. For instance, the talk in Caracas would turn to some piece of downright scoundrelism committed by a native of the city. My mother would express the proper modicum of horror.

"How awful for Guillermo to do such a thing!" she would exclaim. "It's simply unforgivable!"

"Oh, you mustn't say that, Nelly," one of the Latins present would protest. "After all, Guillermo has such a beautiful handwriting!"

And then there was the matter of religion. Nelly Russell de Ybarra, upon whose shoulders everything religious sat with feathery lightness, used to get exasperated, nevertheless, at the serene way with which some Venezuelans lumped all non-Catholics together. To these people, you were either a Catholic or your religion wasn't worth bothering about at all. One delightful Caracas girl, while talking on a religious subject with a group including my mother, calmly remarked: "But, of course, that doesn't concern Nelly, *como Nelly es judía*" ("since Nelly is a Jewess").

"*No soy judía!*" snapped my mother, in sudden exasperation.

"Well, Protestant then," the delightful young lady said, with a bewitching smile of apology. But, probably the very next day, in the midst of another similar conversation, she would be saying: "But, naturally, that doesn't affect Nelly, because Nelly *es judía*." And my mother, beside herself with annoyance, would say later to my father: "If that young woman calls me a *judía* again, I'll. . . ." the rest of the sentence was lost in angry spluttering. And my father's chuckles almost choked him.

Venezuelan accent in the English language could puzzle my mother as much as Jessie Sullivan's jargon. There was a melancholy gentleman of Caracas whose son—known as Bertie—had been sent to the United States to school. My mother had not heard of Bertie's progress for some time; and, meeting the mournful gentleman on the street one day, she inquired politely about his son.

"I think Bairtie go to jail," said Bertie's father.

"WHAT!"

"I think Bairtie go to jail."

"Wh-why, what has he done?"

It was the turn of the melancholy gentleman to look surprised.

"Done? What do you mean?"

"Didn't you say he was going to jail?"

"Yes, I said that."

"Well then . . ."

And then, suddenly, the sky cleared. My mother understood. The idea was to send Bertie from school to Yale.

Certain entries in Nelly Russell's diary indicate that, at times, she shared Jessie Sullivan's ideas about the inherent eccentricity of "them people." For instance:

"Everybody laughing over Conchita X's exploit of going to Macuto in the last stages, and then running to Lucía Z.s house at 4 A.M., and having her first baby there. . . . She was bandaged in half of a drawers-leg of Z.'s, and the baby put in the other half. Luckily, the Z.'s took it beautifully—afraid I should not have been so good. The husband and layette were in Caracas."

THE LANGUAGE OF THE TRIBE

My mother spoke good Spanish, a feat that she owed as much to her natural adaptability as to linguistic facility. Now and then some malevolent form of the Castilian subjunctive would trip her, and, in the accent of her Spanish, there were also occasional signs of unshaken loyalty to Massachusetts.

But she was a marvel compared with some other Americans living in Caracas and helplessly trying to master the local language. Never, for example, did she get so badly bogged in that tongue as did another American lady, also married to a Venezuelan. This lady was trying to explain one day the difference between the Roman Catholic religion and her own, which was High Episcopalian of a particularly high type. Now, in Venezuela, *el papa* means the pope, and *la papa* the potato. Unaware of this important distinction, the young American wife earnestly told her husband's relatives:

"Your religion and mine are practically the same except for one thing: the potato. We disagree only about the potato. Nothing stands between your Catholicism and my Episcopalianism but the potato. If only you people would stop worshiping the potato!"

As for my sister Leonor and my young brother Alejandro, they were as much at home in the language of our father as in that of our mother.

My father was very proud of his English. During one period of exile, in his early married life he wrote—efficaciously aided by his wife—*Ybarra's Practical Method for Learning Spanish*. This book, to its author's intense satisfaction was used for years at the United States Naval Academy at Annapolis. Yet, despite long sojourns in the United States and constant practice in English at home with his wife and children and the phalanx of his wife's Massachusetts relatives and friends, my father's English remained a thing of flawless foreignness. The accent in which he steeped it was as Spanish as Seville.

Some of the things that he could do with English words were incredible. To him, "a woman" was "an ooman," with the first syllable long drawn out, the initial letter "w" being something that he could never negotiate successfully. It was delicious to hear him, a man of martial bearing and virile manner, substitute for "but I didn't" a birdlike chirp of "Bot I deent." Before words like "wash" or "went," he felt constrained to stick a "g" to help him over the hurdle of that dreaded "w"—thus: "Now I go to gwahsh my hahnds" or "He gwent ahway."

Like most members of the Spanish race, he invariably began with an "e" every word in my mother's language such as "start" or "street" or "study."

"Today I estart down the estreet in a brown estoddy," he would announce—to the boundless joy of his irreverent family.

During his enforced stays in Massachusetts, Alejandro Ybarra absorbed a lot about the Pilgrims of Plymouth—in fact, an overdose. I can imagine nothing more alien to a descendant of a Spanish conquistador than a Pilgrim father. At one time, in Boston and Plymouth, we used to see a lot of a very nice cousin of my mother, Jane Goodwin Austin, who had won celebrity with her novels about her Pilgrim forebears. One of the best-known of her novels, *Standish of Standish*, dealt with Myles Standish, prize ancestor of the Russells.

My father heard considerable about Myles. He bore up bravely. Now and then, however, the strain broke down his endurance. Once, at a party in Plymouth at which the subject of Cousin Jennie's book on Myles had been discussed with rather more than adequacy, my father drew my mother into a corner and whispered:

THE LANGUAGE OF THE TRIBE

"Nelly, I am tired of Estandeesh of Estandeesh."

General Ybarra's high ability as a raconteur, combined with the extraordinary accent in which he wrapped everything he said in English, made him a great hit with North American listeners. Once he went on a business trip to Mexico. He traveled at great speed. He hardly had time to eat and sleep. On his return to Boston, one of his wife's cousins asked him:

"Weren't you delighted, General, with the beautiful Mexican scenery?"

With his eyes goggling out of their sockets and his mustache bristling, he blurted:

"*Scenery?* SCENERY? All I know about Mexican scenery is when, on my way back, I jomp into a hot bath at the Planters' Hotel in St. Louis and gwahsh the scenery off myself!"

All through his life, though he considered himself a perfectly good Roman Catholic, he ate as much meat as he wished on Fridays. He justified this on the ground that the Spaniards had received, centuries ago, a special papal permission to eat either fish or meat on Friday, as a reward for having driven the Moors out of Spain.

"But you're not a Spaniard," my mother would object.

"Nelly, were not my ahncestors Espahniards?"

"What difference does that make? You're a Venezuelan."

"Nelly, my ahncestors drove the Moors out of Espain. The roast beef is very good today. Ahnother eslice, please." He would get it, while my mother looked on in disapproval. With a deep sigh of pleasurable anticipation, he would cut himself a piece of meat and remark, as he put it into his mouth:

"Nelly, how glahd I ahm that my ahncestors drove the Moors out of Espain!"

In spite of constant association with his remarkable lingo,

the rest of us would sometimes be mystified as to its meaning. Once, when we were living in Cambridge, Massachusetts, during the régime of some Venezuelan president who would have jailed my father on sight, he arrived from Boston and informed us:

"Tonight eess estrahcahss een Treeneety Chorch."

We all sat bolt upright, imagining a terrible catastrophe at the scene of Bishop Phillips Brooks's locally renowned outbursts of eloquence.

"What did you say?" inquired my mother.

"*Estrahcahss*, Nelly—*estrahcahss* een Treeneety Chorch."

We remained uncomprehending. He began to get peppery, as he often did when the rest of the family were so obtuse as not to grasp instantly the trend of his mysterious excursions into English. Finally, the truth came out. As there had been some sort of big late function at Trinity Church, the Boston street railway company had put on *extra cars* for carrying members of the congregation to their homes. The Ybarra family breathed a sigh of relief.

Despite innumerable indications from those who heard him that his English did not conform to current usage in Boston or London—or anywhere else in the Anglo-Saxon world, for that matter—General Ybarra retained, through thick and thin, his childlike pride in it.

"Have you ever seen a grasp of English like mine?" he would ask me. I hadn't—but not in the sense that he meant. Nothing pleased him more than the arrival of a check from his publishers for royalties on *Ybarra's Practical Method*. No check, to the best of my knowledge and belief, ran as high as fifty dollars. But those checks looked like a million to the author of the book.

THE LANGUAGE OF THE TRIBE

They served to strengthen his already strong conviction that his English was perfect.

If ever there was a fish out of water, it was my father in Boston. The Russells and other branches of my mother's family were interested in him; and they were invariably polite to him. But their interest at times resembled that felt by a visitor to a zoo for the leopard or the monkey; and their politeness seemed, now and then, to be based on the belief that a Venezuelan relation-by-marriage, if subjected to impoliteness, might scratch and even bite.

In and out of Plymouth, my Latin parent wandered; in and out of the homes of Boston relatives-by-marriage and acquaintances; in and out of various business ventures forced upon him by the necessity of supporting his family until such time as Dictator Guzmán Blanco should die—preferably from unnatural causes. But never could anybody thrown with him detect the slightest hint of a change in his Latinism.

Massachusetts never made a dent in him. Every sojourn of his in Boston and Plymouth was an unwelcome interlude. Every return to Venezuela was a blessed release. No boy who ever heard the clock at school strike the hour of freedom was more overjoyed than was Alejandro Ybarra when he realized that, at last, he could sit out in front of his Caracas home, Monte Elena, on the flat *azotea*, or terrace, with the panorama of Caracas spread out before him, and never have to think again of embarkation for the bleak north.

Throwing himself back in a big rocking chair, he would say to his family: "I shall travel no more. I traveled enough when I was younger. From now on, you [he pronounced that word *joo*] can do all my traveling for me. Always, when joo return home, joo will find me here on the azotea and joo can tell me all about the foreign places joo have seen and the foreign people joo have met. As for me, I'll never bodge again from Caracas." And he didn't. At the time of his death in 1918, he had been there without a break for nearly twenty-two years.

When he was first in the United States, at the end of the eighteen-seventies, my father was convinced that whatever was Latin was normal, and all else abnormal, and, hence, to a considerable extent, negligible. So he arrayed himself in one of his many suits of white cloth, the regular garb of the Venezuelan, and sallied forth from his father-in-law's house on Hancock street, quite as if he were in Caracas instead of Boston.

He returned with a string of fascinated Boston urchins behind him. The Russell house rang with the reverberations of his Spanish wrath.

"Are these people not civilized, Nelly? I cannot onderestand why I most be followed on the estreet by estupid little boys because I am esmartly dressed!" My mother soothed him —she was a wonder at that. Soon he was calm enough to join Judge Russell and my grandmother at supper.

In those days my grandfather Russell was prominent in Massachusetts politics. He was often a member of reception committees for big visitors from other states. He used to include my father, whenever possible, as a sort of unofficial committeeman, to the unbounded delight of his South American son-in-law, who was always eager for new impressions.

On one occasion, General Ulysses S. Grant showed up in Boston. He proceeded, duly hedged about by an escort of eminent local dignitaries, to Plymouth, where he was to be the star exhibit at some festivity or other in honor of the Pilgrims. On the train from Boston, my father sat close to Grant. Being

THE LANGUAGE OF THE TRIBE

an exuberant Latin, he never recovered from the memory of the stony silence of the great soldier. It lasted nearly all the way to Plymouth. Finally, even Grant realized that he ought to say something. Pulling himself together, he looked solemnly at the fellow-passengers around him, pointed to the landscape outside the window, and grunted:

"Lots of sand."

He didn't open his mouth again until he was in Plymouth.

There, after a short speech in honor of the big occasion, he again went Sphinx. This perturbed the head of a local boys' school, who had been Grant's chaplain in the Civil War. The ex-chaplain had hoped that the great man would address his schoolboys—who were crowding around the house in which Grant was lunching, eagerly pressing their freckled noses against window panes, in the hope of catching a glimpse of the victor of Appomattox.

"Won't you say a few words to my boys?" he asked respectfully.

"No," said Grant.

Then the schoolmaster begged Mrs. Grant to intercede for him.

"Liss," said Mrs. Grant, "why won't you make a little speech to the boys?"

"Because, my dear," answered her husband, "I have nothing to say." And that was that.

There was no such reticence in my grandfather Russell—to the joy of his Latin son-in-law, who, accustomed to South American volubility, greatly resented its absence from the average Massachusetts make-up. Judge Russell, an excellent speaker, was much in demand in and out of his native state; and many a time, his exotic son-in-law, seated at the speakers' table (though he never spoke himself), drank in an eloquence that, for all its lack of Latin exuberance, must have reminded him pleasantly of the torrential speech of his native Venezuela.

His father-in-law was again and again a speaker at the annual meetings of the Pilgrim Society. I like to believe that it was indeed Judge Russell who, at one of those solemn gatherings, made the following immortal remark—also attributed to Joe Choate and other wits: "Ladies and gentlemen, I want to propose the health both of the Pilgrim Fathers and of the Pilgrim Mothers—for the Pilgrim Mothers not only endured everything that the Pilgrim Fathers endured *but the Pilgrim Fathers as well!*"

In religion, my father was a typical product of Spain and South America. Though he never let any religious observance touch him at any point, he considered himself a perfectly good Roman Catholic.

"I never go inside a Catholic church," he used to say, "but—jost joo try to convert me!" Every Latin Catholic will understand that attitude. No Protestant or any other brand of Catholic will—especially the Irish. My father was sure all his life that Catholics were born, not made.

Once, in Boston, a pious member of my mother's Protestant family tried to convert him to one of the creeds prevalent in Massachusetts.

"General," he said, "wouldn't you like to go with me to my church next Sunday?"

"Delighted," replied General Ybarra, that affable fish out of water. On the next Sunday he attended services at the Protestant place of worship of that northern connection-by-marriage.

THE LANGUAGE OF THE TRIBE

"Did you like it?" asked his host.

"Very moch."

"Didn't you find it simple—dignified—without any extraneous ritual and pageantry?"

"Certainly. It was very kind indeed of you to invite me. I deeply appreciate your kindness."

The other beamed. Conversion, it seemed to him, was just around the corner.

"And now," continued my father, "won't you do me a great honor?"

"What?"

"Come with me next Sunday to my church."

The other was astounded. That wasn't the idea at all!

"I really think he was shocked, Nelly," my father told my mother when he got home—to her great delight and that of my liberal and humorous American grandfather.

My father never drank. In all his life he never put down a straight thimbleful of beer or wine or hard liquor. Though he ran away from home to become a soldier when he was fourteen, he never allowed the dissolute attitude of some of his comrades toward alcohol to get the slightest grip on him. In fact, that attitude was partly the reason for his teetotalism.

As a boy-soldier, he had been deeply shocked by the fate of a favorite cousin. That cousin, also vowed to the military life, was a drunkard. He poured down the burning aguardiente of Venezuela—rot-gut, pure and simple—in unbelievable quantities. He knew his weakness. He fought against it. But he fought only to lose. Finally, he threw himself off a cliff. Near the spot from which he had jumped, a note was found. "No use!" it ran. "I'm beaten." Alejandro Ybarra never forgot that.

But he made one concession. He was extremely fond of rich sauces on food. And, whenever my mother garnished our family commissariat with dishes like kidneys and Madeira sauce, or soup flavored with Sherry, he partook of them in generous portions, with brazen and obvious satisfaction.

"What can I do?" he would protest, with a twinkle in the corner of his eyes, "what can I do if my gwife insists on mixing gwine with my food? It is she who arranges the meals in this house, not I. Nelly—another helping of kidneys, please."

He also used to brew, at long intervals, an awful mess made with a little beer and much sugar, which he called, I don't know why, "bull." The recipe, he alleged, had come to him from an Englishman. He seemed to think that the sugar mixed with this unhallowed concoction robbed the beer of alcohol. Anyhow, he drank the stuff once every two or three years—without competition from any other member of the family.

Once, after one of my father's quarrels with his wife—frequent in our household and entirely without significance—he put on his hat and marched gloomily out the front door. He came back a couple of hours later, still in the geographical center of an awful fit of melancholy.

"Nelly," he rumbled, in his deepest basso, "do joo know where I gwent?"

"Where did you go?" asked my mother, with her usual cheerfulness.

"To the clob. And do joo know what I deed at the clob?"

"What did you do?"

"I ordered a glahss of brahndy—and I totched eet to my leeps!"

He paused dramatically. He expected immediate expressions of shock and horror. But my mother threw herself back in her

General Ybarra in uniform as Military Governor of Caracas

THE LANGUAGE OF THE TRIBE

chair and shouted with laughter. At first, he was annoyed. Then the humor of the thing struck him—he was a good sport. In another minute both of them were chuckling. Theirs was a real marriage.

He never gambled. Gambling, too, he had seen at its worst in rough campaigning; instead of enslaving him, it had touched the steel in his nature, and recoiled, leaving him immune. But he used to like to tell about wild evenings in his early days, when, as military commandant of La Guaira, he had broken the rule of a lifetime and got into games of chance with loose-living local merchants.

"Most exciting, those games," he would tell us, looking wicked. "Very risky. I would think a long time before I made a bet."

"How much would you bet finally?" we would ask.

"One-tenth of a cent."

Always, in my memory, my father stands out as a prince of story-tellers. His stock of yarns was inexhaustible. He loved to garnish an anecdote to the limit, color it up, give it plenty of drama. Yet, along with this, went a keen sense of balance and point that precluded all that was superfluous. As a raconteur, he walked along paths lined with brilliant flowers, but those paths were straight.

And he welcomed with delight the fact that he had a small son who reveled in his stories and begged for more. Indeed, thanks to his yarns, a Caracas that I never knew lives in my memory side by side with my Caracas. And it lives in such clearness of outline and vividness of color that, at times, I cannot believe that I was not really acquainted with its dramatis personae and with the stage on which they played their parts.

rifles! Those letters, don't forget, may be opened by the enemy. Instead of soldiers say cows and instead of rifles say cigars.'

"In a few days the following came from the henchman:

" 'The cows have arrived, but they have no shoes. I have also received the cigars, but there are no bayonets on them.' "

So it would go, sometimes for a couple of hours. Now and then my father and I would get to chuckling wickedly, in hushed tones, as we held one of our sessions in a corner of the parlor. At such times, my mother would call out, from where she was reading:

"Alito, you're telling Tom something he ought not to hear."

"Bot, Nelly . . ."

"Now don't deny it."

More soft-pedaled chuckles confirmed the accuracy of her instinct. But the story continued. She hadn't put in her oar for moralistic reasons. What burned her was that Spanish conventions demanded her exclusion from the party.

Off and on, my father spent about fifteen years outside his native country. But twice as long as that would not have changed the basic Spaniard inside him. The prejudices of that Spaniard used to flare up most unexpectedly, even when North American customs and habits hemmed him in most closely.

Once we were discussing the separation of a Venezuelan wife from her husband. She was living in seclusion in Caracas, providing not the slightest morsel of food for gossip. All that she wanted was to forget. My father did not know the background of the case, whether husband or wife was mainly to blame. Nevertheless, to his Spanish way of thinking, that divorcée was a lost soul.

THE LANGUAGE OF THE TRIBE

"The least she can do," he said judicially, "is shoot herself."

"But, Alito!" exclaimed my mother, in shocked astonishment. She wasn't often jolted out of her philosophical attitude toward life by anything that her wild man of Venezuela said or did. But this time she was. My father, however, stuck to his guns.

"Yes, Nelly," he grunted, with a pontifical nod. "Thaht ooman ought to shoot herself!"

"We must find some more," said Ravelo.

"Perhaps there's a whole bunch of them on the other side of El Calvario," suggested Rauseo hopefully.

But nothing in particular happened after that. It was a hot Sunday afternoon. All the belligerent ardor that had been surging within our bosoms seemed to have oozed out. We bought a few *conservas de coco*, sticky and unsanitary blobs of coconut, held together by brown sugar paste. We drank a lemonade apiece. Then we straggled listlessly back to the city.

Next morning we proudly told the big boys at the Colegio Villegas:

"Yesterday we were in a terrific avance de piedras on El Calvario."

I tell that story to illustrate the essential lawlessness of the schoolboys of Caracas. In my father's boyhood—and in mine—it was the custom for gangs of boys to go prowling around the outskirts, in search of other gangs. As soon as one gang sighted another, its members would fill their pockets with stones, the bigger the better, grab a stone in each hand, and rush into battle. It was nothing for half a dozen of the combatants to get cracked skulls, to say nothing of abrasions and contusions in other parts of their persons. An encounter of this sort was known as an avance de piedras—literally, an advance with stones. It made a snowball fight of the north look like the passing of cookies at an afternoon tea. Fortunately for my skull, my craving for the sport died with my first taste of it.

The Colegio Villegas was established in a spacious old one-story mansion, on the corner of Piñango, three doors from where we were living. Lawlessness was its keynote. Instruction played a certain role there, to be sure; and I suppose that, if you

WILLIAM TELL AND TERESA

searched long enough, you might find traces of organization. Possibly, even, of discipline. But there was no need to go in search of the school's lawlessness. It jumped up and smacked you in the face.

In the classrooms, it sometimes expressed itself in a free fight between teachers and pupils. One day, Coronil, of the teaching staff, lost his temper completely, trying to educate Tailhardat, one of the biggest and most unruly boys. So he went after Tailhardat with his fists. In seeking to elude his enraged mentor, Tailhardat jumped over a long wooden bench, on which half a dozen little boys were sitting in a row. The bench was upset. I'll never forget the outraged and pessimistic look on the faces of those six small boys as they tipped over, their heads moving toward the floor and their toes pointing toward the ceiling. In a few seconds, six little heads hit the floor with a bang in perfect unison—the nearest approach to organization that I ever saw at the Colegio Villegas.

While those lads scrambled and whimpered in the dust on the floor, Coronil continued to chase Tailhardat, and Tailhardat continued to leap over chairs and benches. Finally, old man Villegas himself rushed onto the battlefield, bellowing furious apostrophes to organization and discipline. Coronil returned to his teaching. Tailhardat returned to his seat. Six little boys rubbed the backs of their heads.

Old Villegas took charge of part of my education in person. I cannot remember what he taught. That trifling detail has been submerged by the memories of the stricken fields of battle on which he functioned—with education peeping from bomb shelters now and then, in the usually unjustified hope that the fracas was over. It seldom was.

Coronil, or Mariña, or Dr. Montenegro (who taught Latin) a small troop of little boys marched into one of the classrooms, under the wing of Arias. He promptly locked the door.

"And now," he said, with a grin, "for the paso de aritmética. Who has any money?"

I had a few cents. A couple of the others were similarly endowed. Arias collected. Then he went to the barred window, opening onto the corner of Piñango. He whistled and shouted until he attracted the attention of the man who ran the *pulpería* opposite our school. The man sent a minion across the street.

"Twelve conservas de coco," said Arias. The minion returned to the grocery shop and reappeared with twelve sticky messes, which he handed in between the bars. After levying generous tribute, our self-appointed teacher of arithmetic divided what was left among us small urchins. We spent the next quarter of an hour munching and licking our sticky fingers. Then Arias pulled himself together.

"Now, boys, for the paso de aritmética. Who's got any money?"

Having exacted another forced contribution, he again went to the window and summoned the grocer's minion.

"*Pan de horno*—six," he ordered.

The minion returned with six circular things, like crumbly, dry doughnuts—indigestion in visible, tangible form. We proceeded to eat them.

That, with insignificant variations, was the paso de aritmética. It was held three or four times. Then Old Man Villegas got suspicious.

One afternoon there was a thundering knock on the door. Arias was in the midst of financial negotiations with the grocer's minion. Canceling them abruptly, he unbarred the door. The

WILLIAM TELL AND TERESA

Vice-President of Venezuela strode into the room, his white goatee bristling with unfriendliness. On his face was the look that usually preceded an outbreak of palmeta.

"What's this all about?"

"Un paso de aritmética," explained Arias, in a wavering voice.

Old Man Villegas looked at him. Arias looked at the floor.

"Follow me!"

Preceded by our formidable headmaster, we trooped miserably back to the main schoolroom. The paso de aritmética was never held again. Instead, at the hour when I had been eating indigestible sweets, my ears rang again to enraged shouts of:

"La mano!"

Or, maybe, I was in the elementary Latin class, and Dr. Montenegro, another gentleman of volcanic temperament, was pointing a shaking finger at me, and howling:

"Kneel!"

Which meant that I would have to get down on my knees, in disgrace, on my bench, surrounded by a lot of snickering little boys—just because of some form, unbacked by tradition, which I had attributed to some confounded Latin verb!

Of the boys attending the Colegio Villegas, about one-half were boarders. The rest, including myself, were day scholars. We came around daily from our homes in the city to get our quota of castigation and education, and returned home to eat and sleep. The boarders slept in long, bare dormitories, in the upper story of the school, which stretched along the rear of the old mansion in which William Tell had installed himself. They ate in another big, bare room downstairs, at a long wooden table, just behind the main class rooms. There they stamped and shouted during meals, and threw chunks of bread at one another, and kicked each other under the table, while Coronil and Mariña bellowed for order and dashed about with palmetas in their hands and fury in their eyes.

The school abutted on the house of my grandmother Ybarra, between the corners of El Conde and Piñango. From the rear of William Tell's upper story, glimpses could be had of the rear upstairs balcony of the old Rivas-Ybarra house (the same from which my grandfather used to gaze, in silent reverence, upon the Avila mountains). Glimpses could also be had of my pretty young cousins, Inés Margarita and Ana Teresa, the daughters of my Aunt Inés, going about their maidenly daily round in the home of their ancestors.

This state of affairs was unsettling to the lawless boarders at the Colegio Villegas. They used to ogle. They used to roll their eyes shamelessly when one or both of my cousins became visible. They flipped love notes from balcony to balcony. But that was all. No romantic results came out of these doings—no elopement, or anything like that.

The lawlessness of William Tell's school also cropped out in its journalism. A few of the older boys, not quite such abandoned desperadoes as the average, launched a weekly paper. Its first issue consisted of about a dozen copies, laboriously written in longhand. The underlying idea was to give a dignified chronicle of scholastic doings. Of course, the editors (as they announced in their prospectus) expected also to go into controversial matters—a newspaper not immersed in controversy is something utterly beyond the comprehension of Venezuelans of either sex or any age. The name of the paper was *La Crítica Colegial*.

Hardly had its first issue appeared before a rival was in the field. That rival had one object and one only—to crush *La*

WILLIAM TELL AND TERESA

Crítica Colegial out of existence. Its toughness and vindictiveness were sufficiently disclosed by its title, *El Machete*. So ferocious was the assault of *El Machete* on the dignified *La Crítica Colegial* that the latter promptly folded up. *El Machete*, having accomplished its savage object, followed suit. We were reduced once more to grapevine methods for tidbits of intramural news.

Among the teachers at Villegas's school, my favorite was Coronil. He was an ambitious youth from the interior of the country, who afterward rose to political importance in the régime of Cipriano Castro. But when I knew him he was just a struggling teacher, often strapped and plunged into discouragement. Though I was only eleven and he in his twenties, he took a liking to me and made me a sort of limited confidant. He would describe his home town and his ambitions and the ups and downs of his attempts to get ahead in Caracas. Of all our colloquies, I remember only one. It ran somewhat like this:

"Tom, do you know that little square box I used for saving money?—the one I kept always locked?"

"Yes."

"Well, I've been putting coins into it for a long time. Of course, when I was particularly broke, I used to pry out a few of them through the hole in the top, with a penknife. But I felt sure there were still a whole lot of coins inside. *Ay, Dios mío!*"

"What happened?"

"Last night I got the key to that box out of my trunk. I opened the box. What do you think I found inside?"

"Two dollars?"

"Two cockroaches!"

In drawing on my memories of schooldays in Caracas, I have purposely ignored chronology. For that I have justification, it seems to me. I tried hard, in my early years, to forget as much as I possibly could about the predecessor of the Colegio Villegas in the campaign of my education, the school conducted by Teresa Eduardo. I did this because some of the teachers at that earlier school, including its principal, were women. And that is something that no little boy who ever got attracted, even fleetingly, by rough stuff like an avance de piedras, could possibly want to remember.

Teresa Eduardo was a handsome, middle-aged lady, highly esteemed in Venezuelan educational circles. One of her assistants was Isolina Rodríguez, known, even to the smallest boys, simply as Isolina. Isolina tried to interest me in religious reading. I got interested all right—not, however, in the religious propaganda with which the books provided for me were saturated, but simply in the narrative. If there was plenty of action, well and good. If not, thumbs down. That was my attitude.

There was one grand volume about Christian martyrs at Lugdunum, which I gobbled at a very snappy pace. In my haste to get from one martyrdom to another, without being delayed too long en route by the edifying conversion to Christianity of Roman centurions and such-like, I soon left behind the daily quota. Isolina would ask:

"Tom, where did we leave off in our reading last time?"

Not wishing to let on that I was already halfway through the book, which would have outraged the jog-trot etiquette of the school, I would answer:

"At the end of page fourteen, Isolina."

"Well, begin reading at the top of page fifteen."

Monte Elena, the Ybarra home in El Paraíso, just outside Caracas

LA FAMILIA

"Chuao is not for sale," replied the president of the university.

Guzmán Blanco was furious. As a result of the rage into which he flew, Dr. Ybarra was relieved of his post. And Chuao passed out of the hands of the University of Caracas into those of the dictator of Venezuela.

I never saw Dr. Alejandro Ybarra. He left the world in Caracas at just about the time I entered it in Boston. But my father kept his memory green. He had a great reverence and affection for the obstinate savant who, like himself, had dared to defy El Ilustre Americano. My mother also always spoke highly of her father-in-law. Behind the stories told by both my parents about him, I see a spare and courtly Spanish caballero, who set intellect above emotion, knowledge ahead of politics. In Caracas they used to suggest to him that he go out on the streets without a hat.

"Why bother to wear one?" said his fellow-citizens. "You can never keep it on your head more than a minute at a time. Everybody knows you. And everybody takes off his hat to you."

In those pre-Tom days, when Nelly Russell met the savant who was to be her father-in-law, she also made the acquaintance of another member of *la familia*, who commanded even more respect among his fellow-citizens than the president of the University of Caracas.

This was old General Andrés Ybarra. He and his brother Diego had been favorite aides-de-camp of Simón Bolívar, the Liberator. They had accompanied Bolívar on his memorable campaigns in Venezuela, Colombia, Ecuador and Peru. Through victory and defeat, glory and exile, they had stuck to him.

transpired, had no chance against the flashing eye and dominant mien of his rival. Ana Teresa showed plainly that she was unwilling to let her engagement stand in the way of marriage with the man of the hour in Venezuela.

Incensed at this flouting of tradition, her fiancé rushed around in high dudgeon to his father-in-law-elect. He argued his case with eloquence and called for instant action, worthy of the race that had always upheld the sanctity of plighted troth. Don Andrés listened calmly. But, in this case, he proved again, as he had already in that of his rude cousin, that he believed Spanish tradition to have limits. When the young suitor stopped for breath, the old veteran said:

"My boy, all this is very interesting. But it is not a matter between you and me. It is a matter strictly between you and Ana Teresa."

Shortly afterward, his daughter's engagement to Antonio Guzmán Blanco was announced.

I never saw Dictator Antonio Guzmán Blanco, El Ilustre Americano, on his native heath. This was because, during the years that we might have met in Caracas, his arrival there had a way of coinciding with my father's departure thence, or vice versa. The only time I ever saw Guzmán was in Paris.

That was in 1894, when I was fourteen years old. My father, still in the flood tide of hostility toward the man who had tried to prevent him from marrying my mother, had parked the rest of his family in Munich and was on his way with me to Boston. Not long before, my Aunt Inés had espoused her big, bearded Corsican-Venezuelan Doctor-General Juan Pietri, who had been made Venezuelan Envoy Extraordinary and Minister Plenipotentiary to France and Great Britain. As the great ma-

LA FAMILIA

jority of Venezuelans would have done under like circumstances, Pietri interpreted his duty to mean that he must live in Paris eleven months of the year and one month, if absolutely necessary, in London.

My father found the Pietris installed in grand style at the Venezuelan Legation in Paris, not far from the Champs-Elysées. My Aunt Inés was very fond of my father and he of her. Unfortunately, General Crespo, Pietri's boss, had shortly before booted Andueza Palacio, whom my father had backed, out of Venezuela and put an awful crimp in my father's political-military career. Nevertheless, my father decided to partake of Pietri's hospitality, magnanimously agreeing to forget the swift kick he had received as a result of the Crespo-Pietri triumphal entry into the capital of Venezuela.

On one thing, however, he was inflexible. He would grasp Pietri's hand, for the sake of his affection for his sister Inés, then in the full bloom of her Spanish beauty. But he would *not* have anything whatsoever to do with Guzmán Blanco, or any member of the Guzmán Blanco family—who, at the time of my father's appearance in Paris, were also living in Paris in tremendous luxury. The ex-Dictator had married one of his daughters to a French duke (vintage of Napoleon III) and another to a French marquis (out of the Faubourg Saint-Germain). He was riding high on what was left of the millions that he had derived from his eighteen years' ownership of Venezuela.

My father's intransigence about Guzmán was embarrassing to my Aunt Inés. You see, she was maintaining the same close relations with the Guzmán tribe that she had maintained for years —her deceased first husband, Roberto Ybarra, having been a brother of the regally good-looking Ana Teresa, Guzmán Blan-

queror. He was of good family. He was a man of education—in the limited sense in which that term was understood in the Venezuela of his epoch.

To these characteristics he joined a considerable breadth of vision, a way of doing things that had scope and a certain grandeur. After his triumph over his foes in 1870, which made him supreme in Venezuela for nearly eighteen years, he decreed reforms of a most ambitious kind.

All this, however, he marred by incredible vanity. Many Venezuelans are vain, but few ever equaled Guzmán—and none ever had such opportunity to flaunt their worship of self. In addition to erecting statues to himself and bestowing upon himself the title of Illustrious American and causing it to be used constantly, in all seriousness, on official documents, he surrounded himself with flatterers. For him no flattery was too gross or blatant. His vanity grew upon him until, as he approached the end of his long dictatorship, it became almost pathological.

His good traits were also marred by greed. Eventually he acted as if Venezuela were his private plantation and the national treasury his personal bank account.

He did much to corrupt Venezuela. After his dictatorship, the good part of that country's inheritance from Spain never bulked so large as it had before. Writing once from Europe to my father in the United States about the growing deterioration among Venezuelans of post-Guzmán years, my mother said:

"I do not see how they are going to stop the corruption now. It has been coming little by little for a long time. It began in 1874, when we went there, and saw the luxury with which Guzmán surrounded Ana Teresa; one can see year by year the progress the disease has made. The women are also guilty.

LA FAMILIA

Am I not the only wife of a Minister who had absolutely no jewels and no fine clothes? And did not even so sensible a woman as Inés, your sister, find it awful, and beg you to buy me diamonds, and pay them off so much a month? That evil has such deep roots that I am afraid it will be difficult to cure. . . .

"It is an awful state to which to have brought a country, but Guzmán did his best. Without drinking himself, he did all in his power to make others do so. Do you remember, he took the duty off French wines, to induce Caracas to stop drinking water and be *chic* and take claret?

"The women in Caracas could do much to stop the behavior in public of the men. . . . But while they continue to accept them socially, to talk about their amours . . . and talk before young girls of all these things, just so long will men go on misbehaving themselves. The tone of the women in Caracas is very much lowered, too. . . . I remember when X. was shut out of society because he lived with a Frenchwoman he had brought from Paris. . . . The whole tone is corrupt, and the young girls can tell you things, innocent old *militar* that you are, that would make your hair stand on end. And it's so all over the world."

Despite the way he rode high in Paris, Guzmán Blanco, in his last years there, was a lonely and disappointed man. He yearned for Venezuela. But he never summoned up the nerve to return there after his downfall. In the midst of his life of European luxury, he constantly took aside visitors from Venezuela, to ask them eagerly:

"Do you think the Venezuelans would harm me if I went home?"

Irrespective of what the visitors answered, he never took

the plunge. From 1887, when he embarked on his last trip to Europe, to 1899, when he died, he remained an exile in Paris—thinking, in the midst of wealth and position, of distant, beloved and unattainable Caracas.

In addition to his brother Luis, my father had another brother, Francisco. And there was also his sister Inés. Those three were all that survived of a family that had once totaled nine children. I never had much to do with my Uncle Francisco and don't remember much about him. But my Aunt Inés was a most important ingredient of my early life in Caracas.

She was a beautiful woman. She had an oval face, of ivory pallor. Her eyes were black—and how they flashed when she felt strongly about something! Her hair, also black, curled naturally in little ringlets over her ears. She had a good figure —and a rippling laugh that made a way for its lovely owner wherever she went.

Aunt Inés had character. Despite her basic sweetness, she was neither over-pliant or wishy-washy; into her velvet voice would come ringing tones when she was aroused, which sent chills of fear through malingering servitors and inspired sudden spasms of obedience in her misbehaving children. Nevertheless, her essential characteristics—the ones that stand out in my memories of the Aunt Inés of my childhood—were an adorable gentleness and an irresistible desire to be friendly. She wanted to like everybody and wanted everybody to like her—and I must say that, in almost every case, she had her wish.

My mother and she took to each other instantly. From the very first moment of her first meeting with Nelly Russell, beautiful Inés Ybarra brushed aside every cobweb spun by religious prejudice and racial difference, and struck straight to

LA FAMILIA

the core of a genuine friendship that lasted right through her life.

Much of her time she spent in a *bata*, that floppy and formless dressing-gown that Venezuelan women of my childhood adored—and my father detested. But when Aunt Inés was made up à la Parisienne, and attired in full feminine panoply, she was regal. She stands out in my memory as a vision of glorious Spanish loveliness—and all Caracas thought the same way.

She was my *madrina* (godmother). I have never known just what the duties of a madrina are supposed to be, nor just what she is expected to achieve, but Aunt Inés took her godmotherhood very seriously, and never failed to remind me of it. Whenever I started from Caracas to foreign parts, she gave me little amulets, duly blessed, to guard me from harm during my travels. And, if she heard that I was doing well, at school or college or as a journalist, she would take to herself much of the credit for my performances.

"*Ya vés, Tom, he tenido buena mano*" ("You see, Tom, I have done a good job"), she would tell me.

She showed a liberality of outlook that, in view of her era, environment and upbringing, was a constant and delicious surprise. Once she found in the room of her son—who had lived long in Paris—a photograph of a famous Parisian demi-mondaine. The photograph was conspicuous for two things: the superlative good looks of the lady depicted and the fact that she was depicted without a stitch of clothing.

Aunt Inés gave her the once-over, missing nothing. Then she said, with that radiant, golden, full-throated laugh of hers: "After all, if a woman is as beautiful as that, you can't blame her for getting photographed like that."

My father and Aunt Inés adored each other. When we were

living at Monte Elena, in the suburb of El Paraíso, he used to go to the city invariably every Sunday morning, dressed in his best—the high-water mark of which was a big Panama hat. And, no matter where he might *not* go, he always made a formal call on his sister. That tradition he never broke. It was a pleasant experience to see that handsome man and that beautiful woman embrace each other with an affection that nothing, in the long years that might have alienated them, ever diminished.

At my father's funeral, Aunt Inés sat alone, in a corner, her eyes wet with tears. When I crossed the room, to pat her shoulder in silence, she murmured—and kept on murmuring:

"There were nine of us. There were nine of us."

Another branch of la familia consisted of the widow and sons and daughters of a brother of my father whom I never saw. His widow had the lugubrious Spanish name of Dolores—which, when she was out of hearing, my young sister Leonor and my young brother Alejandro and I translated literally into Aunt Pains.

One of the sons of Aunt Pains, Santiago, was my favorite cousin in my boyhood, when we both resided in Caracas. During the first world war, he visited the United States; and, from the pinnacle occupied by a relative ten years older than myself, he solemnly observed my antics as a New York journalist.

Some time before, a lot of light verse of mine, which had appeared in the New York *Times* and elsewhere, had been published in a book. Apropos of this, Santiago remarked gravely:

"There are now three authors in our family. Your father

LA FAMILIA

wrote a *Practical Method for Learning Spanish*. You have done a volume of verse——" Here he paused dramatically.

"Who's the third?" I asked.

"I am."

"What have you ever written?"

He looked hurt.

"Why, don't you remember? Am I not the author of that Venezuelan classic, the *Treatise on How to Learn to Play the Guitar*, by Santiago Ybarra?"

He was. Santiago had won fame in his native land as a most excellent guitar player. He also used to be (maybe, still is) an enthusiastic *gallero*, or partisan of fights between gamecocks. But I have never heard that he ever wrote a treatise on cockfighting.

The witty sallies of his fat brother Carlos were quoted all over Caracas. Once Carlos took his mother, my Aunt Pains, out for a carriage ride. Being exceedingly nervous, she was thrown into a panic by the high speed developed by the two little horses attached to the diminutive victoria in which she and her son were seated. She began, in her anguish, to pray.

"Oh, Lord Jesus Christ, please come down and help me! Please, Holy Mary, Mother of God, come here to protect me! Oh, blessed San Antonio, holy San Pedro, merciful Santa Teresa, divine Holy Ghost, gather around to save me!" Carlos stood it as long as he could. Then he said:

"Mother, I wish you would stop. Suppose your prayers should be answered—how are we going to get all those people into this carriage?"

In my boyhood, Carlos had a job at a soap factory. He used to ride around town on a mule, collecting bills. This bored him. So, in accordance with an old custom among Venezuelans who

years. At the end of that period both the parties concerned got married at last—*to somebody else!*).

Estéban too, never married his fiancée. Having spent uncounted hours at her reja, making leisurely love, he died without taking the plunge. Meanwhile, he did himself very well indeed in his bachelor quarters adjoining Altagracia.

I used to go to late breakfast with him Sunday mornings, when I was about eighteen. A man servant in a white suit served excellent food in abundance, including wine, while Estéban discoursed on his hobbies; he had a neat wit and a humorous outlook on his fellow-men. One of his hobbies was his bathroom.

At a time when that sort of thing was still sketchy in Caracas, he had a bathroom so modern that he ought to have charged admission to those allowed to see its splendor. It had fine mosaic tiles on its floor and glazed porcelain walls. Its most remarkable feature was the absence of all sharp corners on the edges of the bathtub and everywhere else. Estéban was very proud of this feature and would discourse upon it lengthily.

"Try to find a sharp corner," he would say. "You can't. Sharp corners in bathrooms are very dangerous. You can hurt yourself badly, while you are bathing, if you slip and hit one." I am not surprised that he felt strongly on this point. As he weighed well over two hundred pounds, a collision with a right angle fashioned in porcelain might have done for him on the spot.

Estéban of the Long Engagement used to talk in waggish disparagement of matrimony. What particularly irked him about it was the accepted form of marriage announcements.

"Aren't they absurd!" he would exclaim, as he stowed away some of his good victuals at one of his Sunday breakfasts.

LA FAMILIA

"Could anything be more ridiculous than all that stuff about 'Señor and Señora Fulano de Tal beg to announce the wedding of their daughter Zutanita to Señor Mengano de Perenzejo, on Thursday the twentieth of May, at noon, in the church of Altagracia.' Why beat around the bush? Why doesn't the bridegroom simply send around a note like this: 'Mengano de Perenzejo informs you that he and Zutanita de Tal are going to start a baby factory on the twentieth!'"

In the early Latin phase of my life, the tutelary divinity of la familia was the widow of old Dr. Ybarra, Doña Mercedes Rivas de Ybarra, my Venezuelan grandmother. Though she lived right through my early childhood in the old Rivas mansion, only two doors away from our residence in Caracas proper, my memories of Misia Merced have a curious meagerness and lack of substance.

She was aloof. I don't think she liked me or my sister or my brother. She rather conveyed the impression that she expected Protestantism to leer out suddenly from our eyes. Once, I recall, this aged lady handed me, when I was about ten, a printed prayer to Our Lady of the Rosary. This, she assured me, would be most beneficial to me if I recited it at bedtime. I did. But I never checked on what benefits it brought.

Every day my grandmother used to sit at the head of the family table. True to the old Spanish custom prevailing in my Caracas, she kept open house. Any relative or close friend was free to blow in at midday and take a seat. Always there was food enough for twice as many persons as there were regular members of the household. Sometimes Misia Merced would eat in the company of three sons, one daughter, three sisters-in-law, four daughters-in-law, eight or ten grandchildren, and

Rivas house. One by one they died, while I was a child; and each time I went to the funeral, and knelt, saddened but deeply interested, while the priest chanted the death service and the acolytes swung their censers and the bodies of each of these wrinkled old women—who, for many years, had known only solitude and unhappiness—were carried away to the grave.

At a time when my mother was living in the old family house, during one of my father's enforced absences in the United States, one of the trio, my great-aunt Pancha, long an embittered old maid, was inveighing against marriage. Her views on it were even more uncomplimentary than those of Cousin Estéban.

"A ridiculous institution!" she sputtered. "I can't see any good in it. There's no meaning to it! Absurd!"

"What do you suggest in place of it, free love?" asked my mother. For a couple of days they weren't on speaking terms.

Chapter XV

More of My Caracas

UNTIL I was twenty, I shuttled back and forth between the United States and South America. And, every time I stayed north of the Caribbean, I drank deeper and deeper of Anglo-Saxonism.

I went, for one year, to the Roxbury Latin School—where, in 1775, Joseph Warren, then a schoolmaster, had dismissed his class, shouldered his musket, and gone to his death on Bunker Hill. I attended the Cambridge Latin School for three years. I brushed elbows, as I walked to my studies there, with Harvard men on their way to eat at Memorial, or learn at Sever, or idle in Harvard Square, or cheer the University's athletes on Soldiers Field. Always, everywhere, I could sense the presence, in the background provided for me by my mother, of inflexible Pilgrim ancestors.

Every few months, when I was in the United States, I visited Plymouth. There I drank in anew the tales about Myles Standish and Elder Brewster, Carver and Bradford and John Alden, Samoset and Massasoit and Priscilla, on which, since my earliest childhood, I had been reared and nourished.

Again and again I stayed at Hillside, my great-uncle Marston's home—which, all through my youth, stood out in my consciousness as one of the few fixed points in my life of instability and change. The grounds at Hillside had been laid out by Marston Watson's close friend, Thoreau (the Watsons, years afterward, found in an attic the plan made by Thoreau, the unknown surveyor, framed it, and hung it in a place of honor out of deference to Thoreau, the famous writer). Again and again I occupied the room where Emerson had slept when he visited his friend Marston Watson; again and again I contemplated the picture of Emerson in that room, which William Ellery Channing (when he, in his turn, was a Hillside guest) invariably turned to the wall before he went to sleep because, he told the Watsons, it was the worst picture of Emerson he had ever seen.

If my visit to Hillside happened to be in the winter, I would come down to breakfast from the Emerson-Channing room—or from some other, equally fragrant with memories of the sages of Concord or their Plymouth and Boston counterparts—to find that my cousin Lu Watson, or her sister, my cousin Ellen (daughters of Marston Watson) had put beside my plate five grains of corn. While I drank coffee and munched toast, and bacon and eggs, and muffins of alluring appearance and unimpeachable succulence, those grains of corn would remain by my plate—and by every other breakfaster's plate. They were there to remind us, gathered around that bountiful table, that once, during the first terrible winter in Plymouth, the Pilgrims had been reduced to exactly that ration of corn for days—until, at last, the relief ship arrived with provisions from England.

With such a northern background, what chance had South America to win over for itself the soul of a boy already deeply tinged with the gray hues of Massachusetts, already firmly based on Plymouth Rock?

Yet, for some time, it was a toss-up whether the United

States or Venezuela would annex me. Finally, in my twentieth year, the decision came.

Three years before, my father had gone back to his native Venezuela—never to leave it again, as things turned out. I knew that the rest of the family would soon follow him southward. The thought of staying alone in the North did not appeal to me at all. So, the year after my father's departure from New York for La Guaira, I, too, boarded a steamer bound across the Caribbean for Venezuela. For two years after that I lived in Caracas. And that was the time that my Latin self might have triumphed definitively over the Bostonian inside me and tied up my life once and for all with the southern half of this hemisphere.

But that inner Bostonian of mine put up a terrific fight. Whenever warm and glamourous Caracas seemed about to take me over permanently, he hoisted the banner of Boston, summoned his reserves, and drove home a charge that left my Latinity groggy. He was invincible. Never did he let go his clutch on my soul.

Shortly before my twentieth birthday, a great-aunt of mine in Plymouth left me a legacy. Prompted by that Bostonian intrenched in the citadel of my innermost being, I told my father that I wished to use the money to go to Harvard.

He knew perfectly well what that meant. He knew that he had lost me. He knew that, if I went north, it would be the death-blow to his hopes that I might turn out, after all, a Venezuelan like himself. But always, all through my life, he had made it clear to me that, when it came to making major decisions affecting my future, I was the court of last appeal.

He had dreamed that I might become an international business man; prosperity and satisfaction in business, he felt, must necessarily come to one conversant with English and Spanish, capable of using his knowledge of both North and South America to climb the ladder of business success.

But my mind was made up. I did not wish to live in Venezuela. I did not wish to go into business there or anywhere else. With my definite repudiation of my Latinism had come an unshakable determination to write for a living—and to write, in English, in the United States and Europe.

My father, he of the short temper and volcanic eloquence when aroused, uttered not a word of protest or anger. Like a good soldier, he knew when a battle was lost.

"It is for you to decide," he told me. "Go to Harvard, spend your legacy, and, when the money is gone, I will supply enough more for you to finish your course."

That settled it. Ever since, Venezuela has lived for me only in the glamour and vividness of my memories of the sunlit boyhood that I spent there. But how glamourous and how vivid they are! And what a fight they put up for the mastery of my soul! And how hard, in that fight, Latinity pressed the winner of the final victory, the Bostonian inside me!

"How about a horseback ride?" my father would say to me.
"All right. I'll have our horses saddled."
Such a ride was sure to be a thing to remember. For the eyes of my father looked not only on the Caracas of reality that was visible to the half-North American son by his side; they looked also on another, earlier Caracas indelibly etched into his memory. For instance, we would pass a big house, with balconies jutting from its upper story, close to the Guanábano bridge, in the northern part of the city—a house sunk in a deep dream of peace, sleepy and unwarlike.

MORE OF MY CARACAS

"When Guzmán Blanco stormed Caracas in 1870," my father would remark, "that house was taken and re-taken three times. Those balconies were filled with sharpshooters. That sidewalk in front was covered with blood."

Riding through another part of the city, he would tell me (as I sat the horse to which I had been promoted now that I was too old for Don Rodrigo): "Just about here was where I picked up Leoncio Sarría, with three bullet wounds, and had him rushed to the hospital—and right here was where I found his uncle, Julio Sarría, all hacked by machete cuts, and had him loaded into the dead-cart."

Then he would go on to tell me that Leoncio, whom he thought he could save, died on the way to the hospital, whereas Julio, whom he had checked off as dead, was still living thirty years after the battle.

I knew Julio Sarría well. He had seventeen wounds. When you went up to shake hands with him, he stuck out his left hand because his right had been maimed by a machete thrust in one of the innumerable fights in which its owner had taken part.

It was said of him that he had a magical attraction for bullets and sabers. At the very outset of a fight, the odds were that he would be stretched out on the ground, unconscious and bleeding, a few minutes after the start of the thing. Yet seventeen wounds had not been enough to polish him off. He died in his bed—where he consented to receive the last consolations of religion, unlike his fiery kinsman Leopoldo, commander of the Battalion of the Guard in those childhood days of mine when I was an habitué of the various barracks of Caracas.

There was another incident in the storming of Caracas in 1870—known, among the victorious liberales, as the *veintisiete de abril* (twenty-seventh of April)—which my father tended to soft-pedal, since he had afterward married an American.

He and his soldiers were fighting their way into the city from one of the suburbs. On their way they climbed over a wall behind a Caracas home and started—in the informal way of those engaged in battle—to push their way, through the rooms of the house, to the next place of contact with the defenders of the city.

But they were suddenly confronted by an angry gentleman vigorously waving a flag. That flag was the Stars and Stripes. The angry gentleman was the United States Minister to Venezuela (a predecessor of Judge Thomas Russell). In language of much severity, he told the intruders to climb back over the wall and cease to trespass on premises that were technically American soil.

At this point, according to the legend current among the Ybarras in my boyhood, my father walked up to the Stars and Stripes with drawn sword, politely pushed it aside with the point of that weapon, and signed to his soldiers to continue their advance. Leaving the Star Spangled Banner and the indignant United States Minister behind them, they proceeded through the front of the house to the street outside, where they resumed direct connection with the battle for Caracas, still in noisy and bloody progress.

My father also used to point out a certain street corner and say: "It was here that Martín Vegas surrendered to me."

And then would come this yarn:

Martín Vegas was one of the principal commanders of the godo defenders of Caracas on that April day in 1870 when the Liberals, under Guzmán Blanco, fought their way into the city. Finally, they hoisted the banner of liberalism on the cathedral tower. Seeing that further fighting was hopeless, Martín Vegas, who had been making a last stand, stepped forward, as my father and his men rushed what was left of the enemy's line, held out his sword in token of surrender, and said: "I am your prisoner."

That put my father in a quandary. Fighting was still going on in a dozen places. The attackers of Caracas were in such a frenzy of excitement that anything was likely to happen to those of their opponents on whom they might happen to lay their hands. What was Martín Vegas's young captor to do with his captive? How could he best insure the latter's safety? Vegas was well known to his Liberal foes; some of them might be only too willing to take summary vengeance on him.

Suddenly my father had an idea.

"General Vegas," he said, "I am going to send you under escort to the home of my father and my mother. (Old Dr. Ybarra was as ardent a Liberal as his son.) There you will be perfectly safe. Ask them to give you dinner and a bed. I'll come around later to see how you are getting along."

The prisoner bowed gratefully. Escorted by a squad of soldiers, he was taken to the old Rivas-Ybarra house, where the unmilitary section of the family had been lying low during the street fighting. True to his word, my father appeared at the house just as soon as he could get away from his routine duties as a conqueror. He found Martín Vegas quite at home, seated at the dinner table, discussing politics with old Dr. Ybarra, officially his bitter enemy.

My Caracas was very proud of the *Teatro Municipal*, its leading theater, one of the many ornate buildings decreed by Guzmán Blanco after his great victory of the twenty-seventh of April, 1870. Having soaked Caracas in blood on that day, he atoned later by adorning it lavishly with stucco and cement, statues and parks, in the intervals of assiduous nest-feathering. The Teatro Municipal was—and is—an imposing edifice for a small city. It was erected in imitation of European opera houses of its period; and, in spite of over-ornateness, it has an air. It still keeps its head high in a city, which, since the days of Guzmán, has acquired other places of amusement of a more modern sort.

When I was a little boy in short trousers, there were red-letter nights at the Teatro Municipal when a company of Italian grand opera was performing there. Then it was filled—grand-tier boxes, orchestra seats, balcony, gallery. The Caraqueños would go perfectly wild with enthusiasm if a singer pleased them; and they would howl with rage if he or she did not.

There was one visiting Italian soprano in the eighteen-nineties, Madame Turconi-Bruni, whose trills threatened Caracas with mass apoplexy. After singing the mad scene in *Lucia*, she was sanity personified compared with her audience. They shrieked. They tossed their hats in the air. They pounded with their canes against seats and floor. They hugged each other in a frenzy. They wept.

But it was quite another matter when an Italian tenor—who had eaten something which had disagreed with him, or fallen out with his girl—acknowledged a curtain call by shrugging his shoulders disdainfully and walking off the stage.

That almost started a revolution. The Caracas opera-going public stood on street corners discussing whether that tenor should be allowed to live or whether his affront to Venezuelan honor must be atoned for instantly in his life-blood. The newspapers seethed. Eventually the tenor apologized, and all was

A view of Caracas from El Calvario

MORE OF MY CARACAS

forgotten. It was grand, though, while it lasted—and I reveled in the lack of New England poise displayed by all concerned.

The citizens of Caracas, in my boyhood, also flocked to another theater, the *Teatro Caracas*. It was much older than the Teatro Municipal. And it was the dirtiest theater I ever saw. But, as I developed early into a theatrical fan, I serenely ignored dust and smells and cockroaches. That down-at-heel temple of dramatic art gave me more pleasure per square foot than any I have known since in far bigger cities.

My favorite fare was Spanish operetta. In those days, Spain specialized in this branch of the drama, and exported it copiously to Spanish America. Most of the pieces were in one act. Three one-act operettas, as a rule, made up a complete matinée or evening's entertainment. Each piece, known as a *tanda*, was charged for separately. You went to the theater for one hour or two or three, paying for as many tandas as you wished.

To tempt the public, there were sometimes performances at reduced rates, even *tres tandas por valor de una*, a three-part program at the rate usually charged for a single short piece. On Sunday mornings, there was often a short performance consisting of a single tanda. As it came at eleven A.M., the hour when Caracas men-about-town liked to toss off an apéritif, it was known as *la tanda del Vermouth*.

Spain was also busily exporting to Spanish America something else beside operettas and actors and actresses to perform them. Every few months a cuadrilla of Spanish bullfighters turned up in Caracas. When these included in their Spanish-American tours important bullfighting centers like Mexico City and Lima (and Havana, when it was still under the Spaniards), they were likely to be headed by a really good *matador*. As a rule, however, Caracas only got second-rate or third-rate material. Its purse was too slender to allow of payment, except on very special occasions, of the fancy prices demanded by the haughty leaders among the *espadas* of the Spanish bullfighting art.

But the fans of the Caracas bullring refused to let this handicap dampen their enthusiasm. Those second-raters, those third-string killers of bulls, got ovations, when they delivered the goods, which were frenzied. When they did not (as in the case of the brother-artist, the Italian tenor beset by stomach-ache or crossed in love), they were subjected to the most terrific collective denunciations by the *aficionados*.

Caracas bullfights were fought in strict accordance with the traditional unbreakable ritual of Spain, except for one thing: there was no *picador*. For some reason, the Venezuelans of those days, who were certainly not conspicuous for kindness to animals, drew the line at having horses gored to death in the bullring. Otherwise, the ritual was followed religiously step by step.

There was the stirring bugle call at the beginning, to the accompaniment of savage yells and stamping of feet from the public in the cheaper seats, and more dignified proofs of internal excitement from those who had paid more for their tickets. There was the colorful parade of the cuadrilla, headed by the matador; the formal bow to the presiding officer, usually the Prefect or Police or some such dignitary. There was the thrilling hush before the opening of the bull-pen; the gasp of joy as the bull came rushing into the arena.

Then the picturesque and blood-stained drama progressed in obedience to the immutable rules laid down generations ago at Seville and Madrid. After the *suertes de capa* and the *banderillas*, the bugle signaled for the kill. If the matador killed competently, that meant hats in the ring for him, and cigars and coins, and roars of approval from fans temporarily insane from admiration. If he botched the job, that meant, instead, insults of a vileness and cruelty incredible to us of the north.

I have seen a Spanish bullfighter literally walking on air in the Caracas bullring, picking up hats and returning them to their cheering owners, with a grin like that of a delighted schoolboy on his gypsy's face. And I have seen another with the tears running down his cheeks, dashing back to meet the bull in crazy disregard of safety, preferring anything, even sudden bloody death, to listening any longer to the vituperation beating down on him from the crowd, suddenly transformed into fiends of hatred.

My father's attitude toward *los toros* was a marvel of quibbling. His stays in the north had done their bit—though it was only a very little bit—to cool the ardor of the bullfight fan within him. Or, if not quite that, those stays had at least made him feel the advisability of concealing somewhat his truly Spanish ideas about Spain's national sport. He had a way, at times, of talking about bullfighting as if a Massachusetts clergyman were standing at his elbow. But, when it came to acting in the matter, there was no holding him—Bishop Phillips Brooks himself, and the whole ecclesiastical staff of "Treeneety Chorch," could not have kept him from attending a *corrida*.

"Tom," he would say to me, with that inimitable Latin twinkle in the corner of his eye, "if I were the supreme authority here in Caracas, the first thing I would do would be to forbid bullfighting. Bullfighting is wrong. I know that. But—I am *not* the supreme authority in Caracas. And, since I am not, I am powerless to prevent this afternoon's bullfight. That being the case—what do you say, Tom, to telephoning the office of the *plaza de toros* and getting a couple of good seats?" Utterly unable to find an argument against this scheme, I would hurry to the telephone.

A few hours later my father and I are in the front seats of a front-row box. The whole traditional spectacle of color and cruelty, pageantry and blood, unrolls before our eyes. The band is playing Spanish bullfighting two-steps; the crowd whistles and shouts and rocks back and forth in hungry anticipation. And my cousin Santiago, that aficionado beyond redemption, leaps to his feet in a nearby box, and yells across the intervening space to my father:

"Alejandro! *Empezó la barbarie!*" ("Barbarism has begun!")

If my father is going through one of his spells of political prominence, the matador bows low in front of our ringside seats. He flourishes his sword, with the red cloth of the kill wrapped around it, and dedicates the bull about to perish to "*el muy distinguido General Don Alejandro Ybarra*"—finishing the dedication with a nonchalant toss of his black headgear in our direction.

That is a great honor, of course. But it comes high. My father bows politely. He observes the various stages of the kill with even closer attention than usual. If it is done according to the Spanish equivalent of Hoyle, it is incumbent on him to applaud with special vigor. And then comes the painful part of the ceremony for the man thus highly honored.

The matador, having made the round of the ring to the cheers of the crowd, comes to a stop, a stop full of expectancy, in front of my father. With a deep sigh, my corpulent parent digs into a side pocket of his extensive white vest. Out of it come a couple of gold pieces—seldom plentiful in our family

MORE OF MY CARACAS

exchequer. These he tosses in a lordly manner to the reckless Spaniard in the arena below. The Spaniard makes magnificent obeisance. The crowd gives a special cheer. Sinking back in his seat, my father groans:

"Another twenty pesos gone!"

My Caracas had horsecars. Two sets of them. One set was owned by a company called *Tranvías Caracas*, which operated several lines reaching out from the Plaza Bolívar in all directions. The other company, known as *Tranvías Bolívar*, ran only one line, but that one was so strategic and important that it yielded its sponsors enough profit to keep them going right through my early boyhood.

The little two-horse vehicles of the Tranvías Bolívar started from the main railway station—consisting of one shed for the English railway to La Guaira and another for the German railway southward. Thence they bumped across the Plaza Bolívar. Then they went jolting and clanking down the busy thoroughfare known locally (though its official name was *Avenida Este*) as *la calle de Candelaria*. The line's terminus was the station of the other English railway company, the Ferrocarril Central de Venezuela (the one that took me on the first stage of my journey to El Cedral). This railway, in spite of its impressive name, had the greatest difficulty, in the opening years of my life, in getting itself beyond Petare, some six miles from Caracas.

Once, torrents of rain destroyed a bridge some miles beyond Petare, causing the engineer who had built it for his bosses in London to throw himself on the bank of the creek it had spanned and burst into tears. On other occasions, revolutions would carry off singers of the Venezuelan equivalent of "I'se been workin' on the railroad" and make soldiers out of them. Meanwhile, the road's Board of Directors in London would inform disgusted stockholders that the company was one step nearer bankruptcy. At last—years after I had ceased merely dreaming about becoming a North American and had started working at it—the Ferrocarril Central de Venezuela pushed its rails right into the valley of the Tuy and began to cash in on its long years of struggle.

The horsecars of the Bolívar company were painted light blue. They had four benches apiece, with seats on each bench for three passengers. All passengers faced forward. Standees were allowed on the platforms. If a horsecar carried as many as twenty people, it was loaded almost to capacity.

When the company began operating its cars, they were marked *Empresa Bolívar*, which means Bolívar Concern or Company. But my childish mind failed to grasp that. Already (I was about six when the one-line horsecar company began to operate) I had heard much of the glory and eminence of Simón Bolívar. So it was easy for me to assume that the word "empresa" was connected with the imperial eminence of Venezuela's Liberator. From that assumption it was only a short mental step, in view of the feminine ending of empresa, to figure out that the lettering on the horsecars passing the house where we lived in that early era was in honor of Bolívar's imperial consort, the Empress Bolívar. I propounded this theory to surrounding grownups and was deeply hurt by the ensuing hilarity.

One of the horsecar lines of the Tranvías Caracas ran from the Plaza Bolívar to the station (or, rather, shed) of still another railroad, the Ferrocarril del Valle. The diminutive locomotives of this concern (there were, at least, three) puffed

MORE OF MY CARACAS

and groaned through El Portachuelo, the southern gap in the mountain-wall enclosing Caracas, to the agreeable village of El Valle, some four miles distant. Another horsecar line climbed the sharply inclined streets north of the Plaza Bolívar to the aristocratic section of Altagracia and around the Caja de Agua. Thence, up still steeper inclines, it extended to La Pastora, clustered around the big church of that name, not far from the entrance to the city used by Sir Francis Drake on his marauding expedition to the Caracas of centuries ago.

Horsecars of the Tranvías Caracas, operating on still another spur from the center of the city, crawled southward, along the proletarian Calle San Juan, to our suburb of El Paraíso. The final stretch of this line ended on the Avenida del Paraíso, the central boulevard of the leading "development" of the Caracas of those days.

In my boyhood, the Avenida was just a bare stretch of muddy roadway, flanked by trees in their infancy, and a few suburban villas of daring pioneers. Today, it is shaded by the leafy branches of a double row of big trees, which almost meet overhead, and it is lined by dozens of pretty dwellings. It knows no longer the clop-clop of the iron shoes and the rattle of the frayed harness of badly fed little horses, pulling ramshackle little streetcars. Long ago an Englishman, Mr. Ludford, electrified both the Caracas horsecar companies. Rest in peace, tired little horses! In my memory you and the rusty, unpainted rattletraps behind you, which you patiently pulled, though your muscles sagged and your ribs stuck out, still live, in deathless reality.

The cars of the Tranvías Caracas, unlike those of its rival company, had their benches back to back. They, too, seated twelve passengers apiece; but, instead of all facing forward, some of the passengers contemplated either three of their fellows or a limited view of the route extending beyond the rear platform. My sister and I dubbed these vehicles, in good, irreverent Anglo-Saxon, "chicken coops."

At one time, my cousin Félix Rivas was general manager of the company. That job brought him unending chaff from fellow-citizens. They blamed—or pretended to blame—Félix for all the company's shortcomings, which were many. If a horse was particularly thin: "But, Félix, don't you *ever* buy horse feed?" If a car threatened to grind itself to pieces en route: "Félix, *hombre de Dios*, can't you afford even *one* can of lubricating oil?"

After Félix had relinquished his post, matters failed to improve. The passengers on our El Paraíso line, including ourselves, took to bantering the horsecar crews, especially a witty driver named Norberto. From Norberto you could always be sure of a comeback. Here is a typical morning conversation between Norberto and my father, one of his regular passengers, just before the driver whipped up his horses to start cityward.

"Handsome new suit you've got, Norberto."

"Glad you like it, general."

"Of course, it's a present from the company, isn't it?"

"Of course."

"WHAT?"

"Well, part of it is, general."

"Which part?"

"The sleeves of the vest."

I look back from the world of reality in New York to the world of memory in South America. Velvet darkness falls over my Caracas. The stars are out in thousands. The Milky Way stretches its mysterious belt of whiteness across the heavens. The Southern Cross shines. The little city of my boyhood is sunk in slumber.

At the entrance of each house the big *portón* that gives access from the street has been closed and barred for the night. Inside, each family lies in sleep.

Now and then a victoria, drawn by its two small horses, goes rattling over cobblestones or *adoquines*. A reveler, who has drunk much more than is good for him, leans out from the vehicle and addresses an alcoholic whoop to the world in general. The victoria whirls around a corner.

Silence again.

From the tower of the cathedral come the notes of the chimes, announcing what time it is. They announce it in a simple four-part melody. If it's a quarter past, you get only the first part. On the half hour, the bells play two parts. If it's a quarter before something, the bells toll three parts. And, on the hour, they play all four parts of the melody, bringing it to well-rounded resolution.

Now they are giving all four parts. After that, the biggest bell of all tolls out the hour, in harsh and heavy strokes.

BONG. BONG. BONG. BONG.

Four o'clock in the morning.

From the next corner sounds a sharp signal from a whistle. From two blocks up the street comes another. Then there's a third, from a couple of blocks down the street.

The policemen of my Caracas are calling to one another. As each one, standing, wrapped in his cobija, on a lonesome corner, hears the bells in the cathedral tower, he puts his whistle to his lips and sends out its shrill note into the darkness. It's just to pass the time of night—a friendly Caracas custom. Silence.

Down the middle of the roadway plod a dozen soldiers in single file. They look sinister in the flickering light of the street lamps. Beside them rides an officer, on a horse. The rifles of the soldiers are thrown across their shoulders. The officer has a sword girt to his side. The shuffle of a dozen pairs of alpargatas blends with the thud of the horse's hoofs, as it ambles along, with its big, bored eyes.

That's the *jefe de día* (officer of the day) with his escort. His duty, in spite of his official title, is confined to the night. He and his soldiers go from barracks to barracks, all through the hours of darkness, and to every place where there is a military guard, to see that all is well. At each place of call they are brought to a halt by the challenge of a sentinel, peeking through a small aperture in the big outer door.

"*Alto! Quien vive?*"

"*Patria!*"

"*Que gente?*"

"*Jefe de día.*"

"*Avance, jefe de día!*"

The officer dismounts. The sentinel unbars the door of the prison—or the military hospital—or the powder magazine—whatever it is that he is guarding. The *jefe de día* enters to confer with the officer on duty inside. In a few minutes he comes out again, vaults into his saddle.

"Shoulder arms! Forward march!"

Off he goes, with his men clumping behind him, to visit the next military post on his list. Or, maybe, he heads for some disorderly dive, where soldiers on leave from their barracks

MORE OF MY CARACAS

are likely to be drinking and roistering and brawling—possibly stabbing and shooting.

The cathedral chimes sound again.

A quarter past four.

Again the whistles of the policemen shrill through the darkness.

Silence.

Chapter XVI

More Revolution

I NEVER saw General Crespo, successor of Andueza Palacio, while he was President. This was because the relations between Crespo and my father were similar to those of the latter with Guzmán Blanco. In other words, Crespo's arrival anywhere was likely to be the signal for my father's departure for somewhere else.

But I saw much of another President of Venezuela, who succeeded Crespo: General Ignacio Andrade, whose administration lasted from 1897 until the autumn of 1899. Andrade, a man of peace, was sandwiched in between Crespo, who was a roughneck, and Castro, who was another.

Crespo ran Venezuela from 1892 to 1897. We spent that entire period in Munich or Massachusetts. Then Crespo relinquished the presidency to Ignacio Andrade, fully intending to pull the strings behind the scenes and come back to power later on, in the Guzmán Blanco fashion. But fate played Joaquin Crespo a dirty trick.

Andrade's entry into the Yellow House inspired El Mocho Hernández, that chronic revolutionist, to stage a rebellion against the new government. Crespo, the power behind the Andrade régime, sallied forth in command of the government forces to bring El Mocho to book. He established contact with the enemy somewhere on the plains south of Caracas and was promptly stretched dead on the field by a *Mochista* bullet—almost the only casualty in the skirmish. So Andrade, a man of peace and without initiative, found himself out on a limb.

He had expected to be President in name only; now he was President in fact. That was no job for him. Mild men usually failed to get far in the Venezuela of my youthful days. Nevertheless, Ignacio Andrade tackled the task. And presently Alejandro Ybarra, back again in Caracas from Boston, offered to help. The nervous President, early in 1899, put my father in charge of the state of Guayana, on the great Orinoco river, the capital of which was Ciudad Bolívar, née Angostura—where the bitters got their name.

As the political situation was not exactly stable, my father went to his new post without his wife and children. The only Ybarra he took along was his nephew, Santiago.

Santiago was attached to the staff of the new Guayana executive as a sort of hybrid half-military, half-civilian aide. It was on that assignment that Santiago realized the extent of his uncle's anti-nepotism. On his return to Caracas, he declared, with deep feeling, that his job had been made by my father twice as arduous as it would have been if he hadn't been related to his chief.

Though neither my mother nor any of the family small fry accompanied General Ybarra to Ciudad Bolívar, he received there an unexpected visit from one of his North American in-laws. This was Dora Russell, my mother's younger sister, she who had been thirteen at the time of the irruption of the Russell family into Venezuela, and who was now in her late thirties. She added to a stay with us in Caracas a side trip to the domain of her brother-in-law on the great Orinoco.

Always an adventurous traveler, my Aunt Dora transferred

herself at the British island of Trinidad to a primitive Venezuelan river steamer, which took her hundreds of miles up the Orinoco. From its deck she contemplated alligators and other tropical products, unknown and discountenanced in New England, with Massachusetts equanimity. At Ciudad Bolívar she got a reception befitting her temporary eminence as the sister-in-law of the "president" of Guayana. And, having looked things over with judicial Boston severity, and pronounced them, on the whole, good, Aunt Dora returned to Caracas.

When President Andrade ruled in Venezuela—and for years afterward—paper money did not enjoy the high importance with which it has since become endowed there and everywhere else. Gold was king. Paper bank notes circulated, of course. Also large quantities of silver and copper coins. But gold was constantly visible to the naked eye of anybody at all near solvency.

It wasn't just a symbol. It wasn't a nebulous intangibility. It wasn't merely a resident of exclusive places like Fort Knox, Kentucky. It was securely intrenched in everyday life.

It glittered in Venezuelan coins worth five and ten and twenty dollars. It winked, out of a South American past of conquistadores and buccaneers, from old yellow Spanish *morocotas*, covered with Spanish inscriptions sometimes as illegible as the abbreviated Latin on ancient Roman coins—interspersed with the heads of dead Kings of Spain and the coat-of-arms of the proud Spanish monarchy. It was even handed over the counters of humble corner pulperías, in exchange for loaves of *papelón*, the national brown sugar, and black beans, and candles, and one or more of the chamber-pots, which in those days invariably figured as the main decoration on the shelves of a pulpería.

Yet, despite this ubiquity of gold, I never failed to get a kick out of it. While my father was doing his stuff as boss of Guayana, he used to make exceedingly welcome remittances, subtracted from his official emoluments, to my mother in Caracas.

The telephone at our house would ring.

"This is Blohm & Co.," a voice—sometimes with a strong German accent—would say. (The House of Blohm, heavily Teutonic, was even more important in Venezuelan mercantile circles at that time than the great House of Boulton, heavily Britannic.) "Have I the honor of speaking with *la señora del General Ybarra?*"

"You have," my mother would reply.

"Good morning, señora. We have the pleasure of informing you that we have received instructions from our Ciudad Bolívar branch to pay you the sum of one thousand pesos."

"How nice."

"Will it be convenient if we send a clerk with the money right away."

"Convenient is putting it mildly."

"Very well, señora."

About half an hour later, one of Blohm's younger employes (perhaps Henrique Brandt, descendant of a Teutonic officer of Simón Bolívar in the Venezuelan war of independence, and a great crony of mine) would gallop his horse up to our front door, dismount, enter our drawing room, and bow politely to my mother. Then he would hand her a cloth bag bulging with bullion.

"Please count it," he would say.

My mother would pour out on a table a river of shining gold coins—with the head of Simón Bolívar on one side, and the Venezuelan coat-of-arms on the other. How pleasantly they chinked as she counted—*cien, doscientos, trescientos*—— Then the golden stream would be duly canalized back into the cloth bag, my mother would give Henrique Brandt, or whatever collaborator of the House of Blohm might be standing before her, a formal receipt—and offer him a drink of whisky or brandy or wine. And, for weeks on end, the finances of the House of Ybarra would ride a sharp upward curve.

My main memory of President Ignacio Andrade is inextricably mixed up with my clerkship at the American Warehouse in Caracas, which has a chapter to itself farther along in this book. The incident involving Andrade and me at the Warehouse was far richer in color and movement than the average happening connected with that mild and soft-spoken Chief Executive. He was a sort of Latin American Caspar Milquetoast, whom fate sandwiched in between rough Joaquin Crespo and tough Cipriano Castro.

Andrade was tubby and squat. He wore an apologetic sort of beard. How, even in Venezuela, he had managed to become a general, I never could fathom—perhaps that title settles as naturally on the names of Venezuelans as a fly does on their noses. It may be that Andrade got to believe that the title of general in his native land was like a pair of pants—a man really oughtn't to go around without it. Perhaps that's the way he talked to his political sponsor, Joaquin Crespo, until Crespo saw the weight of his protégé's arguments and caused still another name to be added to the mighty roster of that multitudinous assemblage, the generals of Venezuela.

The Pantheon in Caracas where national heroes, including Simón Bolívar and two members of the author's family, are buried

MORE REVOLUTION

The second time that I made a close approach to a Venezuelan revolution in actual operation was when Cipriano Castro, seven years after my El Guayabo adventure, was leading a rebellion against the government presided over by Andrade. Castro, one of the hardest-boiled macheteros ever produced by Venezuela, had made a spectacular march from his native province in the Andes, far to the westward of Caracas, to the vicinity of Valencia, the republic's second city, uncomfortably near the capital. A government army marched forth from Caracas to support government troops already in touch—to put it mildly—with the formidable rebel from the Andes.

My father had just returned to the Venezuelan capital from Ciudad Bolívar. He rode along (with no definite job at first, as I have already remarked, then as chief of operations of Aragua) in the entourage of President Andrade—who, though emphatically a man of peace, had decided to beard Castro personally in battle.

We all got as far as Maracay, which has since become famous as the official residence for many years of the late Dictator Juan Vicente Gómez. There, Andrade and my father and their whole retinue were welcomed by a strange local celebrity, a man of dense whiskers and unbelievably voluminous paunch, whom Andrade had made the boss of the district. Around him buzzed a swarm of daughters.

"General," he said to my father, pointing out four or five of them, "I want to introduce these children of mine to you. They are good girls, General, very good girls—but as you have undoubtedly observed, they are uglier than the Four Horsemen of the Apocalypse."

Shortly after this bizarre comment—with Andrade and my father and a whole batch of high governmental dignitaries still guests in his house—this individual hoisted his huge person onto a horse and rode away blithely to join Cipriano Castro. That act, on the part of that obese individual, has always made me feel that I have actually seen and touched the invisible, intangible abstraction known as treason.

Andrade, who had ridden well ahead of his main forces to Maracay in the belief that the father of the Four Horsewomen would provide suitable protection, suddenly realized that he was marooned in Maracay with no more than sixty cavalrymen—not including my father and a squad of other generals. At once, Andrade decided to hurry back to the main body of his army, approaching Maracay from Caracas.

So we all galloped to the Maracay station, where a large blond German was in charge—for that railroad from Caracas to Valencia was operated—and still is—by a German company. We clamored for a special train. The German found an engine, providentially unemployed at the moment, in the yard, had it hitched to a passenger car, and sent it whirling away.

As long as I live I'll never forget that ride.

Our engine went shrieking through the night, with that lone car rounding curves at such an angle that it seemed that not more than one wheel could still be on the track. Fortunately, the trip didn't last long. At the station of Turmero, deep in the beautiful valley of Aragua, embowered in coffee trees, we found the main body of Andrade's forces. What a blessed relief to see those long lines of soldiers, their big straw hats almost hiding their swarthy faces, their rifles gleaming through the darkness!

On the station platform, President Andrade greeted their commander, Luciano Mendoza—a man who, throughout his military career, was qualified to enter any competition for picking the toughest general in Venezuela.

I can see Luciano now—one of the smallest among those thousands of men—in front of that little station, surrounded by officers with revolvers dangling from their belts and machetes swinging at their sides. He himself, however, was attired in a black suit, resembling the clothing of a peaceful clergyman in the United States; and he was armed only with a little rattan whip. Luciano Mendoza was always like that. He was the last man whom you would pick out as a tough guy. Rather would you choose for that honor his ferocious brother, Natividad, much bigger than Luciano, always armed to the teeth, closely resembling a bandit chief. Through years of fighting, he followed Luciano like a faithful dog and executed every order of his diminutive brother without question. Natividad, by the way, was at Turmero that night—a terrifying spectacle, as usual.

Feeling a big accession of courage because we were under the wing of Luciano and Natividad and their regiments, President Andrade and my father and myself, and the rest of those who had ridden earlier that night on that blond Teuton's train, returned from Turmero to Maracay. And then it was that I, as a budding militarist, was plunged for the second time into ignominy.

My father and many other martial spirits (not including, by the way, President Andrade) proceeded westward, around midnight, in long trains of freight cars, provided by that same German station master at Maracay. Their intention was to reinforce the government troops already at grips with Castro on the field of Tocuyito, outside Valencia. And once again, as at

Rincón del Valle, my father suddenly spied me hanging unobtrusively around, in the hope of smuggling myself into the campaign. He growled sternly:

"You must stay here. If you don't, Nelly will be worried."

"But——"

Into his eyes came the look that always spelled doom to contradiction. I stayed in Maracay.

But my ignominy, I soon learned, was nothing personal or exclusive. Arriving at the station, early next morning, preparatory to boarding a train for Caracas and home, I found, to my amazement, that my father was also there. Neither he nor anybody else in the President's entourage had got within miles of Cipriano Castro. Before they could bring their forces into action at Tocuyito, Castro had won an overwhelming victory over those other troops of the government that had tackled him. Evidence of this victory was now to be seen on the Maracay station platform, in the form of government soldiers escaped from Tocuyito, disconsolately trailing rifles behind them, with their heads tied up in bloody, dirty rags.

As for my father, he had already consigned Andrade (and rightly) to the limbo of eventual complete defeat and exile. Striding up and down the platform, he talked excitedly of Castro, now Venezuela's man of the hour, the victor of Tocuyito.

"He is a Porfirio Diaz!" exclaimed my father. Castro wasn't. But he was destined to prove himself tough enough to run Venezuela for nine years.

That night, I was back in Caracas again, as in the days of El Guayabo.

After my return, I tried to piece together the parts of the

MORE REVOLUTION

decisive Andrade-Castro campaign, which circumstances beyond my control had caused me to miss. I used to seek out Besson, a young warrior attached to my father as secretary, and bedevil him with questions suggesting answers of a sort calculated to satisfy a romantic young worshiper at the shrine of Mars.

But Besson simply would *not* play up. He was an earnest and lugubrious youth, absolutely devoid of vanity and showmanship. His worship of the goddess of truth transcended even mine of the god of war.

Besson, I soon learned, had been present, with the unlucky Andrade forces, at the battle of Tocuyito. That information acted on me as a match on a fuse.

"Tell me all about it, Besson," I would request eagerly, panting with desire to acquire first-hand knowledge of war in the raw.

"About what?"

"About Tocuyito."

"Well, what about it?"

"Tell me just what happened—your own adventures—exactly what you heard and felt."

"Well," muttered that un-martial and disappointing soldier, after a judicial pause to collect his somber thoughts. "I ran—without stopping once—for ten miles!"

"Is that all?"

"That's all."

I had to leave vengeance on Besson to our parrot. That graceless bird, a remarkable mimic, took to imitating the voice used by my father when he was looking for Besson with some job of secretarial work.

"Besson!" the parrot would grunt, in a guttural tone of awesome depth. Besson, dropping whatever he had been doing, would rush out into the patio.

"*Sí, general!*" he would say. "What do you wish?"

"But I haven't called you," his puzzled superior would remark.

Besson would apologize and go back to his lugubrious meditations.

"BESSON!" Another imperious summons.

Again Besson would tumble out of his room—out of bed, sometimes, where he had been stealing a siesta.

"*Sí, general!*"

"But I haven't called you."

Out of some hiding-place near by, a shriek of satanic laughter would resound.

To return to Luciano Mendoza: for all his peaceful appearance, he was as rough as they came. Forty years before he swam into my ken he was already prominent in the social register of civil strife in Venezuela. Unlike his brother Natividad and others of the latter's stripe, who were roughnecks and nothing else, Luciano combined with military qualities (as these were understood in the Venezuela of last century) a capacity for serpentine political maneuvering that had earned for him the reputation of a Machiavelli.

One seldom knew exactly where Luciano Mendoza stood. He would think one thing, say another, and do a third. On that night in Turmero we all supposed that he was heart and soul with the Andrade government. Yet, a few days later, he was already plotting with Cipriano Castro. And when Andrade was tumbled from the presidency shortly afterward, Luciano

MORE REVOLUTION

didn't fall with him—trust Luciano for that! He managed to fix up matters with Castro in such a way that Andrade was out and Castro in and he himself neither in nor out, but doing very nicely, thank you.

When I witnessed the triumphal entry of Castro into Caracas, shortly after my Maracay campaign, the streets leading to the center of the city were lined by the soldiers of Luciano Mendoza, seemingly as much at home as allies of Castro as they had been as his opponents. Venezuelan politics are fearfully and wonderfully made.

Luciano had acted along similar lines some years before during the short interval of chaos between the flight of President Andueza Palacio and the entry into Caracas of the victorious revolutionary forces that had ousted him.

Just before that, Luciano had instituted mysterious negotiations with the advancing rebels and, at the same time, financed himself by telling the leading merchants of Caracas how much he needed and leaving it to them whether to pay or repair to prison.

After Crespo had finally marched into Caracas, Luciano proceeded to occupy a twilight zone between vanquished and victors, according to his devious wont. And, with the proceeds of the "loans" that he had extracted from Caracas captains of commerce, he tided himself over until the next opportunity for combining Machiavelli with machete.

He had another side to his complicated character. Quite unexpectedly, he would indulge in bursts of shining magnanimity. During the longest of all bouts of civil warfare between the Liberals and Conservatives (known as the War of the Federation), which lasted, without a break, from 1858 to 1863, Luciano Mendoza made his début as a Liberal leader.

Watched by a crowd of the natives, the President appeared at the American Warehouse shortly after the lunch hour. He was followed by half a dozen grandly uniformed aides-de-camp, with clanking swords and glittering accoutrements. Our second in command, in a succession of courtly bows, which I can still see across a gap of forty years, ushered Andrade into the offices of the Warehouse. There, the rest of the staff, with set smiles on their faces, bowed low and mumbled politely: Director Rudolf Dolge, from upstate New York; Paul Christoph, from Minnesota; Don Heisler, from Pennsylvania; and the Venezuelan contingent, which included, beside the second in command, a man who had been an officer in my father's favorite half-battalion of artillery in those earlier boyhood days of mine when militarism was threatening to engulf me.

Nodding affably right and left, mild-mannered President Ignacio Andrade advanced into our inner sanctum. There, after more preliminary obeisances and mumblings, I was pulled forward and seated at the typewriter. The Director's chief assistant began dictating a lot of fulsome and sonorous Castilian. Everybody, from the President of Venezuela down, clustered around me and my writing machine, in expectation of astonishing achievement.

Unfortunately, the pressure of the occasion was too much for me.

I went all to pieces. Out of a possible thirty mistakes I turned in a score of thirty. I misspelled the President's title. I botched his first name. I gummed up his last name. I put in capitals where lower case was indicated. I typed lower case where its presence was eminently undesirable. I got my fingers stuck between the keys. *hIs eXceLLencY geNEraL igNacIO*?? anDr-&aDex,preSIdegg?(OfXVenE:zuE@La* That sort of

EARLY BUSINESS LIFE

thing. The innate Spanish politeness of the President and his aides was put to a cruel test. But they did what they could.

"Wonderful!" "What skill!" "Such accuracy!" "Congratulations, Ybarra—your father and mother must be proud of you." "This will bind still more closely the ties between Venezuela and the great republic of the North!"

Yes, they did what they could. But, as for my boss and the rest of the Warehouse staff, I am surprised that they did not brain me where I sat.

That is my main memory of President Ignacio Andrade. It is only one of many memories of the now defunct American Warehouse in Caracas.

When I was in my seventeenth year, my father had decided, in Boston, to take advantage of the burial of hatchets implied in the accession of Andrade to the presidency of Venezuela. So he had left the United States to dive once more into Venezuelan politics. Soon afterward, I postponed indefinitely my entry into Harvard and joined my father in Caracas. Some months later, the rest of the family turned up there. For nearly two years we saw the United States no more. For three years my enrolment as a Harvard undergraduate was deferred. And what exciting years those were!

Upon arrival in Caracas, I became a clerk of low degree at the American Warehouse. Its director and my father were on excellent terms. Always keen to have me utilize the dual nature of my heritage, my North Americanism combined with my South Americanism, my father had arranged with Mr. Dolge to have me employed at the Warehouse. My remuneration was $30 monthly, I think.

The American Warehouse in Caracas was under the wing of the National Association of Manufacturers, with headquar-

allowed to get even the slightest foothold at the American Warehouse in Caracas. So he thought up a set of rules to govern the office hours of all concerned in the Warehouse's activities. I was instructed to type a list of these rules in Spanish and hand a copy to each member of the staff.

It was an impressive document. The staff member hit hardest by its provisions was Bruno, the porter. Bruno was told, in official writing, exactly when to open the big outer front door and exactly when to shut it. He was told exactly when to shut the little inner street door—built into the big one—and exactly when to open it. These maneuvers were to take place early in the morning, again at lunch time, again shortly before the closing hour, and, finally, at the hour set for suspension of daily business, Bruno found himself confronted with a most exacting task, which depressed him greatly. Privately, I circulated among the lesser members of the staff (unbeknownst to our director) a disrespectful burlesque of the official rules. The complicated instructions to Bruno were lumped together, in my version, thus: "Close the front door when you find it open, and vice versa."

It gave my father great satisfaction to see me caught in the maw of international commerce. In his own strange way, he had rather enjoyed, off and on, being an importer of Venezuelan products in the United States. And he was pretty sure that international business would be my line in the future. So he looked upon me as a budding millionaire—quite a feat of imagination in view of the $30 per month that I was pulling down. But my father was always adept at building a maximum of dream-structure on a minimum of foundation.

Things happened now and then, in connection with my job —nasty northern things—that jarred my father's Spanish soul.

EARLY BUSINESS LIFE

Once, for instance, a large package arrived at the Warehouse for my boss. I was told by him to take it to his house. That rubbed my father the wrong way. Try as he would, he couldn't think of his eldest son as being such a mere cog in the machinery of business as to be eligible for carrying a bundle under his arm through the streets of Caracas—a thing a Venezuelan of our social rating would rather die than do.

"Eet gwass not nice to ahsk Tom to do thaht," grumbled my father at our dinner table.

"Oh, fiddlesticks!" exclaimed my mother. "It won't do him any harm."

"I know, Nelly. I know thaht cahrrying a bondle weell not hort Tom. Bot, jost the same, eet gwass not nice to ahsk heem to do thaht." And no argument would budge my father from that position.

Working at the American Warehouse in Caracas gave me my first opportunity to bring out into the open a personal trait that has stuck to me right through my life: viz, a superb inability to understand anything whatsoever about any known kind of machinery. I don't know why an automobile moves. I don't know why an airplane flies. I don't know why a room is flooded with light when I twist a gadget. I don't know why an elevator rises or a thermometer falls. And I don't care.

This attitude didn't help me at the American Warehouse. When prospective purchasers of American products came in to see our exhibits, I would sometimes be delegated to show them around and explain things. I did fairly well at this as long as I could limit my explanations to pointing at a bottle of whisky and announcing "That is a bottle of whisky"—or directing the eyes of visitors to our gigantic mortuary exhibit and saying brightly "That's a coffin." But when details were demanded by possible purchasers about plows and machines destined to displace manual labor on Venezuelan coffee plantations, I was a flop of the first water.

One occasional visitor, I remember, was my special bête noire. He was a handsome and courteous coffee planter. He thought me a dub. He was right. He would listen, in pained silence, to my floundering analysis of the prodigies that this or that machine would accomplish in speeding coffee berries on their way to coffee cups. To him, probably, it seemed that I was explaining a new dance step. Finally, he could stand my balderdash no longer. With an imperious wave of the hand, he would cut my flounderings short.

"Ybarra," he would say, "don't hand me that line of bunk any longer. If you knew five times as much as you do about that machine, you would still know only one-tenth as much as I know." That was straying pretty far from the rules of Venezuelan courtesy; but, I realize, the provocation was great.

Now and then my father would drop in at the American Warehouse. He liked to feel that he, a Venezuelan conversant with the vagaries of *los americanos*, was a leading protector of the establishment. On one occasion, at least, he proved that his role of protector was no mere fiction.

While Rudolf Dolge was absent in the United States, a terrific quarrel broke out between Venezuelan and American members of the staff. I never knew how it started, or why somebody wasn't assassinated in the course of it. Our ex-artillery officer went perfectly berserk. Standing before the desk of Christoph from Minnesota, he shook his fist and kept roaring, without nuance or modulation of any sort: "Joo are a ——! Joo are a ——!" The rest of the remark was awful.

EARLY BUSINESS LIFE

Christoph, a phlegmatic German-American, kept his temper. "That's all right," he muttered.

I sat petrified at my typewriter—which, despite the fact that we were sedulously advertising utra-modern American office furniture, was perched on a soap box. Any minute, I felt sure, the ex-officer would pull a gun. Young Don Heisler, realizing that the affray could be heard up and down the block, had the presence of mind to go to the windows and pull the postigos tight shut.

When the battle was at its most ferocious point, the man whom our director had left in charge rolled in, filled to the nozzle with booze. Leaping enthusiastically into the fighting, he succeeded in making it worse than ever. Every once in a while one of the combatants would come over to me, as I crouched behind my soap box, and try to interest me in his exclusive story of the war. But I refused to be involved. All I did was to tell Bruno, who was standing, goggle-eyed, on the sidelines, to close and bolt the big front door. I didn't want anybody interested in promoting better American-Venezuelan relations to barge in while the embattled American members of our staff were planning to tear out the entrails of the Venezuelan members, and vice versa.

Finally, everybody went home—amid rumbling threats of coming back next day and cleaning up the whole matter with fire and sword. That evening, our director's wife, who had heard all about the fracas, rushed off a cable to her husband, busily Good-Neighboring in New York and Cincinnati.

Next morning, my father got a frantic message from Mr. Dolge appealing to him to take hold of the situation at the Warehouse before the building was wrecked by the opposing factions, and somebody murdered.

My father promptly came around, with a very purposeful military air, and started an investigation. It soon transpired that the mess was too complicated for a really satisfactory disentanglement. General Ybarra decided to leave both sides, so to speak, in possession of the battlefield. After severe warnings not to let it happen again, he cabled to Dolge that peace had been restored. Nor was the Battle of the American Warehouse resumed.

Down in my lowly category among the members of the Warehouse staff was young Rodolfo Urbano. But the fact that he was just an office boy did not keep him from feeling strongly about the proper etiquette to be observed by an *americano*, no matter how high in commercial station, in dealing with a *venezolano*, no matter how low. Urbano's Latin sensitiveness was badly jarred by the doings around the office of an American stenographer (male) whom we had imported from the United States. This individual was accustomed to abrupt northern ways of doing business—which Rodolfo couldn't see at all.

For instance, our word "boy" sounds almost exactly like the Spanish "*voy*," which means "I go" or "I am going." Time and again, during business hours, while my Venezuela office-boy comrade was sitting beside me, the importation from North America would shout imperiously:

"Boy!"

"*No voy!*" sotto voce, from Urbano.

"Boy!"

"*Venga pues*" ("Come on, then"), in a grunt audible only to me.

"Boy!"

EARLY BUSINESS LIFE

Finally, the disgruntled descendant of haughty Spaniards would heave himself out of his chair and reluctantly go to find out what the americano wanted. But always under protest.

Another thing that grieved him deeply was that Yankee's pronunciation of his name. Urbano is rendered in Spanish with sonorous attention to every vowel—OOR-BAH-NO. But the barbarian from the North had no time for such niceties. He called our proud office boy Errbanner. Constantly we would hear him shouting through the office, to the acute disgust of Rodolfo the Sensitive:

"Errbanner—phosphorus!" ("*fósforo*," in Venezuela, means a match).

"Errbanner—machina!" (this meant that the scion of dead Castilian hidalgos was wanted for the cleaning of a typewriter).

Things might have worked up to a dreadful climax if that tactless stenographer had lasted. Fortunately for the cause of international good will, he went on a magnificent three-day carouse of such commanding proportions that it completely ruined his future at the Warehouse. From start to finish of that monumental orgy, he drank nothing but his favorite blend, unlimited quantities of champagne and crême-de-menthe—mixed! When he came to, he found no job awaiting him. He took the next steamer back to New York.

Another thirsty American bobbed up in the Caracas of those days. He was, I remember, of the type of whom people whisper: "You know, he can't go back to the United States." He used to come around to the Warehouse and regale me with tales of sprees worthy to rank high in alcoholic history. Once, while I listened with popping eyes, he told me:

"The other night I wanted a real snootful. But I only had

sixty centavos. So I decided to drink nothing but Angostura bitters neat—you can get a good slug of that here in Caracas for one centavo. Oh, boy!" He licked his lips.

"What happened?" I inquired.

"I wish I knew," he answered. "All I can tell you is that, when I finally woke up in a zaguán, they had even pinched my socks!"

Rodolfo Urbano was not the only Venezuelan office boy connected with the American Warehouse who was ruffled by the abruptness of North American manners. For a while, we also had another lad whose pride was equally touchy. A couple of years after he and I had worked together under director Dolge, I was in Venezuela on a vacation trip. I made a point of looking up my former office mate.

He had got himself a job at the main Post Office on the Plaza Bolívar. There he worked surrounded entirely by Venezuelans, whom he understood and who understood him—men of feeling and tact and social savoir-faire—there wasn't a solitary yanqui on the premises. He led me to his desk and opened a drawer. Inside was a revolver.

"It's loaded," he said. "Ah, Tom, if only I had been armed with that at the American Warehouse. How quickly I'd have taught those damned *americanos* the proper way to treat me!"

After some months as an employee at the American Warehouse, I seceded to the United States Legation, to act as assistant to the American Minister of that epoch. Details of this phase of my career are set forth in another chapter. The American Warehouse continued in existence for some time; in fact, I resumed work there for a while after my secession.

EARLY BUSINESS LIFE

But it never really put itself over. Those grand exhibits never succeeded in luring Venezuelans in paying numbers. They refused to sit, in life, on the ultra-modern chairs whose prices we diligently quoted, or lie, in death, in the coffins that we offered at most attractive discounts f.o.b. New York. My impression is that the Warehouse did not long survive the downfall of President Andrade, its most distinguished Venezuelan visitor.

Incidentally, director Dolge was just about the last person to whom Andrade talked on the day that he fled from Caracas before the advancing troops of Cipriano Castro.

Under the wing of a couple of hundred soldiers who were still loyal, he started from the Yellow House, soon after dawn one morning in 1899, and hit the old, old trail of Venezuelan politicos out of luck, the road over the mountains to La Guaira and Curaçao and New York and Paris. The Dolges lived in the northern part of Caracas, in the shadow of the Avila mountain slopes. As the President and his soldiers approached, Rudolf Dolge and his wife rushed into the street. To their eternal credit, they showed not the faintest sign in their demeanor that the luckless Andrade had taken the supreme Venezuelan political tumble.

The President reined in his horse. He politely acknowledged the greetings of his American friends. He looked tired and sad.

"Might I have a glass of water?" he asked. It was instantly brought to him. He drank, bowed, gave the signal to his escort to proceed. They wound their way dejectedly up the steep incline toward the mountain wall.

Andrade returned, not long afterward, from exile and ended

his days on jobs more congenial to his peaceable nature than that bucking broncho, the Venezuelan presidency. That was most emphatically not the place for him. He proved himself no Teddy Roosevelt.

Chapter XVIII

From Machete to Peinilla

I SAW Cipriano Castro make his triumphal entry into Caracas in the autumn of 1899, after he had driven Ignacio Andrade from power. He came into the city at the head of thousands of pallid and sinewy soldiers, brandishing *peinillas*, the cruel curved blades that are the counterpart, in the Andean regions of Venezuela, of the machete of the rest of the republic. In their ranks, as they surged through the streets of the capital, were many women, also armed with peinillas and carbines and revolvers; I remember well standing on the sidelines of Castro's parade of victory and seeing the unkempt and muddy wenches of his soldiery waving their weapons over their heads, amid uninhibited whoops of triumph.

Castro himself reached Caracas in a train of the German railway from Valencia. From the railway station to the Yellow House, vacated by the luckless Andrade a few days before, he rode in an open carriage behind two galloping horses. As he whirled past me, he was standing erect in the middle of the vehicle, with his arm raised high over his head. What impressed me most about him was his dead-white face under its thatch of jet-black hair.

Castro introduced into the politics of Venezuela a new note. Until his advent, most of the leaders in that republic (what a quaint name for the turbulent, constitution-flouting land of

all some miles distant from Caracas, in the hills around Los Teques, on the way to the valleys of Aragua.

As soon as my father, sitting on the fence in Maracaibo, heard the news of the revolt of Hernández—who had been a godo all his life—he climbed down from the fence, in a sudden burst of martial activity, and threw in his lot with the new Andino régime. His attitude toward los godos was something like that of the Irishman, in the days of Ireland's bitterest bickerings with England, who said: "If England should go to war against hell, it would be the duty of every Irishman to be pro-hell!"

Apropos of El Mocho: He got his nickname because part of two fingers of his right hand were missing. His admirers said that he had lost them in heroic battling against los liberales. But his enemies, pointing to the fact that, in early life, he had been a carpenter, insisted that he had himself sawed off those missing portions of his fingers, because, as they caustically put it, "he was as rotten a carpenter as he is a general."

Once, in my youth, I met El Mocho when he was living in political exile (pretty much his normal state) on the British island of Trinidad, off the eastern coast of Venezuela. I found it strangely fascinating to shake hands with a man who lacked two fingers, and I lost no chance of doing so. But my mother hated to shake El Mocho's maimed hand—it gave her the shivers—and missed no chance of not doing so. There's no accounting for tastes.

At the outset of the Castro régime, before my father had made his peace with it, the advent in Caracas of the ferocious Cipriano, at the head of his victorious army, presented the Ybarra family with a fresh set of difficult situations. But,

FROM MACHETE TO PEINILLA

though Castro and Alejandro Ybarra were technically enemies for some time after the former's occupation of Caracas, the Andino chief did not molest my mother and the rest of the family, in residence at that time at our suburban home, Monte Elena.

Some of Castro's soldiers were quartered in a big building, formerly a girls' school, only a stone's throw from the foot of the little hillock on which Monte Elena stood. As a result of the lively campaign that they had just helped Castro to win, and the prospect that the adherents of El Mocho Hernández and other anti-Castrists might rush them without warning, the soldiers next door to us were pretty jittery.

Their commanding officer used to station outposts directly in front of our hillock, at the intersection of two roads leading from Caracas proper. One night I took my sister Leonor to the theater. On our return, we caught the last horsecar headed out our way, which went as far as a terminus several blocks from our house, on the El Paraíso avenue, then very sketchily lighted.

While we were walking the remainder of the distance to Monte Elena, I stumbled over the sleeping form of a soldier, stretched, with his rifle beside him, right across the sidewalk. At the same moment, Leonor inadvertently kicked the slumbering body of another. Under our feet, several more, rudely awakened, grumbled testily. A sentry, close at hand, eyed us with malevolence. A scowling officer walked up to us.

"What the hell?" he growled. "Who are you?"

I explained in conciliatory tones that we lived in the big house up there on the hillock and were peacefully returning home from the theater.

"The idea, barging in on us that way!" he scolded. "Don't

you know that this is a *fila tendida?*" (that's the technical Spanish military term for what we would call an outpost).

My sister and I assured him that, up to that moment, no fila tendida had ever entered our lives.

"Well, be careful next time," he admonished us. We hurried away—while the fila tendida, or that part of it which was stretched out on the ground, rolled over and went to sleep again.

On another occasion, when the two of us were again returning to Monte Elena at night, we were suddenly hailed, in a loud and angry voice, by a sentry posted somewhere inside the barracks that had been a girls' school. We didn't know the proper reply prescribed by the Emily Posts of Spanish-Venezuelan military etiquette, so we just scuttled up our hillock and into our house as fast as we could go.

Again the sentry challenged. Nobody in the house—by this time we had been joined by my mother and my small brother and Jessie—uttered a sound.

There was a third peremptory yell from the former ladies' seminary. More reticence from us. Then—BANG—a shot split the silence of the night. A bullet went whistling down toward the spot from which our voices had reached the ears of the sentry.

The whole Ybarra family crept silently to bed. There was not a single word of further conversation. We even didn't say good-night to each other.

After a while, the sanitary arrangements—or, rather, their absence—at the barracks next door impelled me to pay a visit of complaint to General Pulido, Castro's Minister of War. He was installed in the offices where my father used to officiate in the same capacity, in one of the wings of the Capitol.

FROM MACHETE TO PEINILLA

Pulido, who had roughed it with my father in many campaigns, was one of the most famous wits and saltiest characters in Venezuela. Entirely ignoring the fact that he was still officially arrayed against his old comrade, he jumped into a carriage and came rushing out to our house.

He assured us that the sanitary situation at the barracks alongside Monte Elena would cause us no more annoyance. So our minds were set at rest, and my mother offered General Pulido a swig of his favorite tipple, Scotch whisky (though my father never drank a drop of anything alcoholic, we always had a variegated supply on hand for uninhibited visitors). General Pulido accepted the swig with enthusiasm. He had a way of repeating over and over again some of the words in the sentences he uttered, one of the many droll personal tricks that had brought him renown and affection in Venezuela. After a pull at the whisky, and a deep grunt of satisfaction, the old general wiped his lips and his muttonchop whiskers with a gnarled hand and grunted:

"Señora Ybarraybarraybarra, did you knowknow that the favorite drinkdrinkdrink of Queen Victoria is whiskywhiskywhisky. Ha!" He took another pull. "Queen Victoria and I, Señora, have the same tastes, the same tastes, the same tastes." After a chuckle worthy of Tony Weller, he tossed off the rest of the drink and bade us farewell.

Before becoming Cipriano Castro's Minister of War, old General Pulido had been through all sorts of political complications, which he took in his stride, with his deep chuckle, like the old campaigner that he was. Once, when he was reputed to be conspiring against the government of the day, a policeman was installed at Pulido's door, with instructions to watch the general closely. In a few days, that policeman went to his superior officer and indignantly asked to be relieved of the assignment.

"I can't stand it any longer," he complained. "General Pulido is the limit. He comes to the door, where I sit with my carbine across my knees, hands me a few copper coins, and says: 'Hey, run down to the corner and get a loaf of brown sugar.' Or he gives me a bolívar and says 'Go to the tobacconist's and get me a packagepackage of cigarettes, cigarettes, cigarettes.' I won't stand for it! I'm a policeman, not an errand boy! Such things are unbecoming to the dignity of a member of the Caracas police force!"

Pulido's experience with that ruffled policeman reminds me of another similar case of a similar general in the turbulent history of nineteenth-century Venezuela. He was a scarred old veteran, named Machado, who, like Pulido, was at outs with the Venezuelan government. The President was pretty sure that Machado was plotting against him. But he had a spasm of magnanimity. He didn't lock Machado up. Instead, he sent him this message: "I give you the city for a prison." When the old veteran read that presidential message, he grunted: "You do, do you? Well, just wait until I'm on top. Then I'll give you the prison for a city!"

The most celebrated yarn concerning General Pulido was the one about the time when he first saw his wife after she had left him. The Pulido separation had rung a bell of reverberating scandal in Caracas, where such things, even to this day, are rare and sensational, One day, the old general was standing in the Plaza Bolívar with some cronies. A few paces away, coming straight toward Pulido, were the wife from whom he was separated and the man in the case. The general's cronies knew well what a fire-eater Pulido was. They also knew that, like

FROM MACHETE TO PEINILLA

practically all Venezuelan generals of the period—except Luciano Mendoza and my father—Pulido carried a gun.

The couple drew near. They came abreast of the group around Pulido. They passed. All the time, without a word, Pulido stared at them. While the two were still well within hearing, he turned to his cronies and grunted:

"That man deserved a better fate!"

During the years that followed the burial of the hatchet between Castro and my father, the Andino dictator bestowed two important posts on his new coadjutor. The first was the "presidency" of the "state" of Trujillo, to which my father was appointed very soon after Castro's triumph. A few years later, my father became Minister of Foreign Affairs in the Castro administration. This latter position brought him into close—and unpleasant—contact with Teddy Roosevelt, then President of the native land of my mother—but that is another story.

In the earlier part of the Castro régime, the United States Minister to Venezuela was the Honorable Francis B. Loomis. The Loomises and the Ybarras were on cordial terms. During the absence on vacation, early in 1900, of the regular Secretary of the United States Legation in Caracas, Mr. Loomis asked me to act as his assistant.

"Your official title, Tom," the American Minister told me, "will be Legation Clerk. But, as a matter of fact, you will be Secretary of Legation." I was delighted. *"Que honra para la familia,"* I said to myself, quoting an old Spanish saying. And I jumped blithely into my new duties. And I felt all puffed up about them, for I was not yet twenty years old.

One of my main jobs was to act as interpreter between President Castro and Minister Loomis. Now, the United States

Minister, like a good Anglo-Saxon, spoke bluntly, straight from the shoulder, without frills or circumlocution. On the other hand, the President of Venezuela, like a good Latin, draped his talk, particularly when it was supposed to come under the head of diplomacy, in flowery masses of rhetoric. I soon figured out that the principal part of my interpreting would be to decorate the speech of Loomis and deflower that of Castro.

Here is a rough outline of one of our three-cornered confabs:

"Tell him," the American Minister would instruct me, in a deep voice, nodding toward Castro, "that the government at Washington is so sore about those unpaid American claims that, if he doesn't pay them p.d.q., there will be fireworks!"

"What does *el señor ministro americano* say?" Castro would inquire eagerly.

"He says," I would reply, "that the government at Washington fully appreciates the difficulties of Your Excellency's position. But, at the same time, it feels itself compelled, though most reluctantly, to consider the position of American claimants. Therefore, the government at Washington would esteem it a great favor if Your Excellency would take up again the possibility of paying at least a part of these claims—merely, of course, as a token of good will."

Castro would bow politely in the direction of Mr. Loomis. Then he would give an answer something like this:

"Tell His Excellency the American Minister that I deplore from my heart the losses unfortunately incurred by certain citizens of the great and noble republic of the North, owing to the cruel exigencies of that glorious and spontaneous national upheaval that made me President of Venezuela. And tell His Excellency that, in view of the great friendliness toward the

FROM MACHETE TO PEINILLA

United States that throbs in my bosom, I shall give orders at once that the claim against the republic of Venezuela made by the American citizen, John Doe, is to be reconsidered immediately."

"What does he say?" Mr. Loomis would ask impatiently.

"O.K.," I would reply. And Mr. Loomis would bow to General Castro, and General Castro would bow to Mr. Loomis, and I'd feel that, as a decorator-deflowerer, I wasn't half bad.

Cipriano Castro was crazy about dancing. Though badly handicapped as a dancer by the fact that, at the battle of Tocuyito, his mule, when mortally wounded, had had the bad taste to fall on top of him and die there, Castro didn't let the consequent lameness keep him off the dance floor. He used to come out to our house in El Paraíso and go galumphing about, in a rhythm all his own, with Simian perseverance. No woman relished dancing with him—but there is a special etiquette governing relations with Spanish-American dictators, which may be summed up in the words "grin and bear it."

Owing to this, Castro found no lack of dancing partners. After he had whirled his lame leg about for hours, the indefatigable Andino would dash off to the Puente de Hierro, where he got Terpsichorean and other satiation until the small hours.

Old-timers will remember well Cipriano Castro's furious quarrel with Teddy Roosevelt. Shortly after his accession to power in Venezuela, the victor of Tocuyito developed ideas about how the "Colossus of the North" should be treated, which were, to say the least, unorthodox. He spoke and acted for a while as if Venezuela and the United States were pretty much on a par militarily and navally and every other way—with the edge, if any, on the side of Venezuela.

This did not appeal one little bit to Teddy. American-Venezuelan relations became badly strained. Snappy official messages were transmitted from Washington to Caracas. American naval vessels buzzed in and out of Venezuelan waters, ready for trouble.

Venezuelan hotheads paraded the streets of Caracas, calling loudly for the blood of los yanquis. A former crony of mine, very popular in his set, was appointed leader of a nebulous but nonetheless bellicose anti-American organization of youths. They were sworn to defend Venezuelan soil to the last gasp against Teddy's minions. They were also obligated (I think) to occupy and devastate New York, if opportunity offered, but I'm not quite sure.

Fortunately for all concerned, nothing came of the mess except the appointment of a commission to investigate Venezuelan debts to Uncle Sam and straighten them out without recourse to force. Meanwhile, Castro had become embroiled also with Germany, Britain and Holland—but, for subtle diplomatic reasons, the Germans, British and Dutch, like Teddy, resisted the temptation to skin him alive.

When the United States-Venezuela bomb exploded, I was living in New York. My burning desire to become an American writer had finally projected me—after graduating from Harvard—into New York journalism. I remember sitting in the old West Thirtieth Street police station, while I was covering the Tenderloin for the New York *Times*, and saying to myself disgustedly: "What has the telephoning of police raids on bathouses to do with literature? I think I'll go back to Venezuela

FROM MACHETE TO PEINILLA

and get the old man (General Ybarra was then Castro's Minister of Foreign Affairs) to let me help unscramble the foreign department of the Castro administration. Surely there's enough work there for a battalion of assistants!"

But, shortly afterward, I was taken on the staff of the New York *Times* Sunday Magazine, which was not interested in the Tenderloin bat-house situation. So I calmed down and decided to stay an American journalist.

Eventually, after brandy and women had almost done for Cipriano, he decided to have drastic repairs made on himself in order to keep from aiming a premature kick at the bucket. He was told that the best doctor in the world for his particular daisy-chain of ailments lived in Berlin. Castro cabled to that doctor:

"Kindly come to see me at once."

The Teuton replied:

"Sorry, but my patients come to me."

Castro wired back:

"Name your own price for coming to Venezuela."

The Berliner answered:

"Sorry, but my patients come to Berlin."

So Castro went to Berlin. As pinch-hitter, he left Juan Vicente Gómez. Gómez waited until Castro was safely on the operating-table. Then he nonchalantly stole Castro's job. That was at the end of 1908. Never again did Cipriano see Venezuela. He knew perfectly well that his return to his native land, if Gómez had anything to say about it, would precede his demise by, at most, five minutes.

He died in exile—under the protection, by a supreme stroke of irony, of the flag of the country which he had dared to defy in the days of his dictatorial arrogance, the Stars and Stripes.

As for Gómez, though he gave Venezuelans excellent chances to bump him off by staying dictator of their country for a full twenty-seven years, he died peacefully in his bed. What's more, he left scores of children. What's more, he did it without ever taking time out to get married.

In 1935, when I was running about the Near East for *Collier's*, I was staying at Shepheard's Hotel in Cairo. There, one morning, my breakfast and a local paper printed in English were brought to me by a gent in a red fez and a white nightgown. Instantly this headline caught my eye: "FATHER OF 150 DEAD."

"My God!" I gasped. "Juan Vicente Gómez has cashed in!" I was right. He had.

Chapter XIX

Under Fire

IN the Venezuela of my boyhood, where imprisonment for political reasons was a commonplace, my father had a distinction almost unique among those who dabbled in the game of local politics: never, in his lively career, was he ever landed behind prison bars. It looked for some time as if his son Tom would have an almost equally distinctive record: that of never having been under fire.

I did not get under fire when I tried to crash my way into the battle of El Guayabo; nor when I marched forth with President Andrade to confront Cipriano Castro. But, when I tried a third time, late in 1899, at the age of nineteen, I finally heard bullets whistle and scream.

My father had just decided to co-operate with Castro. The latter, in token of his appreciation, had made my father "president" of the "state" of Trujillo, in the Venezuelan Andes. Trujillo was merely a province dependent on the central government in Caracas, like the other "states" of the supposedly federated, but, as a matter of fact, highly centralized, republic of Venezuela. In the course of his long political career, my father was chief executive of half a dozen Venezuelan "states." This inspired one of his favorite jokes: "I haff bean pressident of Venezuela aht retail bot never aht wholesale."

At the time of my father's new appointment, I was bored

with life in Caracas; already a desire was stirring inside me to get out of South America for good and become a North American for keeps. So my father, hoping to calm me down, invited me to come along with him to his new billet, as a sort of unofficial aide-secretary.

To go from Caracas to Trujillo it was necessary to embark at La Guaira for Curaçao, the principal island of the Dutch West Indies, and there transfer to a small American steamer plying between New York and Maracaibo. At the latter port we were to connect with a light-draught steamboat, cross the "lake" of Maracaibo—in reality a shallow arm of the Caribbean Sea—and make the rest of the journey on horseback over mountain trails.

On the morning after leaving La Guaira, we steamed between the two little toy forts of Curaçao. Over them flapped the banner of the Netherlands. We cast anchor in the deep roadstead that bisects highly picturesque Willemstad, the island's only town. We were accompanied by Colonel Montiel, a most solemn individual, attached to my father as private secretary. Montiel and his chief were in civilian clothes. But each of them had brought along a sword. As we steamed into the harbor of Willemstad, both came on deck holding these weapons, with handsome yellow-blue-and-red tassels twined around the hilts.

Presently a little fat Dutch police official came aboard to look us over—the Dutch authorities in peaceful Curaçao always keep a vigilant eye on temporary visitors from bellicose Venezuela and feel jittery until those visitors have been eased off the island again. That Dutchman immediately caught sight of the swords in the hands of my father and Colonel Montiel.

UNDER FIRE

"Can't go ashore with those things," he informed them, in the Spanish language as spoken in Amsterdam.

My father bristled. Montiel temporized. The upshot was that the police officer strutted off with the two swords under his pudgy arm, leaving behind him a formal receipt. "Received from General Alejandro Ybarra and Colonel Felipe Montiel, two swords. In the name of Her Gracious Majesty, Queen Wilhelmina of the Netherlands. Signed: Hendrik Willem Van Hoogstraaten"—or something like that.

We went to a hotel. It was run by a Venezuelan called Carvajal, temporarily in exile from his native land for intricate political reasons. The great feature of Carvajal's hotel was a cocktail-mixing machine of which he was immensely proud. I never understood how it worked, or why it existed. When in action it made a noise such as one would expect from the natural child of a steam riveter and an earthquake.

When that machine got to work, customers in Carvajal's café-lounge abruptly laid down their knives and forks and dropped cups with a clatter. Then somebody would explain reassuringly:

"It's the cocktail-mixer. I just ordered a Martini."

After lunch, the president-designate of the state of Trujillo, faithful to his horror of nepotism, decided to put me to work, no matter how many people unrelated to him spent the afternoon loafing.

"Here are a couple of dispatches," he told me. "They must go to Caracas in tonight's mail. Run up to your room and write out clean copies."

I obeyed. While I was gone, a tremendous rumpus broke loose in Carvajal's hotel. One of the guests was a renowned

Colombian writer who owned and operated a ferocious temper. He, like his host, was in enforced exile, because the Colombian government of the moment included some of the men that he liked least in the whole universe. He objected to something said in Carvajal's bar. I never ascertained just what happened after that. All I know is that, on my return from upstairs, with the clean copies of my father's dispatches ready for his signature, I walked right into the middle of excited stories of a row that had included overturned chairs and broken glasses and other disorderly details. Copying those dispatches was the one stroke of work done by me on that whole trip—and it was just my infernal luck that I had to copy them while the battle of Carvajal's Bar was on!

Next day, my father and Montiel and I went aboard the steamship *Maracaibo*, of the Red D Line, which had poked its way at dawn between the two little Dutch forts, with the Stars and Stripes floating over its stern. On deck we met that fat little Dutch police officer. Under his arm were two swords. He bowed stiffly to my father and his secretary.

"The receipt, please," he requested. The document was handed over. Then came the official restitution of the weapons. Then Hendrik Willem Van Hoogstraaten, or whatever his name was, waddled solemnly down the gangplank, conscious that he had done his duty to Queen Wilhelmina and the House of Orange.

Twenty-four hours later, or thereabouts, we were tied up to the wharf at Maracaibo.

Today, that Venezuelan city is known to hundreds of Americans attracted by the immensely rich oil deposits discovered in the surrounding district. The Maracaibo of the present is endowed with golf links and country clubs and other typically

UNDER FIRE

American gadgets necessary to a high standard of living. But the Maracaibo on which I gazed at the end of 1899 was a sleepy, sullen, unlikable town, broiling in a sizzling sun on a sandspit jutting out into the "lake" named after it.

At that time, Maracaibo lived by clapping big customs duties on hundreds of thousands of bags of Colombian coffee and coffee from the Venezuelan Andes, transshipped every year on its stewing waterfront from the craft that had brought them from the rich plantations of the hinterland to steamers scheduled to take them to New York and Europe. "Maracaibo coffee" was famous then, as it is now, all over the world; but scarcely one Maracaibero in a hundred had ever seen a coffee plant.

We could have gone on to Trujillo the night of our arrival in Maracaibo. But my father wanted to show me the town where he had been governor a short time before. So we went ashore for dinner at the Hotel del Lago, a primitive hostelry directly on the shore of the "lake."

"Plantains!" ordered my father, as soon as he had set foot in the hotel. "Plantains. Many plantains. My son has never been in Maracaibo before and doesn't know anything about the favorite fruit of the Maracaiberos. Plantains!" Off went the waiter to mobilize plantains.

We dined. The favorite local fruit tasted good. After dinner, my father went off to call on various high dignitaries, leaving me to digest my dinner at my ease.

Suddenly an ear-splitting fusillade broke out. It seemed to call from all directions.

Bullets, zipping over the Hotel del Lago, went screaming through the air, one after another, until they finally plopped loudly into the water. *Whe—ee-ee-EEE-plop!* Everybody looked at everybody else. *Whee—ee-ee-*EEEE-*plop!* The plantains I had consumed at dinner turned over in my stomach.

Soon the bullets over the lake became so frequent that the proprietor of the hotel and his guests went, in a body, to the veranda on the inland side of the building. There we all sat on chairs and tried to be nonchalant—no easy matter, in the view of the lively punctuation provided by recurrent *wheeeeeee-plops*. The veranda fronted on a big square yard; at the opposite end was a big wooden portal, opening on the street.

Suddenly this portal was flung wide open. An officer with drawn sword, followed by a squad of soldiers, with rifles and bayonets, crowded into the yard. They lined up before the astonished eyes of our group on the veranda. In a loud, masterful voice, the officer inquired:

"Is the son of General Ybarra here?"

I was seized with an overwhelming craving to say no. But the eyes of the proprietor and the guests had all turned to me. Rising shakily from my chair, I announced, in the voice of a mouse:

"I am General Ybarra's son."

I rather expected those words to transform the officer and his men into a firing squad. To my great relief, he merely announced:

"A revolt has broken out against the government. Your father is at the customs-house. He has sent me to fetch you. Kindly come with me."

I joined him. We proceeded along dimly lighted, cobble-stoned streets toward the waterfront. At every corner a soldier crouched warily, his rifle stuck out in front of him. At sight of us, he would straighten up, lift his rifle to his shoulder, and aim at our group. But, each time this happened, our officer would shout *"Gobierno!"* (government), and the soldier, with a grunt of disappointment, would let us pass and then crouch down again, in readiness for something more exciting.

In a few minutes we reached the customs-house, a little building of imitation-Moorish architecture on the shore of Maracaibo Lake. My father was there, surrounded by a group of other adherents of Cipriano Castro.

I learned that friends of El Mocho Hernández had staged an uprising and taken the government's supporters by surprise. My father and I went aboard the *Maracaibo*, which had just brought us from Curaçao, tied up at the side of the wharf opposite where the little steamboat was moored that was to have taken us onward toward Trujillo.

The fusillade continued all night. By morning the government authorities ashore were reduced to defending a barracks, the main police station, in the central part of the city, and the customs-house, at the shoreward end of our wharf.

From all points of the compass the rebels were closing in. From the deck of our steamer we could see them taking potshots, from windows in near-by buildings, at government soldiers crouching at the windows of the customs-house or behind coffee sacks on the wharf. One soldier of Castro, shot dead directly alongside the *Maracaibo*, lay there for hours, in the stifling heat of the forenoon.

In the early afternoon, reinforcements for the government defenders arrived from the fort at the Caribbean end of Lake Maracaibo and disembarked on the wharf. The sight of them filled my father with martial excitement.

Remembering that, only a few weeks before, he had been

boss in Maracaibo, he hustled ashore from our American steamer and began giving orders to the reinforcements—with me following modestly in his wake. He harangued the officers in command of the newcomers—there was impressive talk of "deploy outside El Milagro" and "take them in the flank."

I walked up and down the wharf in the company of a soldier of most villainous countenance, wearing a dirty uniform that stank to heaven. He trailed his rifle in the dust behind us and yelled enthusiastically about what he and his comrades would do to the Mochistas as soon as they could get at them. Our belligerent promenade was abruptly terminated by Roberts, a young American fellow-passenger on the *Maracaibo*, who leaned, with a wild look in his eyes, over the steamer's rail and shouted to me:

"Come aboard, Ybarra, you damned fool, don't you see they're shooting at you!"

A *wheeeee-plop* at that moment made me see the relevancy of Roberts's words. I went aboard. As for the soldiers dispatched shortly afterward by my father to land at El Milagro and execute decisive flanking movements, we learned later that they landed all right and then returned in a body to civilian life. They were more philosophers than warriors.

Within a couple of hours after their departure, fighting ceased around the wharf. A detachment of ragged Mochistas rushed into the custom-house, cheering wildly and waving their rifles over their heads. Already governmental resistance at the barracks and the police station had been subdued. The rebels had won.

And that meant that my father and his son and Colonel Montiel, his private secretary, were in a pretty mess. We couldn't proceed to Trujillo, because the rebels in control of the city would sink us. We couldn't go ashore. And we couldn't go back to Curaçao yet, because the *Maracaibo* was to be loaded with some thousands of sacks of coffee before it could get out of port. There was nothing for it but to sit aboard the ship as calmly as possible—a minimum calm in my case—and see what would happen.

Then it was that my father had reason to thank his stars that he had married a North American and learned the strange language of North America and made himself adept in the art of ingratiating himself with the citizens of her exotic country. The American Consul came aboard—he had been a good friend of my father for years. With the captain of the steamer—also a friend of long standing—the Consul and my father went into a huddle.

"As long as we can bluff them, General," said the Consul, "you're all right. I'll put up the damnedest bluff you've ever seen. You're a friend of mine and an officer and a gentleman and I'm not going to see those God-damned Mochistas yank you and your son and your secretary off to a stinking *calabozo*, where you'll be lucky if you don't die of suffocation, and where you'll get nothing but rotten plantains to eat." The captain nodded vigorous assent.

"I've already told the Mochistas ashore," continued the pugnacious Consul, "that, if they touch a hair of your head, general—or of yours (with a nod to me) or of yours (with another to Colonel Montiel)—I'll have the *Wilmington* steam up to this blasted town and blow it off the map!"

These words had sound and fury, but they signified nothing. The United States gunboat *Wilmington* was somewhere in the vicinity of the seaward end of Lake Maracaibo, but she drew too much water to get herself over the sand bar there. Nevertheless, the defiant oration of the Consul put heart into Montiel and me.

As for my father, he remained perfectly calm. His usually exuberant manner had given place to taciturn sang froid. That day he proved himself a true soldier, capable of taking things as they came. Turning to the rest of us, he said—quite as if he was bored by too much social chatter at an afternoon tea:

"Gentlemen, as for me, I'm going to take a nap. If the Mochistas come to fetch me ashore, please wake me up." A few minutes later he was snoring.

One Venezuelan aboard the steamer was far less philosophical. That was Rufino Blanco Fombona, who has since become one of the most renowned of South American writers. He had arrived in Maracaibo at the same time as my father and Montiel and myself. He, too, was going through a militaristic phase. He was acting as an aide to General Tosta Garcia, who had been appointed by President Castro to the governorship of Maracaibo.

But the sudden uprising of the Mochistas had completely upset the plans of Tosta Garcia and his literary aide. The general, rudely surprised at his headquarters ashore by the outbreak of the rebellion, had made tracks for a Venezuelan gunboat anchored out in the lake. And Rufino Blanco Fombona, also forced to get to a place of safety at top speed, had managed to reach the customs-house. When that got too hot for him, he had boarded the American boat on which the Ybarras, father and son, had taken refuge.

There, also, he soon felt unsafe. So he climbed down the

side and into a flat-bottomed craft, manned by several humble Maracaiberos, that was lying alongside. Rufino, always a man of violence, pulled out a revolver and aimed it at the heads of the boat's crew.

"Row me out to that vessel at once," he ordered, pointing to the gunboat to which his chief had dashed, "or I'll blow your brains out."

They rowed him to the gunboat.

Through three long days we lay alongside that wharf, in the hellish heat of Maracaibo. Hour after hour we loaded sacks of coffee. In the meantime, the rebels chiefs in control of the nasty little city sent a formal request to the captain of our ship calling for the immediate delivery into their hands of General Ybarra, his secretary, and his son.

But the captain stormed about what the *Wilmington* would do, and that doughty American Consul, our resolute champion ashore, pranced in and out of Mochista headquarters shouting so loudly about the prowess of Uncle Sam and the capacities for dire vengeance inherent in the Star Spangled Banner that nobody dared to try to remove us by force.

"You know, General," the captain would say to my father, "if these devils send down an officer and ten men to fetch you, the jig is up. We can't do anything more for you, or for (another of those disquieting nods in my direction) your son. But, until they call my bluff, I'll keep on bluffing."

"Thank you," said my father gravely. "And now I'm going to take a nap."

I was in no state for sleep. Instead, I buried my nose in *David Harum* and tried desperately to concentrate on its pages. A short time ago I opened that book again. As I turned its pages, I could smell the coffee piled up on that rickety South American wharf; and taste again the heat pouring down on that pseudo-Moorish customs-house; and hear once more the voice of Colonel Montiel (a most unpleasantly pessimistic warrior) muttering to me:

"Tom, I have a presentiment."

"What is it?"

"Tonight they'll send down here to fetch us ashore and lock us up."

"But, wh-why, Colonel?"

"Oh, I don't know. Just a presentiment, that's all."

But no Mochista officer, with a squad of disreputable soldiery, came marching along the wharf for our undoing. That bluff of the American Consul and his accomplice, our captain, worked magnificently.

The representatives of El Mocho confined themselves to sending two guards aboard to watch over the movements of my father, Montiel and myself. I got quite chummy with those guards. They were affable, hookwormish individuals, with ragged sandals on their brown feet, frayed straw hats on their matted hair, and sweaty shirts over their fragrant torsos. They used to give us all the lowdown about doings ashore. And they would accept drinks from me. Once, in the hope of shocking my mother and having her transmit the shock to Boston and Plymouth, I had myself photographed by young Roberts, standing beside those two unwashed guards, just like a genuine prisoner in the shadow of execution.

At the end of three days—composed, it seemed to me, at a conservative estimate, of seven hundred and twenty hours—the last of the coffee sacks was dumped into the hold of our steamship. Our whistle tootled the news of our imminent departure.

UNDER FIRE

A large crowd of residents of Maracaibo packed themselves onto the wharf to witness the getaway of Alejandro Ybarra and his suite. I waited, invisible, below, until I felt perfectly sure that the last hawser had been cast overside and that our ship was backing out into the lake. Then I walked boldly onto the upper deck.

As soon as the crowd caught sight of me, there were cries of "There's Ybarra's son!"—mingled with jeers and derogatory salutings and remarks reflecting adversely on me and my family.

I took off my Panama hat and bowed from the waist, with sarcastic courtesy. The crowd roared insult. I glanced apprehensively over the side—yes, the last hawser was gone, we really had severed connection with the wharf. So I bowed again. And again—holding my arms, with my Panama in one hand, far apart.

The jeers redoubled. Horrid Spanish curses came hurtling through the sun-baked air. Noses were thumbed. In another moment, the *Maracaibo* had swung out into the lake and pointed her nose toward the sand bar and the Caribbean.

Next day, we were back in Curaçao. My father teamed up with other generals of Castro's government bent on reconquering Maracaibo. In a few days, at the head of a considerable force, crowded aboard a flotilla of schooners and other small craft, they all sailed away. They reconquered Maracaibo without much trouble. That left my martial parent free to proceed to his gubernatorial duties in Trujillo.

But—ah, me!—I wasn't in his entourage. On the eve of his departure from Curaçao, he had turned to me and announced, with great severity:

"You must go back home. You are a hoodoo. And, besides, Nelly will worry."

I returned to Caracas. My third direct contact with Venezuelan revolutions, like its two predecessors, had ended in ignominy.

Chapter XX

Customs of the Tribe

HENRY SEIDEL CANBY, that most distinguished author and critic was, when I first met him, many years ago, merely an undergraduate at Yale. He appeared in Venezuela on a visit, accompanied by a Yale pal, John Rice. Canby's mother had been an intimate friend at Vassar of an American girl who, in later years, like my mother, married a Venezuelan. After her son had grown up, Mrs. Canby thought it would be pleasant for him to see a bit of South America from the inside and get acquainted with Caracas, the South American community into which her old friend of Vassar days had married. Hence the visit to Venezuela of Henry Canby and John Rice, during the reign of Cipriano Castro.

They were both promptly projected into the inner life of Caracas. They were introduced to a large number of assorted Caraqueños, including the Ybarras. For Canby and Rice (my mother dubbed them Canby and Can't-be), horses were procured; and, in my company and that of other local youths, they cantered all over the city of Caracas and contiguous portions of the beautiful mountain-girt valley in which the Venezuelan capital nestles.

Late one afternoon, while the two Yale undergraduates and I were out horseback riding, we were caught in one of the torrential rains that frequently pour down, without warning, upon

YOUNG MAN OF CARACAS

the valley of Caracas during the rainy season. Fortunately, we were near Monte Elena, in El Paraíso, the lair of the Ybarras. So putting spurs to our steeds, we galloped up to the stable, beside the big house where my family was then living (once the residence of a sugar-planting family, whose former plantation had been turned into building lots). We handed over our horses to Manuel—for whom, I suppose, the proper title is groom, though he looked more like a dissolute scarecrow—and went into the house in search of the rest of my family. The downpour continued. So Canby and Rice were invited by my mother and father to take potluck at dinner.

We all sat down to table in the big dining room on the ground floor of the old plantation house, which had walls I don't know how many inches thick, and deep windows opening on an open corridor. This corridor ran along the front of the house and afforded (in the daytime) a fine view of the red roofs and green plazas and white church steeples of Caracas, sprawling over its lovely valley, a couple of miles away, with the towering Avila range of mountains shutting it off from the sea.

Soup was served. My father made polite conversation in English, in that indestructible Spanish accent of his, to our guests from Yale. He was aided and abetted (in English free of Castilian accretions) by my mother, my sister, my brother and myself. It was all very social and very correct and very formal.

But things seldom stayed that way long in the lair of the Ybarras.

Suddenly there was a rustling noise from somewhere close to the floor. We noticed the eyes of Henry Canby and John Rice take on a wondering look. From some point under our feet came a throaty, greasy, ornithological chuckle. Then, from beneath Canby's chair, our parrot stepped forth—fat and green, with yellow and red patches distributed effectively over his person. He saluted the assembled company with a deep gurgle of greeting. That was a regular occurrence at our house and ordinarily would have aroused no attention from anybody. But my father, with those two American guests present, was feeling painfully formal.

"Yessie!" he exclaimed petulantly. "Tekk thaht parrot ehweh!"

"All right, General, just a moment, I must change Missybarra's plate," said Jessie Sullivan, upon whom formality never settled even on the most ceremonial occasions. In her own good time, Jessie removed the parrot. Guests and family, again in the grip of social etiquette, applied themselves to the next course—amid talk of a strange and stilted sort—for that was the tone which my father was bent on setting.

In the midst of a grave oration by him on the economic resources of Venezuela, the eyes of Henry Canby and John Rice again assumed a puzzled look. Despite desperate attempts to live up to the formality exuding from my father's discourse, their attention seemed to be wandering.

For, from the direction of the kitchen, a long-legged apparition, with gaudy feathers and a voluminous neck, had appeared in the doorway and halted there, apparently entranced by the statistics pouring out of my father.

"Our pet heron," explained my young brother affably to the two gentlemen from New Haven.

"Yessie!" shouted my father, "tekk thaht theeng ehweh!"

"Just a minute, General, I must serve the black beans," said the unperturbed Jessie Sullivan.

Eventually the heron disappeared. Heavy ceremonial again descended on the Ybarra board—until Messrs. Canby and Rice abruptly laid down their knives and forks and goggled at the doorway leading to the front corridor. Through that doorway a dappled quadruped, with soft brown eyes, had just put in an appearance.

"Our pet deer," remarked my sister.

"Yessie! Tekk thaht beast ehweh!"

Jessie did. And, with "thaht beast" vanished the last shred of formality. Thenceforth, the meal became the usual blend of insouciance and hilarity characteristic of the Ybarra home—with my father, now that he had done his bit to appease the courtly gods of Spanish hospitality, joining, with the zest of a boy, in the revelry.

After I started writing this book, I ran across Henry Canby at a literary banquet in New York. I asked him whether he had any objection to my mentioning him in connection with the parrot-heron-deer episode at our house.

"None whatever," he said. "But," he added, "aren't you mentioning Roosevelt the Cat?"

At my blank look, he told me that, according to his memory, the Ybarra cat, named after Teddy Roosevelt, had also enlivened that dinner at our house, and snapped up any morsel of food that came within reach. I confess that I don't remember Roosevelt the Cat; but there were so many variegated pets at Monte Elena that I haven't the slightest doubt that, in this case, Henry Canby's memory is better than mine.

That was typical of the Ybarra household at the turn of the nineteenth century into the twentieth—and, for that matter, of that same household at any other period during my early years in Caracas. But there were times, despite strong pulls in

CUSTOMS OF THE TRIBE

the opposite direction, when the Ybarras went society. Such lapses were particularly prevalent when I was a little boy and we were living in the city of Caracas itself, and not in El Paraíso. At our residence, between the corners of El Conde and Piñango, formality again and again raised its cold head.

Those were the days when my father held high military office. Diplomats used to dine with us—monocled Britons and talkative Frenchmen and Americans usually homesick for the North—sprinkled with individuals bearing letters of introduction from Massachusetts relatives, who had ventured down to Caracas to get a glimpse of the exotic milieu into which Nelly Russell had married. But even such parties could not entirely repress the anti-society atmosphere permeating the Ybarra lair —not even when my father was Comandante de Armas or Minister of War.

Once, I remember, the table in our city residence was set for a dinner of tremendous formality—with twenty covers or thereabouts, and flowers in the center, and olives at every plate. Yet, unimpressed by all this pomp, my pretty little cousin Ana Teresa, who lived down the block, and I (both of us too young to dine in such state) sneaked into the dining room before the start of the party and ate thirty-two olives! My share, I regret to confess, was twenty-seven!

Even out at Monte Elena there were spasms of ceremonial eating. In the course of these, even Jessie Sullivan was repressed, and from soup to nuts not a parrot or heron or deer hove in sight. During these spasms, the most conspicuous feature was George.

George was a Negro lad from Trinidad, in the British West Indies. My father hired him with the express stipulation that, when on duty, he should wear a white coat. A spotless white coat. George lived up to his contract faithfully. As a result, our meals took on an unwonted air of etiquette, greatly resented by the family Bolsheviki—my sister, brother and I. We were never quite comfortable under the eye of George.

Fortunately, George didn't last long. He was lured away by the head of an American exploring expedition that was about to snoop around the region of the Orinoco. My father was so incensed at George's defection that he refused to re-hire him on his return from the jungle—though George applied for his old job in a coat so white that it hurt one's eyes. Joyfully, the Ybarra small fry again frolicked at meals, with Jessie Sullivan's running comments an integral part of the table talk, and birds and beasts moving about, uninhibited.

Informality was at its mealtime high in the days of Marcus.

He, too, was a British West Indies Negro boy—from Barbados—and no power on earth could graft formality onto him. His clothes were always dingy and floppy, his footgear unpolished, his hair matted. And he spoke a brand of West Indies English that fascinated the lesser Ybarras.

One day at lunch, in accordance with the affable mealtime code of the family, my sister and I egged on Marcus to tell us about life in Barbados. He did—at considerable length—with much animation. But we couldn't understand a word he said! The language employed was unquestionably English—but what English! The Bolsheviki listened, entranced. For all we cared, Marcus could have run on, in incomprehensible lingo, until siesta time. But, finally, my mother—thinking that the leveling of the classes had gone far enough—severely ordered Marcus to pass around the potatoes.

This chapter so far may have given the impression that ours was a household of many domestics. It was. But in the profusion of our servitors there was nothing uncommon or ostentatious. We were simply being typically Venezuelan.

Domestics, especially the females of the species, were as plentiful, in the Caracas of the days of my youth, as mangoes or plantains. And they attached themselves to households with a calm casualness—and remained attached with a tenacity—that made retinues of numerous servitors a most ordinary phenomenon of everyday Caracas life.

For instance, when we hired a new cook, she would probably arrive, on returning from her first day's marketing, with a little son or nephew—maybe, also a daughter or niece. These children would furtively join our domestic force—quite uninvited. Nobody hired them. And as they hadn't been hired, nobody could fire them. There they were. They just sat around, creeping modestly into corners when my mother invaded the kitchen. Presently, my mother or Jessie or my father or I would send one of these casuals on an errand, whereupon their status at once became immutably official. After that, there was an end to efforts—if any had been made—to get rid of them. They were fixtures.

Then there were the hangers-on who might be called domestics by inheritance. Of the staff at our house, the example of this species most prominent in my memory is Rosarito. Rosarito was a cantankerous old female—venomous, in fact—who, so far as anyone in the household could remember, had been employed at some time or other in my grandmother Ybarra's establishment. Therefore, in accordance with the unwritten feudal code of the Venezuela into which she had been born, she felt perfectly justified (if she could get away with it) in attaching herself to a son of old Misia Merced, her former employer.

When I first became acquainted with Rosarito, all hope of getting her fired had been given up by even the least feudally inclined members of our family. We had resigned ourselves, from my father and mother downward, to providing her with bed and board until she should shuffle off this mortal coil—with no quid pro quo, on Rosarito's part, discernible with anything short of a microscope.

The most delicious point about the situation was that Rosarito scorned all that was not Venezuelan, and placed, at the apex of her scorn, my mother, whom she had dubbed *la inglesa* —the Englishwoman. Much of her time she spent in grumbling and perfectly audible soliloquies about la inglesa (a Protestant, forsooth!). At any hour of the day one was likely to encounter Rosarito—wrinkled, dour, bent and unfriendly—muttering that la inglesa had done this—did you ever?—or failed to do that—can you beat it?—what properly *educada* Venezuelan Catholic could ever have been guilty of that? None of us minded, however; we went our way, unheeding—even la inglesa herself took Rosarito as a necessary evil, like cockroaches.

Another kind of family appendage was represented by Antonio. Antonio was a man of magnificent mustachios who, in early life, had been a sergeant with troops commanded by my father in various campaigns. After retiring from the military life, Antonio had set up as a carpenter. By some obscure application of the Venezuelan semi-feudal code, he had imposed himself upon my father and the whole Ybarra family as the only human being to whom carpentering jobs could rightfully be entrusted.

If there was a partition to be built, it was "send for Antonio." If a table was to be repaired, or a chicken coop to be constructed, Antonio alone must be summoned to do it.

There was a fatal flaw in this arrangement—pointed out, with Massachusetts clearness of vision, by my mother. It was this: Antonio was a rotten carpenter. My mother simply could not see why he should ever be trusted even with driving a nail. In vain my father talked of those grand old campaigning days, when Antonio and he were risking their lives together for the Venezuelan Liberal party—my father's beloved *amarillos* or "yellows"—against the red or blue godos.

"What's that got to do with fixing the broken chair in my room?" my mother would ask coldly. Relics of feudalism often struck her as mere excuses for masking inefficiency—which they undoubtedly were. My father would shake his head sadly; and for a while, carpenters, with a grasp of the rudiments of their trade, would potter around our house. But, after the storm was over, Antonio would reappear—pulling at his big mustachios in a nervous and conciliatory manner when my mother encountered him.

Antonio lived in a ramshackle shanty in a lowly suburb of Caracas known as *el Estado Zamora*. He had a tired wife, whom he used to beat when he got drunk, and a squad of dirty, grinning children. My father and I went to dinner there one day, after repeated invitations. We were served highly seasoned chicken and garlicky vegetables, while Señora Antonio, in her Sunday best, acted uncomfortably as hostess, and the squad of children, being no longer dirty, were, in consequence, no longer grinning.

It was an unnatural affair, that dinner. But my father was perfectly at ease—he was accustomed to such inroads upon the barriers of class.

One of his favorite stories was about how Pantaleón, who

had been his orderly in civil conflicts years before my birth, came to him, after prospering as a corner grocer on the Calle San Juan in Caracas, a workingmen's quarter, and asked him to dinner. My father went.

At the house of the affluent grocer, the guest of honor found some twenty butchers and grocers and assorted small tradesmen gathered to receive him. Pantaleón, the host, met my father at the door—with a pair of slippers in his hand.

"General," said Pantaleón, "this is going to be a splendid feast. There will be a great deal of food and many liquids. I want you to be comfortable. Nobody can enjoy a good dinner with tight shoes on. Please put on these slippers."

My father put them on. He entered the drawing room, mingled with the family and the other guests. Pantaleón rushed out of the room, returned with a long, loose dressing gown, and proffered it to my father.

"General," he said, "take off your coat and put this on."

"But why?" asked my father.

"Because this is going to be a superb feast. There will be *caldo*. There will be *sancocho de gallina*. There will be potatoes and yams and plantains and black beans and rice and fruit and coffee. You can't enjoy yourself if you keep on that hot, tight coat. Please put on this *bata*. It will enable you to wiggle your elbows. Please put it on."

My father did. After some minutes of social conversation, the whole company—in slippers and dressing gowns—sat down to a repast which, as Pantaleón had promised, was monumental.

When my mother first knew my father, there were, in my grandmother Ybarra's house, two ex-slaves. Slavery, in Venezuela, was officially abolished somewhere about the middle of

CUSTOMS OF THE TRIBE

the last century. They were named Patricia and Luciana. The latter, well over seventy when I first laid eyes on her as a small boy, survived until a year or so after my arrival in Caracas in the early eighteen-nineties.

Luciana, quite as a matter of course, had continued to be attached to the domestic staff of my grandfather and grandmother just as if there had been no Venezuelan counterpart of the Emancipation Proclamation. She was a cross old thing, of whom I and other small members of the family stood in awe; she had a way of bawling us out on little or no provocation.

She would also talk back and lay down the law to adult Ybarras. But, out of respect to the past, they treated her with something almost like deference—after all, was she not a faithful old servitor, practically a member of the family in her own peculiar way? So Luciana, the crabbed old wench, railed and scolded with impunity—retiring off and on to sulk in her room.

This apartment was on the ground floor. It was of considerable size and comfortably appointed, with pictures of the Virgin and several saints over the bed, in approved South American fashion. I don't know just what Luciana did to earn her keep—little or nothing, I feel sure. Somehow, dimly, I see her in my memory as prominently connected with the transportation, to and from the principal bedrooms of the house, of chamber-pots.

Entries in my mother's diary written just short of half a century ago show vividly the attitude of Venezuelans of Misia Merced's time toward domestics like Luciana. On the day that Extreme Unction was administered to the old ex-slave, my mother wrote:

"Went at 11 with Alito to the *administración* of poor Luciana. She is dying. . . . She was given to Misia Merced on her marriage and has always lived with her, 52 years, and even after her freedom considered Misia M. as *mi ama*, as she called her. Luis was her darling, as Alito was old Patricia's. Luciana is 80 and Patricia died at 84. . . ."

For the next day, the diary has this entry:

"Luciana died at 4.30 A.M. Misia Merced is inconsolable. It is the last link with the past, and she was such a companion to her. We have been there all day. . . . There were lots of women, old servants, etc., and all were weeping. Luis came from El Cedral and cried like a child at the news; could not enter the room where Luciana lay dead."

Then comes this:

"Luciana Rivas Tovar, using the noble names of her mistress, was buried at 9 A.M. Many people went to the house . . . many aides and officers [my father was then Comandante de Armas]. Poor Misia Merced has cried and cried. The coffin was carried to the hearse by Alito, Luis, Francisco and Carlos, and little Tom was a chief mourner and *despidió* [took leave of] the funeral party at the Cathedral. It was quite a consolation to Misia Merced to have Luciana receive a military funeral."

Chapter XXI

The Bostonian Returns

It was my mother—I realize it now—who finally turned the tide of my life away from Venezuela and toward the United States—my mother, ably seconded by that latent Bostonian inside me. I cannot definitely recollect that she ever said or did anything directly to influence my final decision. Nevertheless, she it was who, more than anybody or anything else, won the victory for the land of my Massachusetts ancestors.

For it was my mother who incarnated the North American part of me, just as my father was the incarnation of my Latin self. Exactly as she had attracted and tamed Alejandro Ybarra, her ardent Latin lover, in the days of their engagement and early marriage—exactly as she had built up the passionate love of his youth into lasting affection that triumphed alike over difference of race and passage of time—so, later, she lured the son of Alejandro Ybarra back from the stormy seas of Latinity in South America to the solid anchorage of Anglo-Saxonism in North America.

My mother had a personality before which obstacles melted and vanished. All through her life she met enjoyment more than halfway, with shining glance and bubbling words. Always she brought light into other eyes and happiness into other faces. To every situation she adapted herself without effort—or, if there was effort, she concealed it.

YOUNG MAN OF CARACAS

In her mature life, when she met emergency and peril and grief sufficient to crush out every bit of bravery from the bravest heart, she met them with unshakable gallantry. And with a smile. And with a philosophy that had no room for fear and was made up almost entirely of heart.

She had scarcely turned twenty before she lost her first-born son—he lived less than five months. Within the next eight years, she lost three little daughters—two within the space of one week. One of them died on board a steamer bound from Venezuela to the United States, just before it docked in New York.

Not seeing that little sister when I was landing, under the wing of my mother and Jessie Sullivan, I asked: "Where is Mercedes?"

"She has gone on ahead," answered my mother—bravely hiding her desolation. Before the week was out, another sister of mine, gay little Nelita, was also dead, and, two years later, still another, less than a year old.

But nothing in my early memories shows me a mother crushed under terrible grief. Nelly Russell wished to leave in the memories of her children only a picture that expressed joy and radiated laughter. She succeeded. Yet, when alone, in communion with herself, it was different.

I have read her diaries. From them, though only in short flashes, speaks the depth and poignancy of my mother's grief. Chronicling the eighth birthday of my sister Leonor, she wrote: "Leonor is the first of my four little girls to reach the age of eight." Yet, I do not doubt, she turned from the desk at which she wrote that to make a joke for the three children who remained to her, a joke that set them all laughing.

No wonder Nelly Russell's heart—that is, the physical part

THE BOSTONIAN RETURNS

of it—finally failed her. "I shall die," she said once, "from the sudden stopping of an overworked heart." And so it was that she died—while her hair was still brown and her eyes still bright and her joy in life still fresh. No human heart could have withstood longer the tax that she levied on hers in humanity and constancy and valor. She never saw her sixty-second birthday. To me, she was not only never old but never even middle-aged.

I asked for myself only two of her many photographs. One showed her at the age of fourteen, in a sailor's costume—all her life she loved the sea—with boy's trousers and boy's blouse and a boy's natty cap. That was how she dressed when she cruised over Boston Harbor, in the United States revenue cutter, when her father was Collector of the Port of Boston.

I never saw her in that sailor's suit; long before I knew her she had given up the pranks of her happy girlhood. Nevertheless, that early photograph enchanted me. And when, many years after it had been taken, she dug it up, along with two others, also dating back to the eighteen-seventies, and asked me and my sister and my brother to choose one apiece, I threw all ideals of fairness to the winds and put up such a clamor for the sailor boy that it was hurriedly adjudged to me without further discussion, just for the sake of peace in the family.

My other favorite picture of my mother shows her in her late twenties. "Don't you want a photograph of me taken after I had grown older?" she used to ask me. "You never grew older," I would invariably reply.

Her influence over my father was uncanny. She rode the tempest of his worst Latin rages with New England serenity. And every one of those rages seemed, when it was over—and it soon was—to have further solidified the love which the fiery

Venezuelan felt for the pretty girl who had burst upon him out of the North and who remained as exotic to him as he remained to her.

She handled her wild man of Venezuela magnificently. Her weapons were a blend of firmness and understanding, common sense and irrepressible sense of humor. When he lost his temper, she had an exasperating way of getting off one small, stinging remark, in an unbearably gentle tone of voice, and then closing up like one of the clams of Plymouth harbor. After that, no fireworks from her raging spouse could make her open her mouth. One of the most vivid pictures in my memory is that of General Alejandro Ybarra roaring like a bull, and Nelly Russell de Ybarra sitting in a corner, in a silence worthy of Plymouth Rock.

Alejandro Ybarra throve on this treatment, and kept coming back for more. It was the counterpart of the running fight between my Latin self and my inner Bostonian, when Latinity and Massachusetts came to grips. What chance had the Latin in either battle?

How close my parents were to each other—and remained through long years of trying vicissitudes—leaps constantly from their letters during the periods of separation that Venezuelan politics kept imposing on them. When my mother was in the United States or Europe, and my father in Venezuela, his longing for her cropped up incessantly. All his thoughts hovered around the day on which the separation was to end.

"I am having those alterations made in that room downstairs," he would write. "It will be all ready when you return." Or:

"Do you remember my plan for new chicken coops? Well,

THE BOSTONIAN RETURNS

I am going ahead with it. You will like them very much when you return."

As for her, she missed him every minute. Writing from Munich—after she had gone there with us children to join her mother and sisters, and he had gloomily resumed being a coffee merchant in Boston, because he had again picked the loser in a Venezuelan civil war—she wrote to him:

"I miss you very much, not only as Tico but as a man to talk to—you know, you and I have always talked together as two friends and comrades, and I am used to talking with your friends. Do you remember the many discussions we have had on every conceivable subject, ever since the days of the Latin Quarter, when I was first married. . . . I think I am in some ways more of a man than a woman, and since I have been living entirely among women I am astonished to find how different they are in their way of seeing things; a trifle is of such importance and they are so narrow and personal and a man is such a Being in their eyes.

"Don't think I do not like women; you know I do and I am far more liked by women than by men. I am more popular among them, but I think more like a man than they do. Perhaps the reason they like me is because they never have me as a rival and I hate *brollos* [quarrels] so."

Discussing, in the same letter, a play by Zola, much in vogue, she wrote:

"Talk about heredity! Do you suppose circumstances do not alter lives as much as ancestors? Am I at all the same woman I should have been if I had not married you and gone through so many experiences with you? Of course I am not. Poor old Tico, how tired you must be of all this, but I tell you, I miss you to talk to."

YOUNG MAN OF CARACAS

As my father lay on his death-bed—old, wasted and in sharp pain—he clung to Nelly Russell's hand like a child to its mother's; and he kept whispering to the end: "Forty-one years. Forty-one years." That was the length of time they had been married to each other.

Soon afterward, the United States Minister in Caracas drove out to Monte Elena to tell my mother that, by a new law, she was entitled to claim again the United States citizenship that she had relinquished when she had married my father forty-one years before. She thanked him.

On the next Fourth of July—almost exactly one year after my father's death—she caused the Stars and Stripes to be hoisted over Monte Elena, the home my father had given her and named for her. Throughout her long married life she had been loyal to her man, a foreigner; and, throughout her life, she had remained loyal to her country, which was not his. As she watched the flag of her Massachusetts ancestors, fluttering in the breezes of alien Venezuela, she knew that my father, beyond the grave, would understand.

Before the year was out she died.